Wangari Maathai

Lᴀɴᴛᴇʀɴ Bᴏᴏᴋs ᴏɴ Aғʀɪᴄᴀ

Bill Hatcher
The Marble Room
How I Lost God and Found Myself in Africa
288 pp, 978-1-59056-406-6, pbk original

Wangari Maathai
The Green Belt Movement
Sharing the Approach and the Experience
160 pp, 978-1-59056-040-2, pbk original

Martin Rowe
The Elephants in the Room
An Excavation
244 pp, 978-1-59056-387-8, pbk original
978-1-59056-388-5 (ebook)

Wangari Maathai

Visionary, Environmental Leader, Political Activist

*

NAMULUNDAH FLORENCE

*

"It will come to pass."
—*Wanami Lyambila, Bukusu seer*

LANTERN BOOKS • NEW YORK
A Division of Booklight, Inc.

2014
LANTERN BOOKS
128 Second Place, Brooklyn, NY 11231
www.lanternbooks.com

Copyright © 2014 by Namulundah Florence

Printed in the United States of America

LIBRARY OF CONGRESS CATALOGING-IN-PUBLICATION DATA

Florence, Namulundah, 1958–
    Wangari Maathai : visionary, environmental leader, political activist / Namulundah Florence.
        pages cm
    Includes bibliographical references.
    ISBN 978-1-59056-451-6 (pbk. : alk. paper)—ISBN 978-1-59056-452-3 (ebook)
    1.   Maathai, Wangari. 2.   Environmentalists—Kenya—Biography. 3. Women political activists—Kenya—Biography. 4.   Women Nobel Prize winners—Kenya—Biography. 5. Green Belt Movement (Society : Kenya) I. Title.
    GE56.M33F56 2014
    333.72092—dc23
    [B]
                                2014016277

CONTENTS

Contents

To my parents, Victoria Namaemba Lyambila and Benjamin George Lyambila,
who took the road less traveled in educating girls and boys alike

ACKNOWLEDGMENTS

I would like to express my gratitude to Nicole Haas, Margaret "Peg" Snyder, Vertistine Mbaya, Cora Weiss, Stephen Phillips, Matthew Mbaabu, George Oloo, George Naholi, Kiama Gitahi, and Mia MacDonald, who kindly agreed to be interviewed by me over the course of three years (2012–2014), and who also supported me in my research about Professor Wangari Maathai. I would also like to thank Mia for reading the manuscript and providing me with further insights and comments. My editors, Wendy Lee and Martin Rowe, and Gene Gollogly and Kara Davis at Lantern Books were invaluable in bringing Wangari Maathai's story to a wider audience.

Introduction

I never met Wangari Muta Mary Jo Maathai (April 1, 1940–September 25, 2011), but, as a Kenyan woman and an academic myself, I was very aware of her illustrious life and career. People who knew her speak of the awe she inspired, while her close acquaintances recall a rare personal touch from a global celebrity. Coming from a background so similar to Maathai's in some ways, yet so different in others, I can only marvel at her achievements and the acclaim she acquired.

Wangari Maathai grew up in a Kikuyu family of subsistence farmers in the Nyeri and Nakuru Districts, located in the east and central highlands of Kenya, far away from my own upbringing in western Kenya's Bungoma District. Her father, Muta Njuhiga, worked for several years in Nakuru for a benevolent White landowner named D. N. Neylan, including during the Mau Mau grassroots uprising against the colonial administration that took place from 1952 to 1960. According to her memoir, *Unbowed* (2006), Maathai became aware of racial disparities, of the lives of privileged Whites in a predominantly Black country, during her childhood. She recalled the shock of peering into the closet of Neylan's daughter to see a line of clothes, since she herself had only two or three dresses at the time.

I could understand Maathai's reaction. Recently, as I was talking with a colleague at Brooklyn College in New York City where I teach, I couldn't recall any mementos from my childhood. He was shocked. "But you must have had a room, some space to store or hide the things you valued, like dolls," he volunteered. "No," I responded. "We shared the available, limited space and still do." One never slept in the same place or position (near the door, close to the wall, or in the middle) long enough to lay claim to it. I don't even remember locking up my suitcase of boarding-school supplies during the holidays.

My ancestors' encounters with Whites date back to the Bukusu resistance in the legendary Chetambe War of 1895, in which my great-grandfather, Lyambila Omuyaya, served as a human shield (Makila 1978). (Bukusus are an ethnic sub-group of the Luhya people.) Rather than living as a sharecropper on a White-owned farm, my migrant father worked in the towns of Kakamega, Kisii, Nairobi, and Londiani, locations far removed from immediate family and familiar tongues. When I was growing up, there was sporadic strife with neighboring Teso groups over land, cattle, and water sources. Mostly, I was surrounded by people who spoke my mother tongue, Bukusu, until I attended boarding school about 250 kilometers away from home. As the sole Luhya student, I bonded with the sole Kikuyu student in a school dominated by the Luo and Kisii ethnic groups.

Most of all, Maathai and I are linked through the impact of education on our lives. Education transformed village girls like us into college professors, a status far beyond our dreams. We were shaped by Catholic religious sisters, who drew us into a web of knowledge and steeped us in lives of service in gratitude for that which the good Lord endowed us with. Education and international travel epitomized and spurred on our transition to a new identity as Christians and scholars.

Wangari Maathai: Visionary, Environmental Leader, Political Activist charts my search for, and "encounter" with, the Professor. Part of my fascination with Maathai is how she was at once personable and approachable, and yet, to her opponents, could be radical and challenging. Her longtime colleague and friend Professor Vertistine Mbaya told me how much she admired Maathai's ability to communicate with people across social classes. She admitted that Maathai avoided offending people, even though it occasionally meant that she minimized the severity of the offenses these people had committed. Maathai also touted a servant-leadership model embodied in her father and Kenya's freedom fighters; and the regime against which she fought viewed her autonomy as misplaced. In transgressing prevailing social roles and mobilizing the masses, the administration argued, she created social unrest and political instability.

Like the trees she labored to plant out of love and concern for people and the earth that nurtured her, Maathai's achievements continue to flourish. This is a woman who sought out and journeyed along a trajectory of care and activism, beginning with her Kenyan roots, then through her education, her activism, and her role in politics. Her ongoing struggles with the Kenyan regime illustrate the price of these choices.

In my attempt to understand the origins of this compassion and activism, I explore Maathai's heritage and early education in Nyeri and Limuru, and then overseas. I investigate why her university tenure and trailblazing role as the first woman in East and Central Africa to earn a Ph.D. (in 1971) have been overshadowed by her activism. Academic success set Maathai apart from her peers and put her on a course that many found threatening in a woman. During a much-publicized and humiliating divorce proceeding, her former husband, Mwangi Mathai, was reported by the Kenyan media to have accused his wife of being too strong-minded, too successful, too educated, and too hard to control. The fact that Maathai began her political career in 1979, after her divorce, made me want to comprehend how she reconciled her marital life with her career aspirations.

Maathai's life and work demonstrated how a consciousness that allows for political and economic domination and one that permits the exploitation of nature are inextricably linked, and that, conversely, political and economic freedom should be embedded in conservation and sustainability. How intertwined were the political and environmental facets of her life and work is illustrated by the fact that most of the international awards Wangari Maathai received, including the 2004 Nobel Peace Prize, stemmed from her establishment of the Green Belt Movement in 1977. The environment infused her rhetoric: In public statements, she used the imagery of trees rooted in the earth, birds taking shelter in their branches, and fish that flourish in running waters where children play. Hers was, writes Ellen Gorsevski, "the physical, lived world of earthly existence" (2012) that people know and care about. Perhaps more than anyone else, Maathai felt deeply that relations between people mirror similar relations with the environment; the loss of one impacts the other's existence. Like her, I have watched women's identities be transformed as they gain greater influence on land use and its production.

The Green Belt Movement propelled Maathai into the political arena as the voice for generations of independent women who sought greater empowerment. The tree was, and is, the perfect metaphor for individual, grassroots efforts that in their small, peaceful way can bring about social change where top–down government solutions cannot. In her activism, Maathai broke the silence on Kenya's pervasive fear of Daniel arap Moi's government (1978–2002). Her individual courage and activism remain a rare combination in Kenyan politics.

The accolades following Maathai's death in 2011 demonstrate the impact of her life, the Green Belt Movement, and her vision for social transformation. Maathai was true to her roots, which is perhaps why she achieved so much. She understood that activism needs to be a part of people's everyday life—that the only way to be successful is to help people see that their agency can make a difference in their lives. So simple, and yet so powerful.

In addition to my personal search for Maathai, this book explores her life and work within the context of the realities, influences, and pathways opened for and denied to women who triumphed against tremendous odds. I look at women's social, economic, and political situations in Kenya, Africa, and other parts of the developing world (or Global South), and examine gender relations and the access men and women have to political power, natural resources, education, and participation in cultural conversations surrounding these and other issues.

As I show, Maathai's life and career mirrored the complexities of African women as their nation states maneuvered their way from colonialism to independence; the balance between indigenous cultural norms and the attractions and claims of modernity; the shift to and from rural and urban identities; the expectations placed upon girls and women by their class, region, and ethnic heritage; and the always challenging negotiations between genders regarding what is and is not appropriate for girls and women to be or do.

My search to understand Wangari Maathai's life, work, and perspectives draws primarily from her books. In *The Bottom Is Heavy Too: Even with the Green Belt Movement*, based on the lecture she gave upon her receipt of the Edinburgh Medal in 1994, Maathai discusses her professional work within Kenya's patriarchal system. *The Green Belt Movement: Sharing the Approach and the Experience* (2003) charts the organization's development and methods. *Unbowed: A Memoir* (2006) is her autobiography. *The Challenge for Africa* (2009) examines the social, economic, and political bottlenecks that have held back the continent's development and provides a manifesto for change. *Replenishing the Earth: Spiritual Values for Healing Ourselves and the World* (2010) explores the values that underpin the Green Belt Movement and suggests how these can be applied to conscious activism and spiritual growth today (Bassey 2011). These books make clear how deeply Maathai's life in Kenya was shaped by the forces of colonialism, urbanization and migration, cultural traditions, religion, and storytelling.

Maathai's life achievements capture the transition from a rural identity to a cosmopolitan and elite persona, in some ways paralleling Kenya's own shift in political landscape from a cluster of ethnic enclaves to colonial, and then post-colonial, national identity. The end result for Maathai and her country of birth has been an uneasy compromise between tradition and modernity, each appealing to what each considers normative during challenging times—a struggle for cultural definition that shadowed much of Maathai's life and work.

I

KENYAN ROOTS

1

COLONIALISM

No examination of Maathai's work and legacy can avoid the role that pre-colonial and colonial Kenya played in shaping her imagination and life. The "ethnic enclaves" that I mentioned at the end of the introduction were, in pre-colonial Kenya, indigenous cultural and political communities that existed in relative isolation from one another. Maathai's Kikuyu grandparents only had contact with the Maasai, a neighboring pastoralist group in the central highlands. Across the country, ethnic groups engaged in livestock rearing and agriculture, practiced mixed farming or iron smelting. Clans produced spears, knives, swords, hoes, wire, jewelry, arrowheads, and tongs, among other items.

Nonetheless, contact *was* formed with other societies. In the early 1900s the Kikuyu to the north of Nairobi traded wood planks to be used as doors for huts made of woven grass, colobus monkey–skin anklets, spears, feather headdresses, charcoal firewood, foodstuffs, and livestock. The Maasai sold livestock products to buy sheep, goats, and skins. Other tribes made pots and baskets and tanned skins. In *Unbowed*, Maathai recalled that her community exchanged sweet potatoes, bananas, green vegetables, root crops, sugarcane, livestock, and land, and intermarried with neighboring Maasai groups (2006). Commodity exchanges of excess produce among neighboring communities expanded to include imported goods from Somali, Arabic, and Indian traders, as well as slave dealers, and, later, European merchants.

By the early twentieth century, Africans' lives had become increasingly dependent on European settlers rather than the ownership and utilization of their own land, livestock, and agricultural implements. Maathai attributed the loss of cultural sovereignty and the depletion of environmental resources to the arrival of colonial settlers and missionaries who introduced a capitalistic-imperialist and cash-based system that displaced traditional egalitarian structures.

One of the first conflicts between the colonial government and the indigenous populace arose in 1895, when Britain declared Kenya a protectorate, began to appropriate resources (first land, then livestock), and conscripted labor and levied taxes (Kanogo 1987, 2005; Mutiso 1975). These taxes had to be paid in cash (rupees, and, later, shillings). The 1902 hut tax on homes compelled families to congregate in fewer huts to lessen the tax burden. The following year, the administration introduced a poll tax to be paid by all African adults. Meanwhile, settlers only paid three rupees per acre to compensate locals: "In the Kiambu-Limuru areas about 60,000 acres of Kikuyu land were alienated between 1903 and 1906," writes Tabitha Kanogo. She continues:

By 1933, 109.5 square miles of potentially highly valuable Kikuyu land had been alienated for European settlement. A register listed 50 Europeans who were expected to compensate the African owners of the land they now occupied with a total of 3,848 rupees to be shared between approximately 8,000 Kikuyu. A further 3,000 Kikuyu living on the land at the time of alienation received no compensation whatsoever. (1987, p. 9)

Between 1905 and 1918, the Kipsigis lost 130,000 acres (52,000 hectares) of land to European settlement. Kanogo acknowledges there were land shortages before 1914; some landless Kikuyu (known as *ahoi*) voluntarily migrated to the White highlands in search of grazing pasture, while others moved to its agriculturally rich lands. Others relocated after relations soured with chiefs or family members:

By 1918, there were about 8,000 squatter families in the Nakuru District alone. Of a population of 9,116 Africans in the Naivasha District, 6,600 belonged to almost exclusively Kikuyu squatter families. . . . Unlike the Luo, Luyia and Abagusii contract workers, the Kikuyu labour-force brought their women and children to the settler farms, as well as certain items such as livestock and beehives, which could be regarded as indications of the permanent nature of their migration. (1987, p. 14)

Laborers received between three and six rupees, but most Kikuyu squatters were attracted by the "availability of sufficient land for cultivation and grazing" (*ibid.*, p. 23). Squatters had the freedom to set up "homesteads anywhere within the area the settler had set aside for them on his farm," in contrast to contract workers "who were housed in (or rather, herded into) wattle-and-daub labour camps (in lines), which the Kikuyu squatters derogatorily referred to as *maskini* (poverty stricken). This consideration for the squatter's individuality played an important part in enhancing the Kikuyu's sense of self-respect" (*ibid.*, p. 19).

Edward Bever (1996) notes that by 1922, 1,715 settlers owned over 11,375 square miles of the country's best lands, employing 87,000 Africans by 1924. By 1932, settlers' farms averaged over 2,400 acres, and the number of White settlers in the Kenya highlands increased from a hundred in 1903 to two thousand in 1934 and four thousand by 1953. Prior to British rule, land rights within most communities were based on occupancy, cultivation, and grazing. By reverting "unoccupied" lands to Crown land status, the administration alienated fertile lands in the years 1903 to 1911 and the White settlers displaced locals, "including a large number who were forcibly relocated to the Rift Valley," where Maathai's family resided (Maathai 2006, p. 10).

In 1911, there were only 3,175 Europeans in Kenya. By 1948, this number had increased to an estimated 30,000, relative to 98,000 Asians and 5.2 million Africans. According to the Kenya Land Commission, 1,594 families or 7,950 individuals lost their land in Kiambu, and families received compensation of only four rupees for a two-acre plot of land. Increasingly, the colonial office edged out Africans to accommodate the growing White population (Bever 1996; Tignor 1976; see also Coray 1978).

Tabitha Kanogo's interviews for her book *Squatters and the Roots of Mau Mau* (1987) provide a social history of Kikuyu squatters in the White highlands. She shows how colonialism reconfigured the Kenyan landscape and its cultural identity. Government legislation like hut and poll taxes as well as the Masters and Servants Ordinance and the 1920s *kipande* (ID card) system drew in and co-opted the indigenous populace. Initially, the squatters sought to retain their cultural activities, including maintaining their cultivation and grazing practices. However, the 1918 Resident Native Labourers Ordinance (RNLO) transformed squatting from a relatively parallel system of employment to a subsistence subset of the settler government.

Kanogo attributes the political activism of Nakuru squatters, most of whom were Kikuyu agricultural workers, to frustration at the increasingly draconian measures of the colonial government, missionaries, and settlers. During the *kifagio* (sweeping away) of squatters in the late 1920s, the latter lost their livestock. In *Rural Rebels: A Study of Two Protest Movements in Kenya*, Audrey Wipper (1977) suggests that the squatters' taking of the Olenguruone oath of unity and the Kikuyu Central Association oath of loyalty in the years before the Mau Mau uprising were a facet of the squatters' opposition to the government—specifically, the exploitative activities of settlers.

Africans also participated in a money economy in order to purchase mass-manufactured commodities. For instance, Maathai's father, Muta Njuhiga (who was interviewed by Kanogo on November 1, 1976), owned a truck, lands, and livestock. By 1922, Kikuyu farmers from Kiambu and Limuru sold vegetables in Nairobi at higher prices than at local markets. This practice of selling produce in urban centers to a stratified society prevails in the post-independence era.

2

URBANIZATION AND MIGRATION

In indigenous communities, blood and kinship ties create relatively exclusive networks of trust and mutual support. Commenting on the centrality of family ties in indigenous communities, Charles Hobley (1970), an administrator in the British Africa Protectorate, noted: "Family affection is generally a very potent force and, according to the patriarchal system which prevails pauperism is unknown, for any person unable to fend for himself can always look to his blood kin for support, an appeal which will never fail" (p. 182). By the mid-1900s, however, many of these networks of trust and support were under assault from urbanization and an individualized monetary economy. In cities, interethnic interactions and shared living space diffused ethnic separatism.

In the first decades of the twentieth century, settlements sprang up around major cities and towns—Nairobi, Nakuru, Nyeri, Eldoret, Mombasa, Kisumu, and Thika—and along the railway route to which Africans like Maathai's relatives migrated for jobs while Europeans and Asians sought business prospects. By mid-century, 17 towns held an aggregate population of 276,000, including Nairobi and Mombasa, which together comprised 83 percent of all urban residents. The rural-to-urban migration trend persisted and by 1962 urban centers had doubled to 34 with an urban population of 671,000 and an annual growth rate of 6.6 percent.

The 1969 and 1979 population census estimated the number of towns and cities at 48 and 90, respectively, with the highest concentration of people in Nairobi and Mombasa. Nairobi accounted for 70 percent of the total urban population at an annual growth rate of 9.9 percent. The growth rate in urban population in all cities in 1979 registered a 7.9 increase from a decade before. Meanwhile city housing production was below 6,000 units annually between 1969 and 1978 and a total of 7,300 units annually between 1979 and 1984. The urban formal sector provided 44,000 of the 58,000 housing units necessary for residents, typically unaccompanied husbands (many of the bachelor residences still exist). To exacerbate the problems of density and lack of accommodation, the expansion of infrastructure networks—water, sewage, electricity, etc.—lagged behind the provision of housing (Ondiege and Obudho 1988).

The colonial administration seized lands within and surrounding urban centers, citing political insecurity and health hazards. It reorganized indigenous peoples and resources, and redesigned production and distribution processes around international trade rather than utilizing indigenous structures and consumption patterns. By the mid-twentieth century, Kenya's domestic economy had been transformed to make products for European manufacturing industries and to import its consumer goods and machinery.

Nonetheless, city folk maintained their rural connections, traveling to their villages to "collect" food grown by members of their extended families, as a means of supplementing cash income. They also went home in the event of an illness, marriage, or death in the family and, regardless of the occasion, neighbors gathered expectantly for handouts and city news. Maathai's father had his polygamous family, allowed by the African Inland Church to which he belonged, divided between ancestral land in Nyeri and his residence in Nakuru.

John Oyaro Oucho (1988) identifies three primary migratory trends that existed, and continue to do so, in Kenya: rural–urban, rural–rural, and inter-urban. Apart from those from the coastal region (Kwale, Lamu, Taita Taveta, and Kilifi) who move to Mombasa, most migrants settle in Nairobi, Mombasa, and Nakuru (the most industrialized cities). Determined by the availability of fertile lands and economic bases, inter-urban migrations have primarily been from Mombasa, Kisumu, and Nakuru to Nairobi.

Besides the migrations to urban centers, White settlers—growing sugar, tea, pyrethrum, horticultural products, and coffee—attracted workers and squatters to large plantations in the early- to mid-1900s. The migration continued following independence. Between 1962 and 1969, towns holding 10,000–19,000 people increased by 107 percent, followed by those with 2,000–4,999 people growing by 67 percent. Urban centers of over 100,000 expanded by 45 percent. Between 1969 and 1979, the higher pace of migration shifted to cities with more than 20,000 people. These increased by 610 percent, followed by the 5,000–9,999 sized cities, which grew by 117 percent (Ominde 1988). Overall, rural–urban migrations and resettlement schemes strengthened ethnic and cultural integration within Kenya but they also accelerated the commodification of production. The high density of population in one-third of the country that had water, good soil, and forested mountains compounded these features (Maathai 2004).

The migration of families—and especially men—took a toll on the original structures of the family home and community. In her critique of modernity, Maathai blamed sub-Saharan Africa's pattern of "uprooting the African man and forcing him explicitly or by default to seek employment away from his home," as her father was compelled to in the 1950s (Maathai 2009, p. 275), when he was one of 150,000 Kikuyu men who worked as *nyapara* (squatters) in the Nyeri District. Maathai only interacted with him occasionally, since he lived away from the Nyeri rural village. Her father died of esophageal cancer in 1978, but Maathai remembered him as a force of nature: "In his prime, my father seemed like a mountain to me: strong, powerful, invulnerable, immovable" (Maathai 2006, p. 21). Her brother Nderitu, who had some of the father's vigor, could pull cars out of mud spots "*almost* single-handedly" (*ibid.*, p. 12).

Subsequently, associations based on religious affiliations and physical proximity replaced the networks offered by extended families.

Ironically, the Maasai communities, which had limited interaction with administrators and missionaries during the colonial period, now are considered the "authentic Africans" whom tourists patronize (Maathai 2010).

Missionary activity had as disruptive and decisive an effect on communities as did the arrival and land apportionment of the colonial government. In the early 1900s, Christian missionaries isolated converts from relatives and neighbors for fear of compromising their emerging allegiance. Bishop Hanlon, who led the first Mill Hill Missionaries group across Kenya in 1895, created centers that replicated those known as the Paraguayan Reductions of the seventeenth century in which Jesuit missions were designed, Hans Burgman writes, as "huge new Christian communities, where converts built up a completely new world, sufficient unto itself and [with] none of the pagan influences prevalent in the surrounding world" (Burgman 1990, p. 10). The missionaries' policy of separating converts from villagers proved hard to implement in the long run.

The missionaries promoted literacy, which from the outset divided the local communities. Gideon Mutiso (1975) analyzes the origins, development, and interventions among the *asomi* (literate converts, who read the Bible) and non-*asomi* groups in Kenya's nationalism. In the 1940s, Maathai's family was among the *asomi* rather than illiterate Kikuyus who were wedded to local customs and were vilified by the government. What began as an initial skepticism and even hostility between the *asomi* and the non-*asomi* would ultimately coalesce into a solidarity focused on the fight against colonial rule. This distinction has resonance even today, as politicians appeal to the rural and urban underclass, most of them poor and semi-literate, utilizing the rhetoric of solidarity against an elite class that dominates government.

The lives and roles of women were also challenged by the arrival of the missionaries and colonialism—although to what extent remains the subject of debate. Fatuma N. Chege and Daniel N. Sifuna (2006) dispute claims made by the colonial powers that they (the powers) improved the condition of African women, and argue that both the colonial administration and Christian missionaries exploited the prevailing gender hierarchy. In *African Women in Colonial Kenya 1900–1950* (2005) Tabitha Kanogo highlights the overlap between pre-colonial and colonial structures in subordinating women. Men entered the emerging urban jobs market to earn their wages at the expense of the domestic sphere to which most women were confined, mirroring British female domesticity. Missionaries promoted a Victorian femininity that emphasized contemporary Western fashions, etiquette, and housewifery. The educational curriculum for locals primarily consisted of religious dogma and training in manual work (Kanogo 2005; Mutiso 1975): "[T]he boys were taught wagon making and masonry, while girls were tutored in cookery, food preservation, tailoring and laundry" (Chege and Sifuna 2006, p. 27).

Kanogo illustrates a pattern of women's marginality that precedes the colonial era. The Solicitor General in April 1919, Chief Native Commissioner (CNC) John Ainsworth, noted the patriarchal bias in native and customary laws, whereby women never came of age even in marriage. Their lives were similarly circumscribed in Reserves. During this period, the Crown Counsel ensured women's continued marginality in ownership by ensuring that any money they earned went to the parents or the family. Rarely did communities honor women's choices or future aspirations. In 1947, the Local Native Council (LNC) of Maathai's birthplace Nyeri "resolved that 'chiefs should issue orders prohibiting women from entering the Township on Sundays except for the purpose of going to church or for some legitimate reason known to the girl's parents, husband, etc.'" (Kanogo 2005, p. 34).

Kanogo also documents how difficult it was for women to defy the limitations of their society through converting to Christianity and escaping female circumcision, or leaving forced and unhappy marriages. Parents might ostracize them for going to school and entering a public sphere dominated by men. Kanogo tells the story of Serah Mukabi, who took refuge in Thogoto mission station without her father's permission in order to obtain an education; Keran Akoto, who attributed her parents' reservations about education to the threat of modernity, which meant gender equality and human rights; and a Luhya community, which opposed the education of Grace Nyanduga, who graduated as the first Kenyan state-certified midwife in 1957. An educated girl meant that parents lost out on labor and a dowry in later years. Most communities worried that their educated girls would dismiss parental authority and cultural practices, and thought that investing in education was a waste of resources.

Some women did manage to escape poverty, and forced or unhappy marriages, and at times found the freedom that urban centers promised. As a result, communities sought to limit what they considered wayward behavior and excessive liberties in girls and women. Communities and the colonial government retained differences in perspective toward women's empowerment, and proponents and opponents existed in both camps. The colonial government, missionaries, and settler communities avoided confrontations over local customs and laws; yet they weren't entirely unavoidable, since complaints and litigation required settling in the courts.

To some extent, Maathai avoided sanctioned gender roles because of her elite status. However, as Susan Okin (2002) acknowledges, "in many circumstances, oppressed persons, in particular women, are not only less able to exit but have many reasons not to *want* to exit the culture of origin; the very idea of doing so may be unthinkable" (p. 207, italics in original). Women's high levels of poverty, limited access to property, restricted travel beyond the demands of attending family weddings or funerals, and extended family pressures that reinforce a gender ideology further limit their potential to shed prescribed roles. Maathai's Green Belt Movement would serve as an exit point for many rural women. Her educational attainments and campaigns for democracy undermined the prevailing autocratic and patriarchal Kenyan regime.

The period before independence was defined by the anti-colonial Mau Mau insurgency, dominated by the Kikuyu, Embu, and Meru communities. Maathai acknowledged her good fortune in beginning school a year before the onset of the uprising. The resistance that started in 1952 was in response to the displacement and alienation of Kikuyu-majority regions of central Kenya. In its wake, "two thousand black Africans, two hundred police officers and soldiers, and thirty-two white settlers" lost their lives (Shachtman 2009, pp. 26–7). Evan Mwangi (2010) offers higher casualty figures, estimating a loss of 95 Europeans, nearly 2,000 loyalists and 11,503 "rebel" Kenyans. The number of detainees comprised about "eight thousand Mau Mau sympathizers and fighters" (p. 88).

The substantial loss of life among Black Kenyans during the Mau Mau period mirrored the prevailing system of racial hierarchy—remnants of which survive to this day. Colonial Kenya was a three-tiered *de facto* segregated state. Europeans presided over other racial groups. Estimated at 100,000 in number, Kenyan Asians, who occupy the middle rung, currently constitute less than one percent of Kenya's population but play a key role in the economy, dominating the business and retail sector. In the twenty-first century, residences are more integrated, but mixed marriages among Europeans, Indians, and Africans remain minimal. Kenya's 42 ethnic groups comprise about 97 percent of the population with the rest composed of immigrants from Europe, Asia, and other countries.

Maathai (2006) admitted that her elder brothers worked closely with the local Home Guards who repelled Mau Mau infiltration of their village. Charges of collaboration with the enemy dogged Maathai's father because of his close relations with the White landowner D. N. Neylan. At one point, Neylan sheltered Maathai's father from Mau Mau vigilantes. At independence, D. N. Neylan bequeathed Maathai's father 25 acres of land, and may have treasured the friendship of Maathai's father more than he let on. One day, the seventeen-year-old Maathai was arrested and detained as she traveled from her school in Limuru to Nakuru although she had the required pass book. Her release was in part due to Neylan's intervention. Neylan eventually donated a portion of his land in Nakuru to the Catholic Church, on which was built St. John's Catholic School. Some of Maathai's half-brothers and sisters attended the school. Maathai took partial credit for its establishment, following a chance encounter with Neylan, and she herself aspired to graduate studies at Makerere University. Although her friends and teachers expressed skepticism, Maathai was confident of her skills to excel (Maathai 2006).

3

Cultural Traditions

Maathai's primary cultural exposure and later her formal education provided the language, framework, and contacts that supported her vision for social transformation. Recalling her polygamous family homestead, Maathai spoke fondly of an environment that fostered community and creativity as well as trust. Her home felt "secure and protected" by her father's patriarchal presence, although she also acknowledged "that there were conflicts in [her father's] household, especially between the wives, and that my father beat them, including my mother, because when I was much older, they complained. But I never saw or heard about any of this as a child" (Maathai 2006, p. 19).

Maathai felt deeply the importance of childhood experiences in shaping one's identity. She participated in the rites of birth, naming, courtship, marriage, and burial even as she absorbed knowledge of commerce, homemaking, climatic patterns, games, proverbs, and hygiene from her family and society. Her own qualities of obedience, industry, organization, and attention to detail enhanced her recollection of a peaceful existence among peoples, animals, and a natural environment that was active, dynamic, and inspiring. Maathai recalled an idyllic childhood in the Nakuru District. Her mother, she related, loved the land and her people respected the forests, using specific trees for various rituals.

Socialization

Socialization encompasses organized learning experiences through which members adopt conceptual and behavioral standards characteristic of a primary group. Within groups, socialization patterns comprise generations of human experiences and interactions. Specifically, communities socialize members into the histories and legends of their people and provide knowledge for handling day-to-day issues, as Maathai's family did for her. In indigenous communities, although initiates acquire some knowledge in formal settings, most information comes from participating in family and community structures. Family institutions are central to the social, economic, and political organization of African communities, in most of which "family" is understood more broadly than the concept of the immediate nuclear one of European cultures. Maathai's stories about her parents and siblings, relatives, and long-term relationships that developed over the years disclose this element.

Socialization is heightened for Kenyan communities because of their relative cultural isolation from global media. Kenya comprises a wide range of ethnic groups, each of which consists of numerous families. In general, family structures and gender relations replicate national patterns, with males considered the breadwinners and protectors of women and children. In such societies, women are expected to produce children for the *patria* and can only find their identities in their associations with the male as a father and husband (Yuval-Davis 1993, 1997). Women who marry outside the group exchange membership for their marital identity, and children take on their father's names and clan identities.

Kenyan indigenous communities have viewed marriage and family as foundational institutions, an expectation that persists (Ayiemba 1988). In traditional Kikuyu society, for instance, both men and women braided their hair before marriage and shaved their heads completely once they were married. Those who converted to Christianity in the early twentieth century abandoned these rites. Kenyans still derive their primary identity from membership in a family, kinship circle, or ethnic group. Then and now, marital unions unite lineages, maintain links between a community's descendants, and guarantee the family descent.

Before and during the colonial period, the community surrounded a person's life—birth, youth, marriage, aging, death—with ceremonies.

Among Maathai's Kikuyu communities, couples named their children after the grandparents (starting with the father's father), a practice that cemented relations between grandparents and grandchildren through the years. Besides the gratification a child might feel in raising their "parent," as it were, grandparents, uncles, and aunts were doubly attached to the children named after them. Maathai's parents named her after her paternal grandmother, *Wangari* ("of the leopard"), and she prided herself in being as hardworking as her namesake.

Because of their socialization and eventual acceptance of prevailing social arrangements by adulthood, children are less able to envision alternative modes of existence or influence the direction of the group, "including being able to remedy their status and to achieve gender equality within the group" (Okin 2002, p. 207). Even in the birth of a child, for instance, a gender discrepancy opened up. The community welcomed the birth of a baby boy with five ululations in contrast to three for a baby girl.

INITIATION

In Kenyan traditional communities, adolescence remains a definitive and significant demarcation point for youth as they search for their identity and potential spouses. Some indigenous rituals have retained their essential nature even though they have changed in appearance over time or are expressed differently depending on the region. In most Bantu ethnic groups (Luhya, Taita, Kikuyu, Maasai, Kalenjin), scarification experts etch decorative patterns on male as well as female bodies. Among some peoples (Luo, Luhya, Kikuyu, Kalenjin), women remove two or more of their front bottom teeth. Today, the extraction of teeth among Luo and facial scarifications among Maasai and Turkana as well as some Luhya groups are losing their cultural significance and are less commonly practiced.

Circumcision has long served as a ritual for adulthood as well as a marker of one's membership in a community. Clitoridectomy, female genital mutilation (FGM), or female circumcision "entailed the excision of the clitoris and in some cases the labia minora and part of the labia majora as part of a rite of passage" among diverse ethnic groups, including the Kikuyu, Embu, and Meru (Kanogo 2005, p. 73).

In the early colonial period, boys were circumcised and in some ethnic groups like Maathai's Kikuyu community, including the Meru and Kisii, girls were as well. Maathai grew up at a time when her primary community practiced female circumcision. Kanogo (2005) writes: "In precolonial Kenya, the rite delineated right from wrong, purity from impurity, insiders from outsiders. . . . For circumcising groups, the uncircumcised represented the aberrant, outsider, nonconformist, and the unknown quantity to be kept at a distance" (p. 74).

By the early twentieth century, some girls raised in the Anglican Christian tradition declined to undergo initiation, even though the community considered it a central rite of passage, while many Anglican converts succumbed to the pressure and "backslid" in their faith long enough for daughters to be initiated. The colonial administration linked clitoridectomy to "infant and maternal deaths, difficult childbirth, mutilation, reduced fecundity, immorality, and barbarity" (Kanogo 2005, p. 86). Protestant missions demanded that converts renounce clitoridectomy. As early as 1906, the Church of Scotland opposed female circumcision, citing impaired urination and menstruation and obstructions during childbirth. Before the 1920s, the African Inland Church and the Gospel Mission Society had banned members who circumcised daughters. By the end of 1929, all local national councils except Nyeri, Maathai's birthplace, banned clitoridectomies (Kanogo 2005).

The current controversy over clitoridectomy among parents, children, indigenous communities, feminists, and human rights activists reflects long-standing differences about its role in the cultural identity of African women. In the 1900s, outsiders were stigmatized as kavirondo (a region inhabited by uncircumcising Luo communities), msheni (missionaries), and not karing'a (pure) if they stayed uncircumcised. Female circumcision remained persistent. As early as 1903, the colonial administration was resigned to the rite. In the early 1920s, Catholic priest Fr. Philip Scheffer in Nyabururu, Kisii, tolerated local traditions including the circumcision of boys and girls and ritual celebration, and in 1930 the Fort Hall district commissioner brought in a Dr. Miller to train female operators in a milder form of clitoridectomy.

Dr. Kenneth Allen, the station head of the African Inland Mission (AIM, to which Maathai's father belonged), vowed to stamp out Kikuyu practices, which he regarded as incompatible with Christianity. In defiance of the missionary ban on female circumcision, leading figures of the Kikuyu Central Association (KCA), such as Joseph Kangethe, Henry Mwangi, and Job Muchuchu, maintained the practice as well as the drinking of locally produced beer and polygamy. The Maasai also defied the AIM ban on their cultural traditions, which included the circumcision of girls and pulling out of teeth, as well as earlobe-piercing among boys.

Independent schools and churches like the African Inland Church emerged as an alternative to the mainstream opposition to indigenous rites (Burgman 1990). In September 1929, the secretary of the Kikuyu Progressive Party (KPP) condemned the rite in an editorial published in the *East African Standard*, likening it to the bridal burning of Indian widows, another form of "patriarchal subordination and exploitation of women" (Kanogo 2005, p. 89). For girls, repudiation of the practice made them social pariahs. In 1943, Kanogo reports, the Church of Scotland experienced frequent resorting to polygamy among converts. Although Christians condemn polygamy and clitoridectomy, these practices continue in modern-day Kenya, however infrequently and often clandestinely. Sidestepping the historical controversy in her written corpus, Maathai (2004) called the rite retrogressive in her speech on receiving the Nobel Peace Prize.

In the period immediately before and after independence, the colonial administration focused its opposition on the unhygienic aspect of the ritual, as did the organization of Kenyan women called Maendeleo Ya Wanawake (MYWO), which was dominated by British women when it was established in 1952. The organization still advocates for women's issues in health, education, governance, and economic progress. Nonetheless, on the issue of female circumcision, MYWO's record is checkered. In 1999, Ebla Ali, then vice chairperson of the North Province branch of MYWO, advocated the rite's retention on religious grounds. Yet Ali, a mother of two, endured six hours of labor during her first delivery as she painfully waited for her mother-in-law to tear apart stitches made during her circumcision. Shukri Noor, a mother of seven, supported Ali's choice. The chair of MYWO Central Division, Garissa District, Shukri herself underwent a harrowing four-day labor, where the "baby had a cut on the head as my mother-in-law struggled to create space for normal delivery" (Mothers 1999). A prominent member of parliament from the constituency of Kitutu Masaba in western Kenya, George Anyona, also defended female circumcision as a "hallowed" cultural ritual. In contrast, Sophia Abdi Noor, the Director of Womankind-Kenya, campaigns to have the rite banned. Her greatest obstacle has been to convince women that the rite is marginal to one's cultural and religious identity, a position Maathai appears to have supported.

Some Africans view the campaign against female circumcision as a racist intrusion upon African cultural practices. In Ghana, Mark Wisdom, a Baptist preacher and native Ghanaian, openly waged war against purportedly indigenous rituals:

> Mr. Wisdom's campaign against slavery—not to mention witchcraft, demon worship and ritual sacrifice—is emblematic of a much broader struggle taking place across Africa. Throughout much of the continent, from the ritual slavery of the Ewe to female genital mutilation to polygamy, ancient practices that strike both Westerners and many Africans as abhorrent coexist side by side with modernity, and show no sign of imminent abandonment. (French 1997)

As of 2011, FGM is illegal in Kenya, Ivory Coast, Benin, Senegal, Guinea, Chad, Tanzania, Togo, Uganda, Djibouti, Egypt, Eritrea, Nigeria, and the Central African Republic; however, over 85 percent undergo the practice in Djibouti, Eritrea, Sierra Leone, Ethiopia, Somalia, and Egypt, despite legislation. The Kikuyu rural-based Akorino group known as the turbaned Christians of Kenya still practice circumcision of both boys and girls as infants, although some splinter groups have adopted modern elements such as performing the rites in hospital.

Efforts have been made to find alternatives to FGM. A 1997 report featured Julie Kemunto Maranya of Julekei International campaigning in Kisii, Kenya, against female genital mutilation by creating awareness about its adverse impact on initiates. Maranya's organization promotes an alternative rite, *Ogosemia Gwekiare* or "Circumcision with Words," whereby young women receive counseling, training, and information pertaining to their role in society. Similarly, the *Njuri Ncheke* (indigenous court of elders) in the Nyambene District implemented its first "Circumcision through Words" ritual in August 1996 with thirty families in attendance. The number increased to an estimated fifty families in December 1996 and seventy families by August 1997. Other groups have emerged that delicately try to balance competing worldviews (see Path Press Release 1997 and Kisii Women 1999).

Across the country, communities are re-envisioning initiation rites for male circumcision and female genital mutilation. As of 2012, at the Queen of Apostles Seminary on Thika Road, Nairobi, Martin Simiyu coordinates 328 teenagers (234 boys and 94 girls) who completed their KCPE (Kenya Certificate of Primary Education) to undergo a rite of passage under the tutelage of trained peer counselors at a cost of KSh 10,000 for boys and KSh 8,500 for girls. As more parents settle in urban centers, cultural practices and beliefs are losing their efficacy among youth who are divorced from their indigenous culture and language, and yet require guidelines to navigate entry into adulthood.

In 2004, IRAP (Initiation to Responsible Adulthood Programme) was established by Regina Wanderi and fourteen other family life counselors. Wanderi recalls the concerns of parents about youth "caught up in pornography addiction, drug abuse and irresponsible sexual activities"

(Kiberenge 2012). Candidates attend sessions on the dangers of premarital sex "including contracting HIV and other sexually transmitted diseases, unwanted pregnancy that could lead to unsafe abortions, dropping out of school and even death." Traditional circumcisers are also trained by the group (*ibid.*). Although women are gaining control over initiation rites, the issues of dowry and polygamy pose greater challenges. Nonetheless, these emerging cultural rituals honor historically revered practices and are led by interethnic teams, which grant them credibility.

CONTRACEPTION AND MARRIAGE

Organizations such as the Family Planning Association of Kenya, Maendeleo Ya Wanawake, the Protestant Medical Association, the Kenya Catholic Secretariat, and Family Counseling Services Association provide education, contraceptives, and family planning services. However, cultural and religious resistance has made this task more difficult. In the 1970s, this took the form of demands at once religious (God's mandate to multiply and fill the Earth), cultural (failure to name deceased family members), and affective ("You would not be here if . . .").

Religious and cultural figures were outraged at the introduction of birth control pills through the Kenyan Family Planning program in a Nairobi clinic in 1955 with a second opening up in Mombasa the year after (Karanja n.d.). It was argued that contraceptives would undermine social values by promoting promiscuity in youth. Yet when the male-potency drug Viagra came to Kenya in 1998, there was minimal outrage over its introduction or promotion. Evidently, maintaining masculine sexual prowess is culturally acceptable but not protecting women from the consequences.

That apparent bias for what enhances male interest or that of a regime demonstrates the double standards that exist when appeals are made to preserve a cultural practice. This situation is, of course, not unique to Africa. Japan's Ministry of Health and Welfare approved a controversial birth control pill after a nine-year deliberation. The delay angered many women's groups, particularly when Viagra went on sale in Japan just six months after being submitted for approval. Before approving the contraceptive pill, health officials warned against its negative side effects and stressed its impact on the nation's morals (WuDunn 1999).

Both John Stuart Mill (1869) and Okin (2002) view the family as limiting women's freedom of opportunity and the individual expression of talents, including the choice of spouse. Mill's "The Subjection of Women," writes Nancy Hirschmann, attributes women's subordination to "domestic violence, divorce, women's rights to compete equally in the professions, the benefits to society of their doing so, and the questionable character of most claims about women's 'nature'" (Hirschmann 2008, p. 201). Mill's view supports Susan Arndt's (2000) connection of women's education with empowerment, providing what Okin calls "exit options" from oppressive situations. Without the ability to earn wages from their labor, women are dependent on what their husband gives them to sustain them and the children, a situation that the feminist analysis of Chege and Sifuna (2006) naturally considers problematic.

The reality is that Kenya's social and cultural changes have transformed *both* gender roles and disenfranchised women *and* men. Consequently, empowerment programs need to encompass the family as a unit rather than focusing solely on gender roles, which can be subject to the bias inherent in the conventional separation of the public from the private sphere. Nancy J. Hirschmann (2008) and Okin (1994) question the false distinction between paid labor as productive and unpaid labor as not, while Maathai (2009) called for a partnership in childcare in an "atmosphere where gender equity is respected, and men and women share responsibility fairly" (p. 278).

In her analysis of whether women's degree of autonomy or diverse ways of life can palliate oppression, Susan Okin (2002) critiques the liberal presumption that marginalized groups can really leave a collective. She notes that an oppressive system hinders the ability of some members to express vital features of their nature; that the person requires freedom to exit to another collective with a degree of individual independence; and she or he must have the capacity to get there.

Women have less autonomy than men to exercise the right to exit. Indeed, Okin (1994) views gender as a caste-like system. Socialized from childhood through tradition and religious practices into unequal gender relations, few girls or women can envision an alternative mode of life or possess the means to embrace it. Their ability to leave depends on this understanding of the options to exit. Some women only want to be treated fairly within the primary systems to which they feel attached. Typically, less powerful groups rarely enjoy these liberties, nor may they be aware of the illegitimacy of unequal relationships.

Maathai (2009) lauded the election of Ellen Johnson Sirleaf to the presidency of Liberia in 2005 (the first female African head of state) as an emancipating representation of what is possible for women. Since then, other women have attained power on the continent: Joyce Banda assumed the presidency of Malawi following the death of Bingu wa Mutharika in 2012; in 2013, Catherine Samba-Panza was chosen as the president of the Central African Republic in the wake of politicized ethnic violence in that country; and Farou Bensouda was voted in as Chief Prosecutor of the International Criminal Court in 2012. However few, these women are defying inhibiting cultural expectations in office. Yet this progress is by no means uniform. For instance, in October 2000, Muslim women in Nairobi demonstrated against the Kenyan parliament's Equality Bill, which they considered "anti-Islamic," since by allowing men and women equal right to an inheritance or choosing a husband, it would violate Muslim law and tradition in these areas (Sekoh-Ochieng 2000). Ideological differences such as these hinder the adoption of policies that promote or express gender parity.

A Eurocentric feminism that associates women's economic independence with autonomy and entry into the labor force as the pathway to freedom and equality has been questioned by Chikwenye Okonjo Ogunyemi. She observes that despite the possibly marginalizing effect of motherhood, some women prefer the "career" of wife and mother rather than to work for money outside the home. Nira Yuval-Davis (1997) attributes Third World feminists' skepticism about Euro-American notions of feminism to the belief that the former have been dismissed and vilified by their Western counterparts as "frozen" in the archetypal victimhood of barbaric customs (female mutilation) and violent subjugation by men. Further, some African scholars question the relevance of liberal, radical, and Marxist/Socialist feminist perspectives and theoretical frameworks in the African context, although they utilize existing Western literature and terms. They explore the range and complexity of women's experiences to show the inadequacy of "Western" solutions (Ampofo, Beoku-Betts, and Osirim 2008; Arndt 2000; Kolawole 2002; Mama 2001; Ogunyemi 1985).

Drawing on structuralist and feminist theorists, Fatuma N. Chege and Daniel N. Sifuna (2006) highlight the impact of cultural practices, colonialism, missionary activity, and ongoing educational policies on the marginalization of Kenyan women. They argue that, although uncoordinated for the most part, the tripartite "male-constructed machinery" (Nasong'o and Ayot 2007, p. 170) has legitimized patriarchy by sanctioning socially constructed masculine identity and primacy. For women, statutory, religious, and customary laws impose a triple burden (House-Midamba 1996). The predominance of Kenyan male authors and media journalists as well as their access to formal education betray a similar pattern of emphasizing a male point of view on all social matters.

Yuval-Davis (1997) emphasizes that colonialism didn't only subjugate women. Men, she suggests, have interpreted their feelings of disempowerment following their loss of status within the colonized state as "emasculation and/or feminization" (p. 67). This binary vision is complexified by such relationships as the one that Maathai's father had with D. N. Neylan. At one point, Maathai's father gave Neylan a male goat—a cultural signification of honor among friends. Neither father nor daughter knew what happened to the goat except that Neylan did not reciprocate the exchange by returning the front part of the leg to the donor, as Maathai's Kikuyu culture dictated. There was no mention of social bonding between them. Perhaps Neylan's bequest of twenty-five acres of land to Maathai's father *was* the reciprocity.

Balancing the needs of girls and women and the men of their communities can be difficult. Rebecca Lolosoli offers refuge to children and women fleeing forced marriages and marital abuses in Umoja, Nairobi. A few years ago, she took in a thirteen-year-old bride pledged to her own brother, who was three times the girl's age. The men of the village set up a center across from Lolosoli's house, where they advocated traditional gender roles and charged Lolosoli with undermining their culture (Wax 2009). Okin (2002) underscores the predicament of girls married at an early age to ensure their virginity and to accustom the young bride to her marital family. She notes how they grow up with the burden of patriarchal expectations. They are restricted by parents in their choices and yet they are expected to preserve cultures by helping dependents develop cultural identities. On both the individual and community level, women have fought for equal rights, although few succeed in shifting the debate in the way Maathai did. It is to be hoped that Kenya's recent policies regarding gender parity will offer a corrective to women's underrepresentation in national discourses and formal politics.

POLYGAMY

Nira Yuval-Davis (1997) points out the asymmetrical and haphazard manner of cultural change illustrated by the traditional Kenyan concept of marriage. The French anthropologist Claude Lévi-Strauss linked gender relations to social cohesion. He viewed the exchange of women in marriage as an "original mechanism for creating social solidarity among men of different kinship units as the basis for constructing larger collectives" (cited in Yuval-Davis 1993, p. 623). If we agree that this exchange is at the center of social order, then the right to citizenship is really an entitlement that men enjoy. In the *polis*, men define whom to include and exclude, what is acceptable and what is undesirable. Communities with arranged marriages dictate whom their daughters marry. Parental approval, specifically male sanction, is a less subtle way that men control the marriage partners of their progeny (Yuval-Davis 1993, 1997). Maathai's situation was no different. Her father had four wives. Her mother was the second wife. Maathai's mother moved from Nyeri to Nakuru (1943–1947) as her husband commanded (Maathai 2006).

Maathai was as reticent about polygamy as she was about female circumcision, perhaps because polygamy is practiced across the African continent. Communities sanctioned polygamy because children were guarantors of a kind of immortality and the generational transfer of economic assets. A large family was a tribute to the man and his ethnic group, and some women urged their husbands to marry a second wife to assist them with household chores or to avoid the demands of a sexually active husband who might divorce her because she failed to meet his needs. Even Kenya's first president, Jomo Kenyatta (1962), defended the practice, arguing that Kikuyus were socialized to share love and affection.

Wanjiku Mukabi Kabira (1994) presents a very different picture. She contends that Kikuyu folktales depict a contrary reality to the supposed delights of plural marriage—one of extremely abusive and evil stepmothers whose actions result in tragedy. The increase in "official" monogamous marriages and squabbles in polygamous homes may well portend changes to these socialization patterns. Occasionally, first wives are relegated to the margins, sometimes left to fend for themselves and their children.

The idealization of polygamy in African societies overlooks concurrent abuses of the system. Although the number of polygamous families is decreasing, quite a few Kenyan men are known to have *ndogo ndogo* (transient affairs) on the side or keep one "wife" in the countryside and another in town. In February 2000, Akorino musician Ayub Kamau walked down the aisle at the Foundations of the Prophet Church in Nakuru with a bride on either side, antagonizing mainstream Christians. Kamau's wives, Zipporah Wambui and Miriam Wangoi, had ten children between them. Kamau boasted of the mutuality between his wives and their children. The Church's archbishop, Johanna Mwangi, appealed to the scriptures to defend Kamau's position. In Genesis 25, he noted, the patriarch Abraham married two wives, Sarah and Keturah. Kings David and Solomon had scores of wives. The prophet Samuel was born of Hannah, second wife to Elkanah. Also, Jacob (Israel) married two women, Leah and Rachel. However, when widow Joyce Wambui's two male suitors, Sylvester Mwendwa and Elijah Kimani, chose to marry her and help to raise her twins, taking turns to live with her, the decision caused national outrage in a society that legalizes Ayub Kamau's form of marital union (Smith 2013).

GENDER ROLES

Maathai (2006) self-identified as Kikuyu, although her mother was Kikuyu and Maasai. Maathai's mother attended adult education classes that taught domestic skills, and Maathai worked closely with her, shouldering child rearing and domestic chores as the eldest girl. Like many rural women, Maathai's mother worked on the family farm all her life, both while she resided in Nakuru and upon her return to Nyeri where she grew food crops and raised domestic livestock for family sustenance. Later, Maathai's own garden would remind her of what the work and benefits must have been for her mother.

Maathai found emotional support with, and learned social mores from, her mother, as Maathai's longtime friend Professor Mbaya attested in one of my interviews with her:

> Perhaps one of the most vivid attributes I recall about my friend was her exceptional love and show of deference to her mom. She, more than once, related an episode when her mom was hospitalized at a time when Wangari was very young. In her attempt to attend to the collection of the farm produce from their substantial *shamba* [plantation], as well as prepare a meal for her siblings, Wangari found the whole exercise so tedious she missed a visit to the hospital that day. Her mom was quite disturbed by that omission and enquired about Wangari's absence. Wangari managed to explain the situation to her mom's satisfaction. Even so, Wangari still remembered the disappointment of that day at age 50.

Maathai never disagreed with her mother, a crucial trait in her role as understudy of the patriarchal abode. She took comfort in their amiable relationship. Like Maathai, my mother, Victoria Namaemba, referred to by her profession, *Mwalimu*, instead of her name, was a primary school teacher whose life revolved around the farm, students, family, and the extended family. Before sunrise, *Mwalimu* would go to the five-acre ancestral farm, weeding whatever crop demanded attention—maize, cotton, bananas, cassava, beans, and vegetables—in order to feed the nuclear and extended family that frequently turned up for produce and financial assistance.

Not long after the sun rose she walked back home—hands, feet, and ankles caked with mud. There never was thought of a breakfast or packed lunch for her, both of which required firewood for cooking and limited food supplies. She took a quick bath and hurried to school to arrive before eight A.M. At the close of school at five P.M., she came home, changed into work clothes, ate a bowl of porridge, and then walked back to the farm to work until it was too dark to distinguish weeds from the crops. On Saturdays, *Mwalimu* rose early and worked until the sun was overhead and then came home for a bowl of porridge. Sundays were days for prayer and light work—milking, cleaning the house, cooking, grazing livestock, and washing and drying grains. My siblings and I trudged alongside our mother to join other congregants who walked miles to the three-hour Catholic mass.

During school holidays and before most of us moved on to boarding school, we were sleepily and unwillingly shepherded to the farm by *Mwalimu*, where we staked out sections to plow, plant, weed, or harvest in the open sun. In the plowing season, we worked on section after section of land in teams, taking longer on each portion as *Mwalimu* would complete hers and round back to meet her increasingly exhausted children. Harvest time involved hours of uprooting bean stalks, digging up cassava or potato roots from the ground, piling and separating the cobs of maize from the stalks, and then carrying the produce home, the weight determined by our ages. We would dry, thresh, winnow, and grind grains—maize, groundnuts, beans, millet, and sorghum—before they were ready for consumption.

At home, the girls would take care of younger children, hand-wash clothes, and fetch water from the river, while the boys herded livestock out to the meadows kilometers away. *Mwalimu* shared the chore of milking the cows with the younger boys and girls. The extended family milled in and out of the house the whole day, chatting or requesting favors of one kind or another. Like other women, *Mwalimu* plastered the homes with cow dung and kept the compound clean of livestock droppings on a daily basis. She slumped into bed late and exhausted, rolling the beads of her rosary, aware there was always tomorrow and another day of endless demands.

Many of the relatives who came to help *Mwalimu* (with the aim of testing her capability) were shocked at her stamina. Village women rarely dwell on their emotional and physical burdens, at least not in public, probably because their lives are so similar. Their lot is one of interminable, selfless chores, broken only by occasional chances for camaraderie with other women. The housework is endless: children to care for, meals to prepare, grain to be dried and ground for flour, market trips made for groceries or seed for planting, prices to haggle over to avoid going beyond the limited budget. There is no refrigeration. Cooking requires burning twigs and chopped wood in a smoke-filled, grass-thatched house. If the fire is not tended, it dies out and has to be restarted, which is difficult and inconvenient.

My mother's lot was and is not unique. Women and girls still must search for firewood a mile or two into the nearest bush or forest, returning with more than twenty pounds tied up by tree bark on their backs. They still have to walk to the river, the number of trips dependent on the water the household needs for washing, cooking, and cleaning. The river, however, offers a reprieve. It allows village women to stop and chat with other women. They can bathe and try out each other's soaps, creams, and clothes. They exchange news and catch up on the latest gossip. In a world of few radios and no newspapers, this village talk offers women a glimpse into what men, to whom society allows greater mobility, experience firsthand. Young adult males go to the river to wash their clothes or bathe, but fathers rarely do; water is brought to them.

Despite parallel gender responsibilities in the domestic sphere, men like Maathai's father occupied the apex of authority. They headed decision-making bodies in communities, such as the Kikuyu, that manifested more inclusive governance. Traditionally, men herded cattle; they built homes, granaries, and fences; they dug wells and cultivated lands; and they engaged in carving drums, mortars, pestles, and other implements from wood. Gender role–typing is evident in various aspects of social interaction in work, the family, religion, government, and recreation. Yet Maathai focused her critique on the public sphere in which she operated rather than domestic gender relations.

Women's domestic burdens remain as they have been for generations, managing households and food reserves. Despite the changes brought by modernization, particularly in urban areas, their tasks continue to be the same throughout most of the country. Education and the cash economy have made little difference in most women's daily routines. Their contribution—cooking, cleaning, care-giving, and moral education—is not included in international indices of wealth such as the Gross National Product (GNP) or Gross Domestic Product (GDP) (Hirschmann 2008), even though women today account for 53 percent of Kenya's electoral roll. The omission of tasks, traits, and characteristics that society associates with women reinforces their marginality in the public sphere.

Women, not merely the bureaucracy and intelligentsia, create the nation—whether biologically, culturally, and symbolically (Yuval-Davis 1993). They give birth to children and raise them to become citizens of the *patria*. As homemakers, they produce and feed families as well as nurture children in cultural mores. Agriculture accounts for at least 24 percent of Kenya's GDP. However, while women comprise about 75 percent of the labor force in that sector, only 3 percent hold title deeds to land (Chimbi and Okello 2011). Ironically, educated women reinforce this structural gender bias. They can be overprotective of boys and tolerant of the liberties of men. They excuse men's avoidance of childrearing and domestic tasks. Men are served first at meals. Abusive men are portrayed as frustrated, and philandering is tolerated as a male characteristic.

Susan Okin (1994) roots male supremacy and children's view of their role in society in a "learned acceptance of injustice, enforced by male power" (p. 37). Eventually, children are socialized into this hierarchical gender ideology and accept "as inevitable the power of the male family head over many of their activities and decisions" (p. 36). As we have seen, marginalized members of oppressive systems find exits most difficult and costly. For them, the choice is often complete submission or total alienation (Okin 2002).

Analyzing John Rawls' *Political Liberalism*, Okin (1994) observes that family relations are based on affection but should be regulated by principles of justice. Family relations of "naked power and vulnerability" compel the need for the protection of marginalized members. In patriarchal societies, women's lives are "circumscribed and without authority," in contrast to males (p. 29). Society's unequal relations grant males freedom and equality with fellow men but undermine the unity and justice of society as a whole (Okin 1994).

Yuval-Davis (1997) distinguishes between the equality men enjoy in fraternities or the public sphere from the dominance they exercise over women and children in the domestic realm. In *Justice, Gender, and the Family,* Okin (1994) argues that heterosexual couples are characterized by inequality; they are "unjust in their distributions between women and men of work, power, opportunity, leisure, access to resources, and other important goods" (p. 35). Girls grow up in these unequal relations and acquire a learned acceptance of injustice, enforced by male power. In contrast, boys grow up with a sense of entitlement and of the inevitability of male power within the family. Neither gender develops a healthy sense of justice.

Maathai (1994) was as caught up in the politics of gender as the average Kenyan woman and never got over sexism in her country of birth. She contrasted her experience with gender with that of racism in the United States during the civil rights movement. For her, the racist lines were clearly drawn—White on Black: "Several years later I was in the village of my birth and childhood and I was at home with people who were black like me. I was still not o.k. This time though, it was my gender that was the problem. I have since learnt at the bottom of the pyramid there are very strict cultural and religious norms which govern the birth, life and death of women in society. These age-old traditions make the bottom quite heavy" (p. 9).

Elias Ayiemba (1988), Mark Schoofs (1999), and Luise White (1990) illustrate some of the ways women have escaped stereotypical gender roles and expectations in rural areas and have reinvented themselves in urban centers. Ayiemba states that, although marital arrangements in Kenya are relatively stable in comparison to the developed world, urban areas have higher proportions of "never-married" women than rural areas. From 1976, the proportion of "never-married" women, especially among 18–21 and 26–30-year-olds, increased, although that number decreases in older age-groups, probably due to these women's rising educational levels and the impact of urbanization on people's attitudes toward marriage.

Many single women in Kenya's urban centers are divorcées or widows migrating to cities in search of mainstream employment or to become prostitutes. And although women who remain single beyond a certain age have often been labeled rebels, abnormal, and rejectors of society and its customs, in 1984 24 percent of 20–24-year-olds nonetheless remained unmarried. By 1989, the percentage of unmarried women had risen to 32 percent (Gaggawala 1992). Overall, the proportion of women remaining single and the age at which they are first married have continued to increase. Meanwhile, marital unions have become less permanent and stable, the exclusiveness of the sexual bond between husband and wife has weakened, and kinship obligations and parental control are on the decline.

The complex choices (or lack thereof) available to women are exemplified by the decision some women make to become sex workers. Deviating from conventional debates that associate prostitution with moral degradation, poverty, the depredations of urbanization, or the breakdown of family structures, Luise White (1990) highlights women's control over the extent, intensity, and duration of sexual relations without having to engage with the puritanical morality of Kenyan communities. Such women earn from their work, which enables them to raise their offspring. Of course, some women are trafficked and enter prostitution younger than the age of consent. But in addition to revealing conventional views that women are victimized and disgruntled, criticisms of female sex work echo the myth that prostitution is a problem associated with urbanization and modernity, that rural life is and always has been a bucolic idyll, and that a return to the strictures and patriarchal authoritarianism of rural life would "eliminate" prostitution.

Prostitution has a long history in Kenya. In the 1890s, a series of catastrophes—drought, famine, rinderpest, and smallpox—among the Kikuyu, Kamba, and Maasai destroyed communities, lives, and livestock. Families pawned wives and daughters in exchange for food, and continued to do so, although before World War I many viewed this exchange as a temporary arrangement. The dissolution of communal land rights and changes in family structures increased women's dependency on male spouses and relatives. Sex workers made life less lonely for migrant male workers in 1920s Nairobi.

Women have long diversified their work through lucrative even if sometimes illegal occupations to support their families. Increasingly, prostitution has become a facet of social life. In a series on AIDS in Africa for the *Village Voice*, Schoofs (1999) reviews the lives of women forced into sex work. He observes that the disparity in conceptualizing prostitution is jarring: it is acceptable for parents to sell off their daughters for a dowry, but abhorrent when the woman initiates that sale herself.

Cases of women's agency, such as in certain sex workers, illustrate an ongoing contest among different notions of what is, or is not, acceptable work for which gender, within the inevitable cultural changes that have transformed Kenyan communities. Such examples shatter "conventional ideas about gender" (Felski 2011, p. 39). When marginalized people voice their goals, however "minimal or discrete," they "raise the specter of a more fundamental change in power" (Robin 2011, p. 5). Once they assume agency, women discover "the idea that inequality and social hierarchy are not natural phenomena but human creations" (*ibid.*, p. 53). The very claim unsettles the old regime and its upholders who lose an illusory superiority that depends on "people who are quiet and deferential" (p. 66).

Elizabeth Minnich (2005) advocates the analysis of the past to recover and affirm women's autonomy. In the case of Maathai and her predecessors, "reworking the past exposes its own hybridity, and to recognize and acknowledge this hybrid past in terms of the present empowers the community and gives it agency" (Yuval-Davis 1997, p. 60). On the other hand, societies tend to portray these autonomous women as an aberration; unnatural, if not witches. Many women's achievements are honored only posthumously, if at all.

4

RELIGION

Kenya contains many religious identities. Among Christians, who constitute over 70 percent of the population, are Anglicans, Roman Catholics, Lutherans, Baptists, Presbyterians, Methodists, Jehovah's Witnesses, Seventh Day Adventists, Mormons, Christian Scientists, Quakers, and members of the Independent African Churches. There are also devotees of the Baha'i faith and, along the East African coast, Islam has been practiced among Swahili-speaking communities (Somali, Galba, Bajun, Mijikenda, Pokomo groups) since the seventh century. Competition for membership among splinter groups is intense, and often descends into sectarian mudslinging.

Before the arrival of Christian missionaries, Kenyans in the interior had organized rituals of prayer and sacrifice to a Supreme Being. It wasn't anything like the Ten Commandments, wrote Charles Hobley, remembering his time in Kenya: "Nevertheless, a code, which adjusts relations between individuals, does exist and, many acts, which are obviously antisocial, are taboo, [as are] also many others, the origin of which cannot be easily understood" (Hobley 1970, p. 186). The focus on social cohesion permeated and directed day-to-day attitudes and behaviors. Maathai's decades-long criticism of politicians' abuse of power demonstrates a sense of justice grounded in a commitment to righteousness. The privilege of a few at the expense of the masses—whether White colonialists, missionaries, or Kenyan politicians—was, she felt, antithetical to traditionally cohesive societies with inherent social obligations.

Kenya's different ethnic communities transmitted moral codes through participation and injunctions. The gods, in conjunction with the founders of clans (ancestors), enforced a scheme of governance based on divine decrees. A community established punitive measures and subsequent purification practices, rites, prohibitions, and ablutions for all forms of evil—ranging from misdemeanors to significant deviations, such as theft and murder. Religious and cultural experts consulted ancestors on worship and ancestral links in the event of a family misfortune, and also communicated ancestors' grievances and demands for appeasement. These intermediaries also presided at sacrificial ceremonies, prescribing the process and chanting the necessary incantations. They employed a variety of techniques to diagnose illness or recommend cures for afflictions. Sometimes individuals or families offered sacrifices in gratitude for a bounteous harvest or family/community welfare.

Individuals could face the unexpected without overconfidence but also without undue fear, note John S. Mbiti (1970) and Laurenti Magesa (1997). Ordinary people attributed misfortune or natural calamities to the displeasure of the gods and spirits due to human infractions. Within family and the community, the appropriateness of social relations depended on age, gender, and social ties. Established hierarchies dictated an indisputable chain of command; children respected adult members of the clan. Hill Bravman (1998) notes how among the Taita in the early 1900s any challenge women and younger men made to older men's authority was viewed as wrongful behavior that "upset" the natural order and wreaked havoc on society, which required appeasement through sacrifice.

Hans Burgman (1990) acknowledges that African restrictions and taboos "ensured a fairly strict morality," but is aware of the prevailing dismissive attitudes Whites had towards Africans as displayed by the Catholic priest Fr. Stam's position, articulated in 1915: "[T]heir capacity for understanding first has to be developed before they can grasp my explanations." They had, however, "blind obedience, and they would plant a cabbage upside down" if they were told to do so. To Fr. Stam, the people seemed lazy; he even called them children, and considered that it was best to treat them as such (Burgman 1990, p. 51). To this end, it was the missionary's calling to "eject the devil out of the African: a devil of ignorance and of hunger, of cruelty and of naked immorality" (*ibid.*).

Jomo Kenyatta (1962) and John Anderson (1970) discuss the role of beliefs and practices in indigenous communities, specifically those Kikuyu structures that guaranteed cohesion and harmony. Indigenous groups censored anti-social behavior and attitudes through a shroud of taboos and prohibitions. Kikuyu communities forbade a *kehee* (young man) from building a homestead of his own or participating in raids or hunts. It was taboo for him to wear his hair straight or to have intercourse with a circumcised girl. He was forbidden from eating certain meat joints at feasts but was permitted to eat birds, eggs, lungs, and shank meat.

Some communities didn't permit women to eat with men, which meant they had to eat in private and after the menfolk. Some communities forbade women from eating protein-rich foods so that (contrary to all evidence) they might more easily become pregnant. In the home of Maathai's friend Julia Ojiambo, females ate chicken, eggs, and some wild game in the mid-1900s, a customary taboo within the community. Retired teacher Marciana Munyendo was ridiculed for eating poultry and even rabbit, which were foods prohibited to women (Kanogo 2005). Missionaries dismissed such cultural prohibitions on women's diets as baseless superstition.

Most scholars argue that the introduction of Christianity to Kenya in the mid-1800s created a major upheaval in cultural communities. Drawing converts away from their ethnic allegiance, Christianity introduced new beliefs, intermediaries, terminologies, roles, and rituals, reflecting European rather than African cultural histories and traditions (Mutiso 1975). In contrast, John Mbiti (1970) contends that Africans only acquired a veneer of Christianity and that fundamental beliefs were little impacted.

How did Christianity spread so quickly? In 1846, Johann Krapf and Johann Rebmann, Swiss-German pioneer missionaries with the British

Anglican Church Missionary Society, established the first Christian mission center in Kenya. Krapf later switched denominations and founded a Methodist missionary society near Mombasa. Although not as effective in converting local residents as later groups were, both missionary centers introduced European-style educational institutions. Later missionaries expanded activities inland, employing government protection.

Early converts at Rabai Church Missionary Society (CMS) were runaway slaves from Arab and Giriama masters. In Taveta Mission, they were political refugees or in flight from famine. Some members of the Sagalla community took shelter at the missionary Wray's Centre following the droughts and famine of 1884–1885 and the 1906 outbreak of bubonic plague. In the hinterland, missionaries initially appealed to chiefs to educate sons as a way of boosting enrollment in schools and churches. Later, they attracted the poor and those, such as twin children, who were outcasts from traditional society. A few enterprising individuals willingly joined mission centers (Anderson 1977).

Environmental catastrophes in the 1890s left communities vulnerable to British and Christian influence. Between 1896 and 1914, the African Inland Church (AIC) and the CMS took in famine and war refugees among the Kamba, at one point rearing sixteen orphans whose parents had died in the famine. In 1908, Kijabe Mission absorbed refugees from oppressive chiefs and at the height of wartime recruitment, in 1917, Tumutumu Mission sheltered draft defectors. Adult men converted more easily than women and younger men, who required third-party consent, typically an adult male. Some females did convert, however, risking social ostracism.

In essence, Christianity became a gateway to the emerging economy (Mutiso 1975). Local converts had access to a literate culture, acquiring marketable skills and a Western worldview. Many were employed as porters, interpreters, domestics, soldiers, artisans, carpenters, bricklayers, stonecutters, teachers, and farmhands besides functioning as a native intelligentsia. Western education guaranteed converts like Maathai social mobility, although the novelist and social critic Ngugi wa

Thiong'o (1997) is dismissive of its benefits and opportunities. To him, the good African exemplified the Christian virtue of spineless humility and a longing to be loved by the enemy. Ironically, a similar reductive stereotype is evident in the association of Westernization with cultural decay by scholars like Maathai, although she was selective about what she opposed.

Imperialists were also ambivalent about conversion. In the early 1900s, Christian missionaries and settlers in Kenya boasted of the spiritual and material benefits of formal education, yet educated locals posed an unending threat to White supremacy: "As time went on, the ideas and ideals of the new elite diverged more and more from European hopes. The newly educated were nationalistic, quite ready to drop hallowed customs and trade them in for whatever was part of modern society. They were not at all altruistic, but eager for power, wealth and status. They did not seem to be grateful for the many things they had received, but were rather cheeky and overconfident" (Burgman 1990, p. 191).

Mbiti (1970) attributes the alienation he sees in Africans to the fact that, he argues, they have been torn from their ancestral life with its historical roots and tradition, and thrust into a technological age that for many "has no concrete form or depth" (p. 3). Overall, Christianity and Islam drew people away from their cult of family and kingship gods and aligned them with adherents of a faith outside their primary family, locality, and often outside the ethnic group. Early converts were viewed as colonial "stooges," hated and despised by other community members.

Maathai (2009) herself recognized the joint influences of cultural practices and Christianity, and questioned the latter for its racist undertones. However, she never resolved her contradictory allegiance to Western influence. She deplored the loss of indigenous African values that were denigrated with the onslaught of Christianity, but distinguished nurturing indigenous values from regressive cultural rites like female circumcision. On the issue of identity, she understood her dual provenance as a protégée of both Africa and the West, and tried to balance between local and international allegiances, her elite status and her humble beginnings. She would cite Christian scriptures to reinforce her appeals for community (Christian charity), servant leadership (Jesus Christ as model), and responsible stewardship of the Earth.

In later years, Maathai would credit her value structure to her primary culture although she patronized various religious centers. Her assessment of religion went beyond Christianity's condemnation of indigenous practices. Culture, she argued, comprises oral and material sources transmitted through the tenets, ceremonies, songs, and stories of the triumphs and troubles of its people across generations. It provides self-knowledge and self-identity. People's participation in cultural rituals cements their identity and provides a sense of belonging (Maathai 2009).

For Maathai, the connection between religious belief and cultural knowledge was most intimately seen in environmental conservation. Cultures encoded traditional ecological knowledge from their day-to-day experiences, which were the equivalents of scientific understanding. Communities identified herbs for different ills or ingredients for foods and distinguished edible from inedible roots (chemistry, biology). They built fires before the introduction of book matches and stoves (chemistry, physics). Crop rotation was a mainstay in African communities (biology, geography). Before the introduction of contraception, local people had ways for spacing births (biology, chemistry). Grassroots resistance like the Mau Mau uprising drew upon historical and sociological processes to reject illegitimate authority (political science). Kenyans had their own system of agriculture, law, and education before the advent of colonialism (Maathai 2006). When Christianity introduced its deities and saints to replace local theological ideas and rituals, it was no surprise to Maathai that ecological and cultural knowledge was lost in favor of contemporary culture's worship of "the gods of commercialism, materialism, and individualism" (Maathai 2009, p. 165).

5

STORYTELLING

One aspect of cultural transmission from generation to generation that Maathai considered very important was storytelling (Vidal 2011). She drew upon stories from other religious traditions that displayed a reverence for trees and reflected her own family and community values. And she often cited Kikuyu proverbs and stories.

In the Kikuyu folktale of Konyeki that she relates at the end of *Unbowed*, four women become enamored of a man who is extremely handsome and a beautiful dancer. He invites them back to his home, but he turns out to be a dragon who holds them captive. The girls concoct a plan to escape. To acquire tools, they ask the dragon for an ax to cut up firewood, which they use instead to dig a tunnel. One girl, however, remains infatuated and marries the dragon. Their baby, Konyeki, grows up to become as dragonish as his father. In the end, his mother tricks and wears out the strength of both dragons in order for her nephews to kill them. In another tale from *Unbowed*, Irimu the Dragon, disguised as a handsome young man, lures children and young maidens to their doom.

Like Western fairy tales, such as those of Cinderella and Little Red Riding Hood, to which Maathai compared these indigenous stories and which did not resonate with her, stories such as these emphasize the consequences of bad decisions (such as gullible girls falling prey to seductive men, and pranks that go disastrously wrong) and are morally ambiguous. The stories usually end on a positive note, with humans consistently outwitting scheming and malicious monsters.

In *Unbowed*, Maathai acknowledges that she learned through another oral tradition: the everyday interactions she had with her mother. Through stories such as those her mother and aunt told, a community, she wrote, transmitted its belief systems, successes, and difficulties across generations. Illustrative of her efforts to raise the consciousness of her listeners, Maathai consistently drew upon two primary analogies that bore witness to her background as a teller of, and listener to, stories. In her discussion of the traditional African three-legged stool, whose seat requires the stability of its legs, Maathai linked the campaign for democratic space, sustainable natural resource management, and a culture of peace to a nation's development: without each in place, everything would fall. Yangki Christine Akiteng (2009) elaborates on Maathai's second analogy, the Wrong Bus Syndrome, familiar to most Kenyans who rely on public buses for transportation. One can get onto and stay on the wrong bus in error and lack the courage to speak out thereafter, just as one can elect and support a corrupt politician in ignorance or fear of subsequent reprisals.

Maathai's resilience rested on her communal interactions and the folk stories of her youth, something that still resonates in the African context. Swedish novelist Henning Mankell writing in *The New York Times* (2011) lauds the art of listening in African communities as a guiding principle that "has been lost in the constant chatter of the Western world, where no one seems to have the time or desire to listen to anyone else. . . . We talk and talk, and we end up frightened by silence, the refuge of those who are at a loss for an answer." Mankell associates storytelling with knowledge rather than simply conveying information, insofar as the art involves people responding to each other's "dreams, fears, joys, sorrows, desires and defeats" rather than engaging in the classical interpretation of reality.

Maathai's corpus of storytelling could be accused of romanticizing the pre-colonial African cultures that already by the time of her birth were changing and hybridizing. She lamented the condemnation of Africans and African traditions by missionaries and colonizers. She regretted that after years of being denied an education and the limited access to professional classes, locals who assumed leadership positions lacked management skills and did little to change the colonial bureaucracies they inherited. Those who collaborated with colonial administrators had the connections and education to assume positions of leadership at independence; meanwhile, the masses remained submissive to authority, often for expedient reasons, such as that their ethnic group was in power. Maathai felt that many *wananchi* (ordinary people) assumed, decades after independence, that issues of public policy were beyond their understanding and so left vital areas of governance to elected officials and church leaders.

One of Maathai's (2009) main narratives was to credit Kenya's Mau Mau freedom fighters and African "founding fathers" with freeing their people from the "yoke of colonialism, humiliation, and exploitation" (p. 28)—an appeal to the symbolism of the Mau Mau freedom fighters that Evan Mwangi (2010) questions, given ongoing Kenyan ambivalence toward the group. Maathai advocated servant leadership that empowered followers rather than exploited their dependency and ignorance. She saw selfless service embodied in Kenyan freedom fighters like Dedan Kimathi Waciuru; dignitaries like Nelson Mandela, Julius Nyerere of Tanzania, and Mahatma Gandhi; civil rights leaders like Rev. Martin Luther King, Jr.; religious practitioners such as Mother Teresa of Calcutta and Archbishop Oscar Romero of El Salvador; and the Brazilian environmentalist Chico Mendes. The force of their exemplary lives changed those around them (Maathai 2009).

The allegiance to orally transmitted cultural histories, however, has an aspect that Maathai did not, to my knowledge, address. Holding the wisdom of a tradition for many years could provide elders with authority at the expense of children, youth, and women. No less inhibitive of social change is the belief that cultural authorities have the sole right to promote the right and good within communities. Presidents Jomo Kenyatta and Moi "assumed a gerontocratic stance and regarded themselves as untainted *wazee* (elders)" (Amutabi 2007, p. 211). The imposition of traditional values can easily slide into indoctrination even if no group within a community holds sway. Maathai (2009) downplayed the notion that the passivity of people or their deference to their leaders was an African tolerance for poor leadership.

Maathai not only drew on stories from the Bible to encourage conservation and self-determination, she, perhaps unwittingly, echoed a tradition of storytelling and tree-planting that is evident in many other cultures. Quaker Henry Van Dyke, the legendary Daoist Tam Yang Bun, the remarkable shepherd and acorn planter Elzéard Bouffier, John Barleycorn in England, Johnny Appleseed in America, and the Swedenborgian nurseryman John Chapman all were known for their planting of trees.

These outsized personalities and the claims associated with their tree-planting walk the line between myth and reality, between tall tale and inspirational and aspirational folk-wisdom. Drawing on his Quaker tradition and *Soul Food* by Jack Kornfield and Christina Feldman, Robert Pierson (2011) argues that questions of the factuality of stories do not undermine their significance. Did, for instance, Martin Luther really say that "even if I knew that tomorrow the world would go to pieces, I would still plant my apple tree"? German writer Martin Schloemann (2005) argues that the statement is "Luther gemäß" (i.e. "appropriate" for Luther to have said), even though it may not be strictly true. Indeed, Tamsin Kerr maintains that stories are less about fact and more about metaphor and motivation (cited in Pierson 2011, p. 154). True or not, Maathai's own stories inspired people to plant trees. And she employed them not only as bonds between her and her followers, but to highlight social malaise (Maathai 2011).

II

THE EDUCATOR

6

PRIMARY AND SECONDARY EDUCATION

To understand the uniqueness of Maathai's educational experience, it helps to examine the economic and social context in which it took place. As we've seen, Kenyan societies initially ostracized those who received a formal Western education. Schools competed against informal family- and community-based education, whereby children acquired indigenous cultural values. Educated girls were considered unsuitable for marriage and educated men labeled traitors and conspirators.

These essentialist conceptions of community and cultural homogeneity, however, covered over the internal tensions of social definitions and conventional practices. Cultural critics have always existed within families, communities, and national arenas—and such was the case in Kenya throughout the colonial period and beyond. Indeed, although Maathai's writings could be seen as an apologia for, and romanticization of, pre-colonial African cultures, she herself acknowledged how the hybrid approaches to defining and transmitting knowledge that she experienced provided a more comprehensive view of the natural world and her peoples than she would have otherwise known.

In the early colonial period, European schools largely trained the elite, before increasing land shortages, a growing population, and contact with Whites heightened the demand for schooling among the larger indigenous populace. In the 1930s, independent schools and churches among the Kikuyu in central Kenya proliferated in response to governmental legislation against female circumcision and the dual school curriculum (vocational education for Blacks vs. liberal arts education for Whites and

Asians). The British significantly increased aid for the economic and social development of natives following the Mau Mau revolution in the 1950s, and indigenous groups initially focused on broadening the curriculum to include literary subjects. When such attempts met resistance from missionaries, communities (primarily the Luo and Kikuyu) appealed for intervention from the government. The establishment of independent schools was a last resort to address local demands for Western education (Bravman 1998; Kaplan *et al.* 1976; Tignor 1976; Swainson 1980). The Kikuyu, Maathai's ethnic group, specifically spearheaded the growth of independent schools in order to meet the growing clamor for an education that was not based at a religious mission.

In *The Struggle for the School,* John Anderson (1970) reveals the varying motivations of missionaries, government officials, settlers, traders, and indigenous groups in the growth of Western education in Kenya before and following independence. As with most studies of Kenya, coverage favors the central, eastern, and coastal regions—areas that experienced greater foreign infiltration and economic development. Nyeri, Maathai's birthplace, had a history of missionary activity; growth of independent churches and schools; displacement and local opposition to the British administration's efforts, including the ban on female circumcision; political activism and representation during the Africanization policy after independence; the education of girls; and participation in the modern cash economy. Perhaps it is not surprising that these areas receive more academic study.

Colonial education registered the existing racial class structure. Not only were educational opportunities for African children limited, but per capita spending varied according to racial group: "In 1950, for example, the government allowed one British pound per annum for the education of an African child, while the Asian had 8.3 pounds and the European had 56 pounds spent on education per child" (Chege and Sifuna 2006, p. 26).

The colonial administration used schools to instill its own values and ensure its predominance. Initially, most teachers were foreigners;

students who were either Christian converts or squatters on White-owned farms, such as the one on which Maathai's father worked, had greater access to schools than others. For indigenous students, the choice of education involved a renunciation of traditional practices, so-called primitive rituals in favor of the Christian Bible and its precepts. Besides the diminution of traditional hierarchies based on land ownership, the introduction of education created and perpetuated class distinctions based on book learning.

The exclusivity of opportunities for a liberal education during the colonial era reinforced its perceived status in most Kenyan communities. Mission centers initially secluded Christian initiates to avoid them having contact with ethnic traditions and to minimize the danger of "backsliding." Kenyans later realized the value of education for social mobility, and among Maathai's Kikuyu community, rich and poor alike increasingly clamored for it, aware of the rewards of a well-paying job and potential escape from rural poverty. Since its inception in the early twentieth century, this kind of education has offered access to salaried or high-wage employment, conferring substantial benefits to families who can afford to invest in a full secondary education, and reinforcing class differences within communities.

By 1967, 228,769 students were enrolled across the country, of which 58,612 were from Maathai's central region—compared to 629 in the north, where the Samburu people live. In the chart "Development of Secondary Schools for African Students in Kenya 1945–1968," of the 601 existing schools, the central province had 165 schools (5 government and 94 community-funded schools) compared to the northeast, with a solitary government-aided school in 1968 (Anderson 1970). To this day, regional disparities in development persist despite calls for national unity.

Until 1985, Kenya retained the colonial education structure of 7–4–2–3, which consisted of seven years of primary education, four years of secondary education, two years of high school, and three to five years of university education. Currently, Kenya has an American-style system with eight years of primary, four years of secondary, and four years of college/university schooling. Education remains highly competitive and punitively expensive despite the introduction of free primary education (FPE) in January 2003 (see SACMEQ).

Parents are calling for the abolition of the Kenya Certificate of Primary Education, citing a disconnect between the official curriculum and the demands of citizenship, particularly its relevance or lack thereof for future employment (Okwany 2013). Critics of the current assessment system offer few remedies that withstand public scrutiny. Kenya needs a mechanism for identifying students' abilities and skills in an increasingly competitive school system. Anderson (1970) acknowledges the ongoing battle over aims, methods, and standards of Kenyan education that preceded independence in 1963.

Currently, Kenya spends about 7 percent of its $32.16 billion (est. 2010) on education in a country with per capita GDP of $1,600. Of the government's education expenditure, 55 percent goes to the primary level, 27 percent to the secondary level, and 16 percent to the tertiary level (see UNESCO Institute for Statistics). The Central Intelligence Agency's *World Fact Book* (2011) estimates the literacy rate at 85.1 percent: males at 90.1 percent and females at 79.7 percent. The primary net enrollments are in the mid-70-percent range for both male and female students. Secondary net student enrollments are in the low-40-percent range (see Central Intelligence Agency), as much due to limited capacity and finances as cultural factors.

Student enrollment has steadily increased across educational levels since the introduction of FPE in 2003 (see SACMEQ). The number of girls enrolled in secondary schools rose from 881,328 in 2003 to 1,180,267 in 2007; however, the figure is much higher for male students. According to Millie Odhiambo (2012) the overall gender disparity increased from 34,926 to 98,519 in 2007. In addition, male students perform better on national examinations; female students account for only 34 percent of the top students. Although acknowledging the impact of poverty on women's access to education, Susan Okin (2002) identifies a gender preference within "highly patriarchal traditions and cultural heritages" (p. 217) across the globe. When faced with a choice of which children to educate, parents give priority to sons, making Maathai's early access to schooling, along with the support she received from her family, a very rare circumstance and one that undoubtedly accounted for many of the achievements of her later life.

PRIMARY

Despite considerable increases in school enrollment for Kenyan girls, few reach Maathai's pinnacle of academic success. In 1931, out of a total population of 3,041,000 native Kenyans, only 101,000 were enrolled in both primary and secondary education in Kenya. By 1949, of a total population of 5,406,000, Maathai was one of only 326,000 Kenyan students in primary school. The estimates for secondary school enrollment that year were 6,000. In 1962, when Maathai was in the United States undertaking her college education, 936,000 Kenyan students were in primary education with 27,000 in secondary education, out of a total population of 8,636,000. By the time Maathai returned to Kenya in 1969 for her doctoral studies at the University of Nairobi, Kenya had 1,282,000 students enrolled in primary school with about 115,000 at the secondary level, out of a total population of 10,943,000 (Mitchell 1998). When Maathai was undertaking her college degree in 1963, the primary school enrollment had increased to 891,553; by 1994, that number was 5.43 million. Government expenditure has always been skewed toward primary education (see Kenya—education).

It was extremely rare in the 1950s and 1960s for rural Kenyans, especially girls, to attend school, and Maathai (2006) always acknowledged how fortunate she had been to gain a formal education. Education for girls, however, was not unknown. In the 1950s, the women's non-governmental organization (NGO) Maendeleo Ya Wanawake, which Maathai eventually joined and headed, had a social club in Ruringu, Nyeri. The club promoted basic education with an emphasis on literacy.

Few Kenyans had the pro-education stance of Maathai's family at the time, as evidenced by the fact that at the age of eight she was sent to nearby Ihithe Presbyterian Primary School close to Kanungu in the Nyeri District. Maathai's father was literate in both Kiswahili and Kikuyu, a privilege to which few Kenyans could lay claim in the 1950s. Muta could also communicate with Kipsigis, Luhyas, and Luos, having picked up their languages at his workplace. Maathai's brother Nderitu campaigned for her to go to school and he later attended Kagumo Teachers College. At the age of eleven, a year before the Mau Mau insurgency, Maathai joined St. Cecilia's Girls Intermediate School, run by Catholic missionary sisters from Italy. The school had a reputation for "good teaching and discipline" (2006, p. 54). Nderitu was more than just a role model, contributing to Maathai's school fees and providing school supplies during his own studies at Kagumo High School. Many families found the tuition of one shilling and fifty cents per term prohibitive in the 1950s.

Maathai (2006) recalled the excitement of her first day of school. An older cousin, Jonothan, impressed her with his ability to write. Maathai ascribed the aura of formal education to the novelty of literacy and as Mutiso (1975) reiterates, its perquisites. Indeed, the Kiswahili word *soma* refers to both the act of praying and reading; to that end, "a denomination that ran the best schools would eventually have the most Government positions taken by its adherents" (Burgman 1990, p. 140). The privilege of the literate over oral traditions and ways of knowing persists in Kenyan society. Although Maathai's knowledge base was primarily experiential and interactive, she embraced Western education—its abstraction and basis in theory.

Maathai's initial instruction in mathematics, Kiswahili, English, and geography was in her mother tongue, Kikuyu, with students only beginning to learn in English after the fourth grade. Although the Kenya Colony's 1949 Beecher Committee's proposal recommended integrating local languages in schools to prepare locals for available jobs, some native Kenyans viewed the report as furthering their isolation from modernity (Anderson 1965)—a reinforcement of the three-tiered social system that privileged Whites and Asians, both of whom learned exclusively in English. The separation of races and disparities in access to education were deliberate policies to reinforce the prevailing racial hierarchy (Maathai 2009).

Pedagogy at St. Cecilia's was completely teacher-centered and limited primarily to rote learning. Students ate what was available, however Spartan the fare. Much as in current Kenyan primary boarding schools, students lived regimented lives of study, work, and prayer with periods of recreation interspersed. Students maintained a spotless compound: they cut the grass, swept the paths, scrubbed the bathrooms, and tidied up the dormitories. Few girls attended boarding school and day scholars juggled the responsibilities of education and house chores (Kanogo 2005).

The Catholic missionary sisters punished transgressors and monitored students' correspondence to prevent relationships with boys. Maathai (2006) recalls one nun accusing a student of lying when the latter mentioned "eating fire" in a letter to parents. For her punishment, the girl was served a plate of charcoal for supper although she had simply meant they she and her fellow students were having a great time (*no turaria mwaki* in the Kikuyu idiom). Students were punished for laughing out of turn or when caught speaking their mother tongue, a cultural denigration mirroring the experiences of Aborigines in Australia, Native Americans in the United States, and the indigenous people of the Amazon at the hands of their White educators.

It was at school that Maathai began to see the schism at the heart of local peoples exposed to Western culture and education. After many centuries of colonization and imperialism, she writes in *The Challenge for Africa*, the conquered peoples defined themselves using the "cracked mirror" of a Western bias rooted in the supposedly superior "power, knowledge, and skills" of the colonizer (Maathai 2009 p. 36). The school's dismissal of students' primary cultures "contribute[d] to the trivialization of anything African and [laid] the foundation for a deeper sense of self-doubt and an inferiority complex" (Maathai 2006, p. 60).

Maathai spoke passionately of the long-term effects of the indoctrination by which Africans seemingly accepted their second-class status.

At St. Cecilia's, Maathai became a Catholic and renamed herself Mary Josephine. She was a member of the Catholic Legion of Mary Society, an organization that instilled in participants "a sense of service and the importance of volunteerism for the common good" (Maathai 2006, p. 60). Her baptism as a Christian and exposure to Western education were double-edged swords, both processes awakening her interest in other cultures and worlds. The perception changed during her studies in the United States, when Maathai began to question the conventional wisdom of White supremacy. Later, she was struck by the loss of traditional cultural elements at the time of her mother's death. To her, people seemed increasingly to be divorced from each other and from the environment. Yet she recognized that she herself was a product of the very factors she disassociated herself from.

An attentive listener, Maathai (2006) focused on lessons and regurgitated the information during examinations, like many of her Kenyan compatriots from oral cultures who found literacy fascinating. She graduated at the top of her class at the end of Standard Eight with fond memories of St. Cecilia's. Teachers recognized Maathai's talent and spurred her on.

SECONDARY

Maathai's (2006) secondary education remains an exclusive privilege in Kenya. As late as the 1950s, attending secondary school distanced students from village life. By 1950, only 61 boys had ever sat for the school certificate of examination, with the number increasing to 1,292 boys and 199 girls in 1963. By 1965, the ratio of students who didn't take the exam to those who did stood at 40:1 (Kanogo 2005). Between 1963 and 1994, secondary school enrollments increased from 31,120 to 520,000 students (see Kenya—education).

Being the only Catholic high school for African girls in the 1950s, Loreto Limuru was cosmopolitan. English was the official language, since students hailed from different ethnic groups. Maathai graduated at the top of her class in 1959, and during her studies, one of her teachers, Mother Teresia, drew her into chemistry and biology science projects. The headmistress, Mother Colombière, supported Maathai's academic pursuits and these personal relationships helped Maathai stay focused on her studies. In addition to nurturing Maathai's love of science, the Catholic missionary sisters also instilled in her a sense of God's goodness and the call to service for the common good, the very qualities that infused her commitment to social transformation.

Dr. Julia Ojiambo's friendship with Maathai dates back to 1954 when both sat for national examinations. While Maathai studied at Loreto Limuru, Dr. Ojiambo was in Alliance Girls High School, another school renowned for excellent academic results. Decades later, Dr. Ojiambo recalled the cultural denigration of women in an interview: "To our community, a girl [was] nothing. There is no way any normal man would invest in a girl. . . . [I]n our tradition girls were called frogs" (cited in Kanogo 2005, p. 210).

Dr. Ojiambo is referring to two Samia community proverbs: 1) The harshness of a frog or toad cannot prevent a cow from drinking water (*obwalaba bwe rihere sibwakayira ingombe okhungwa amachi*), and 2) The croaking of a frog or toad cannot prevent a cow from drinking water (*obuyoka bwe rihere sibwakayira ingombe okhungwa amachi*). These proverbs depict power relations between a cow and frog at a drinking well. The latter may be the resident of the site and even croak more frequently but it is insignificant in the presence of a cow; it cannot prevent a cow from drinking water.

Dr. Ojiambo explained how society saw women as "submerged objects," such as frogs in a pool of water. Women, like frogs, make noise in an enclosed environment. They are confined to domesticity, restricted by culture and the expectations of their roles. Women can cry, sing, and talk among themselves in the background of their limited spaces, like frogs in a pool of water; however, they have no political space or social platform to air their views. The analogy debases womanhood and dehumanizes the gender, even though communities benefit from a girl's dowry upon marriage and, later, her employment, although they may refuse to invest in her education.

What further drew Maathai and Dr. Ojiambo together was that they were labeled "boring" and "bookworm-type girls." They prepared for exams as science lovers and excelled (Obonyo 2011a). At the time, those who entered the elite class of educated women had few prospects of a career, which was limited to nursing or teaching.

The visibility and advocacy of women like Maathai have highlighted the predicament of the girl child in Kenya's male-dominated society. Kenyan girls don't go to school at significant rates due to a patriarchal preference for educating boys, and still more girls miss school to avoid humiliation and harassment during menstruation. Eventually, girls drop out of school completely, increasing their chances of engaging in prostitution or marrying early. The limited availability of contraception, as well as ignorance of safe-sex practices, force teenage girls into unsafe abortions, some of which result in infertility and death (Mungai 2011).

Ongoing grassroots and national efforts are addressing the issue in Kenya. In collaboration with the 2006 Girl Child Network, Procter & Gamble launched a two-year program to supply over 600,000 underprivileged girls with sanitary towels through Nakumatt, a Kenyan supermarket chain (see Procter & Gamble 2006; 2013). To be able to attend school during one's menstrual cycle is a privilege long coveted by many Kenyan girls. The Budalang'i District in western Kenya recruited 15 teachers to help students make reusable napkins to reduce the number of days that girls were absent from school (Ogutu 2008b). Extensive lobbying of the government led to the establishment of a budget for free sanitary pads for schoolgirls (Gathigah 2011), although in late 2013 the government put a price on the pads, further inhibiting female students.

7

College and Graduate Studies

A t the tertiary level of education, public and private university enrollment increased from 452 undergraduates in [Nairobi] University College in 1963 to a student population of 40,000 in 1994 (see Kenya—education). In the run-up to independence, the Kenyan government increased access to education, primarily for men, preparing them to assume national leadership (Chege and Sifuna 2006). One crucial factor in opening up opportunities for Maathai and others turned out to be the Kenya Airlift, which sponsored students for studies overseas from 1959–1960 (see Appendix 1).

Plans for the Airlift started well before independence, when the union activist Tom Mboya anticipated the need for educated Kenyans and received support from the Soviet Union, China, and the United Kingdom. In the United States, a private consortium inspired by Mboya and made up of George M. Houser, Harry Belafonte, Frank Montero, Sidney Poitier, Jackie Robinson, William (Bill) X. Scheinman, John F. Kennedy, and Cora Weiss organized to educate Africans at American campuses.

Scheinman established the African American Students Foundation (AASF) with Montero and Houser as vice presidents. Houser, who turned ninety-seven years old on June 2, 2013, first met Mboya in 1956 in response to a request from Michael Scott of the Africa Bureau in the United Kingdom to bring him to the United States. The twenty-six-year-old Mboya, a student from Ruskin College, Oxford, undertook a two-month speaking tour of trade unions and colleges organized by Houser. The two next met at the All African People's Conference in Accra,

Ghana, in 1958, where Mboya was made chairman upon his arrival at the airport!

Mboya returned to the United States in 1959 at the invitation of the trades union movement. On April 15 of that year, at a celebration of Africa Freedom Day held in Carnegie Hall in New York City, 2,700 people paid to attend and hundreds were turned away due to space. Mboya traveled across the country—New York, Boston, California, and Miami, Florida—speaking at about forty colleges to solicit scholarships for promising students from Kenya, Uganda, and Tanzania. On one occasion, Vice President Richard Nixon offered to drive Houser, Scheinman, and Mboya to Howard University, "where throngs of students, faculty, and some community people, almost all black, were waiting" (Houser 1989, p. 88).

Mboya would make as many as six speeches a day, for a total of about a hundred speeches in thirty-five days. On these trips, he met many trades unionists, such as George Meany of the AFL-CIO, A. Philip Randolph of the Leadership Conference on Civil Rights, and Philip Murray, president of the United Steel Workers of America. Years after their first meeting, Houser still honors Mboya for introducing Americans to the Kenyan situation, successfully gaining scholarships to help train Kenyan labor leaders and building a trade union center, and for laying the foundation for the Kenya Airlift to bring African students to U.S. universities. Houser and Mboya attended Kenya's Self-Government (Madaraka) Day at President Jomo Kenyatta's home in Gatundu on June 1, 1963.

Houser's praise for Mboya echoed the impressions of Margaret "Peg" Snyder, who was then the dean of women at Le Moyne College in Syracuse, and Cora Weiss, the former executive director of AASF: "He was young, dynamic, and unusually articulate," said Houser. "His brilliance as a speaker seemed all the more remarkable because of his limited formal education. A disciplined person, he could work long hours without seeming to tire. He had the unusual quality of following through organizationally, and he kept up a remarkable correspondence" (p. 82).

In 1959, 140 applicants competed for 81 airplane seats. Seventy-nine of the students were Kenyan. Two of the 13 women were from Uganda, whose incorporation was due to an East African organization established to facilitate the process. There were at least four or five non-Kenyans in this Airlift, and more in 1960, according to Cora Weiss. Weiss and her associates introduced Mboya to then Senator John F. Kennedy at Hyannis Port in the early summer of 1960. They had decided to involve the senator after having completed the successful first Airlift in 1959. Hundreds of Americans contributed a dollar, two dollars, ten, or more to underwrite the charter of three planes for the 1960 Airlift. Among them was a group of employees of a Bronx post office who responded to an appeal issued by Harry Belafonte and Sidney Poitier by sending in a list of workers with the amount of each person's contribution.

In an interview I conducted with her, Weiss explained how the organization acquired over 800 scholarships to educate 877 students during the three years of the Airlift. Schools like Skidmore College, Lincoln University, the University of Alaska Anchorage, and the University of Hawaii offered two or more scholarships. Little is known about the scholarships that were arranged by a Unitarian minister in Boston. Weiss recalls being criticized for lowering the standards for scholarships in an era when college was attainable only for a privileged few. Nonetheless, the Airlift was revolutionary in making tertiary education accessible to a mass of foreign students.

Weiss remembered Maathai as one of the beneficiaries of a $100,000 grant from the Kennedy Family Foundation, brokered by Senator Kennedy. In spite of the U.S. government's opposition, the Foundation paid for three Airlift flights in 1960 with the rest of the money allocated to miscellaneous students' expenses. That year, 260 male and 53 female students—including Wangari Maathai in the second Airlift, which took place in September— came to the U.S. Although Kenyans made up the majority of the Airliftees, six countries were represented, with far smaller numbers of students by the time of the final Airlift in 1963: "What had begun as an iconoclast[ic], private moral crusade by a handful of committed individuals . . . had metamorphosed, in just a few years, into a regularized mainstream activity funded by the government and its guarantor institutions" (Shachtman

2009, p. 222). Michigan State University retains documents on the Kenya Airlift in its African Activist Archive.

There is a lack of consensus on the exact total of Airliftees from Kenya and other East African countries to the United States—although a number of 779 has been estimated (Campbell 2011; Maathai 2009). I discussed this vagueness with Richard Knight, the director of the African Activist Archive. It's clear that the absence of a centralized data system has complicated the task. Further, although research has focused on university admissions, some students attended high school. There is little data on the latter group. In addition, no full record of scholarships exists that would enable a one-on-one match. A similar discrepancy emerges in the estimates of scholarships and total monies advanced to students. Some donors didn't report all of their contributions, and some money never came through. For example, the U.S. State Department initially offered $100,000, most probably to counter the Kennedy Foundation's grant of a similar amount. Hugh Scott, the majority leader in the Senate, denounced the Kennedys' grant and the government's pledge never materialized.

Maathai, along with Agatha Wangeci and half a dozen other Kenyan scholarship recipients, owed their inclusion to "interchanges between the Catholic bishop of Nairobi, Mboya, and Catholic-run colleges in the United States" (Shachtman 2009, p. 129). Mboya was a protégé of Father "Barney" Traynor at St. Mary's Catholic School Yala in the 1940s (Burgman 1990). The group lobbied for students like Maathai who were products of Catholic religious–affiliated Kenyan schools to attend Mount St. Scholastica College and its counterpart school for men, St. Benedict's College, in Atchison, Kansas. Kenyan students also coveted colleges like Georgetown, Michigan State, the University of Southern California, Bowdoin, La Salle, Iowa Wesleyan, Moravian, University of Pennsylvania, Morehouse, Tuskegee, Howard, Harvard, Spellman, California State University, Chicago's Roosevelt University, and Cascade College. Students appear to have valued faith-based institutions: those placed in religious-affiliated colleges completed degrees at their initial colleges, while those at secular colleges often transferred out.

In 1959, Mboya picked up 451 scholarships on his exhausting and exhaustive speaking tour of U.S. colleges, universities, high schools, and religious organizations. As Peg Snyder testified during an interview with me, Mboya embarked on similar efforts within Kenya. Snyder joined the Airlift vetting team in Nairobi in 1961. Led by Gordon Hagberg of the Institute of International Education (IIE) and working with Mboya, the team processed the students' applications, verified academic qualifications and other eligibility requirements, and helped those who were selected to acquire visas and health clearances in preparation for the overseas trip. Mboya untiringly knocked on doors and met with potential sponsors and traders to raise money to supplement the Kennedy grant. Snyder recalled how Mboya would arrive at the Equatorial Travel Agency, which had invited the group to use their office, put his hands in each of his pockets, and empty the contents on the desk. She also remembered the exuberance at the airport on the nights the Airlift flights took off. Passengers arrived with relatives, friends, and other well-wishers, jubilant at the prospect of the chance at education for their own. Snyder remembered how mothers and sisters and aunts ululated loudly enough to drown out the jet engines of the departing planes.

The Airlift organizers and its recipients formed lifelong relationships. According to her father's request, Susan Mboya was informally adopted by Fred Burke, who headed the East African Studies Program at Syracuse University, after Tom Mboya was assassinated in 1969. Even today, Dr. Susan Mboya refers to Fred Burke's widow, Carol Sterling, as her American mother. In addition, later generations including Dr. Mboya contributed to the education of fellow Kenyans. Cora Weiss recalls how American activist William "Bill" Scheinman, a longtime associate of Mboya and manager of the AASF team in New York, informally adopted Tom Mboya's family and lies buried next to him on Rusinga Island in Kenya.

In 2007, Cora Weiss organized the first Airlift reunion along with Pamela Odede Mboya, Tom's widow, who was part of the first 1959 Airlift. The reunion took place at a hotel in Nairobi where a family member of the management team was the daughter of a 1959 Airlift couple. In one of the pictures we viewed together, Weiss stands next to three Airlift recipients: Wangari Maathai, Pamela Odede Mboya, and columnist Philip Ochieng. In Weiss' 2007 speech to librarians at the African Studies Association meeting she confessed: "No one ever dreamed how this simple, laudatory idea would rock the boat. . . . The editor of the *Pittsburgh Courier*, P. L. Prattis, wrote to us saying 'the Airlift is truly participating in history and you are playing both a helpful and dramatic role. Someday something like *Exodus* will be written about this undertaking.'"

On the continent, relatives, friends, neighbors, local merchants, and church members contributed at *harambees* (fundraising functions) to educate Airlift family members. (These self-help projects initiated by Jomo Kenyatta continued to proliferate and develop, reaching their peak in the mid-1980s at 15,000–20,000 [House-Midamba 1996].) The Kenya African National Union (KANU), the ruling party under Kenyatta, devoted some funds to training prospective candidates for scholarships. In addition, KANU's nemesis, Oginga Odinga from the opposition Kenya African Democratic Union (KADU) party, also organized travel for students who studied in Eastern European countries, often without government permission (Anderson 1970). Most of the Airlift students were the first in their family to go to college and the first Kenyan-born non-Whites to attend any college. In the United States, many students initially had difficulty in classes because of differences in linguistic patterns and accents, and pedagogical disparities, such as critical reflection versus rote memorization (Shachtman 2009).

Nonetheless, education transformed the lives of many Airlift students, many of whom went home to become the nation builders of newly independent East African countries. Among the female United States Airlift recipients were prominent citizens such as Dorcas Noit, Miriam Khamadi Were, Muthoni Muthiga, Margaret Wachira Giithara, Pamela

Odede Mboya, Josephine Ogalla, and Leah Marangu, who became vice-chancellor of Africa Nazarene University in Kenya (the equivalent of the president of a university in the U.S. system). Florence Mwangi attended Smith College before studying at the Einstein College of Medicine and returning to Kenya to establish the first clinic for women there. Edith Gitau studied in Southwestern College. In 1964, she undertook her graduate studies at UCLA with her husband, James Gitau, a fellow Airliftee. Edith joined the Ford Foundation in 1966 where she rose to be the East African regional administrator during her nineteen-year tenure, after which she established the first private elementary primary school in Kenya, called Akiba School, in the Kangemi District, in 1993 (Shachtman 2009).

Maathai stands out among the mostly male U.S. Airlift recipients who remained in academia, including Maina wa Kinyatti, Frederick Okatch, and Peter Muia Makau of Kenyatta University, Geoffrey Ole Maloiy and Johnston Muthiora of the University of Nairobi, Boniface Nyaggah (California State University), Kamuti Kiteme (City College of New York, CUNY), Samuel Okello-Onyango (Brooklyn, CUNY), the Ugandan Mahmood Mamdani (Columbia University), Owino Okong'o (Great Lakes University of Kisumu), Harrison Bwire Muyia (Wayne Community College), Gilbert Odhiambo Ogonji (Coppin State University), and John Andima (Bronx Community College, CUNY). Barack Obama, Sr. was *not* a recipient of the 1959 Airlift, despite claims to the contrary.

Most of Kenya's Airlift graduates were expected to nurture future generations. In recent years, remittances totaling $12 billion in 2007 from overseas-trained Africans and those in the Diaspora have outpaced foreign direct investments (Maathai 2009). In all, "over 950,000 Kenyans have furthered their education abroad with a majority of graduates from India, [the] U.K., Canada, the U.S., Russia, and Uganda" (see Education in Kenya).

Maathai was not alone among her Airlift compatriots in being transformed by their time abroad or falling foul of the post-independence regimes. Her fellow students also "admired [and embraced] American 'friendliness,' 'industriousness,' 'informality,' and 'interest in the individual'" (Shachtman 2009, p. 208). These qualities undermined prevailing social hierarchies based on age, gender, and class and dented the walls of ethnic enclaves.

Generally speaking, however, Airlift graduates fared poorly in the one area where, perhaps, Mboya and others might have expected them to succeed: politics. In 1974, Mark Ofwona failed in his run for a parliamentary post in Uganda, and Maathai's husband, Mwangi Mathai, lost his first political campaign in 1969. Besides Maathai, George Saitoti, Nicholas Mugo, and Beth Wambui Mugo are among the few Kenyan Airlift recipients who successfully ran for political office. These failures weren't solely the fault of the candidates. The Kenyan state has a history of detaining, jailing, and ostracizing intellectuals who question the system, using mass media to deride their positions and critiques as too foreign. Maathai spent much time "in litigation against the state and in police cells" for her political activism (Amutabi 2007, p. 203), a great deal of which was grounded in her educational experiences abroad and her observations about her homeland prompted by that education.

The effects of the Airlift continue to reverberate across the world. Dr. Susan Mboya carries on the family tradition of preparing Kenyan youth in overseas institutions for leadership positions through the Zawadi Africa Education Fund, which she founded in 2002. Recruiting bright but poor students from English-speaking countries including Kenya, Uganda, South Africa, and Ghana, the fund has brought about 80 female students on scholarships to U.S. institutions like Yale University, Xavier University, and Smith College. The students boast an average GPA of 3.70 with 100 percent graduation rates (see Zawadi 2010).

COLLEGE

The impression Maathai provides of her trip and studies overseas is like that of a child captured by the wonder of a new toy. Another image that comes to mind is one of a child at a first sleepover, suddenly experiencing the unimagined, and trying out skills and capacities that had heretofore lain dormant. Like a light switch, frameworks were turned on and off by correspondence from the old country and interactions with fellow *wananchi* (Kenyan citizens). Old norms were transgressed often, like a background tune that cannot be totally ignored but can be pushed to the back of the mind for short periods. Maathai and her Airlift compatriots knew that, like dreams, the magical experience of life in the United States could not last forever.

In *Unbowed*, Maathai describes the journey abroad as a new birth, flying on a plane across places whose names she'd previously encountered only in geography lessons: Libya; Reykjavik, Iceland; Newfoundland; finally New York City. The plane crossed the vast desert, during which time she slept and woke up to a sight of more sand dunes. On a stopover in Luxembourg, the three hundred Airliftees experienced the novelty of airports and formal dinners. Maathai was later shocked to learn she had eaten frogs' legs, assuming the delicacy was chicken. In New York, the group stayed at various hotels in Manhattan, toured the United Nations, and met dignitaries and other newly arrived African students. Maathai compared her New York visit to landing on the moon. She and her friend Agatha Wangeci walked around in awe, amazed at the skyscrapers of twenty to thirty floors, elevators, and escalators, which she thought of as *irimu* (slithering snakes). In one instance, she lost a shoe in her rush onto an escalator. Maathai and Wangeci were astounded to encounter Blacks in America with similar skin tones to theirs and resembling people they knew in Kenya, but who spoke with a differently accented English.

After a few days in New York, Maathai, Wangeci, and another compatriot, Joseph Kang'atu, boarded a Greyhound bus with seven other Airlift students for the two-day trip to Kansas. They traveled through New Jersey and Pennsylvania to Ohio and Indiana, and were further shocked to behold miles and miles of corn, having thought maize was unique to Kenya. In Indiana, a small café prohibited the ten patrons from sitting at the counter for a drink. This racial segregation was an eye-opener for these foreigners.

Edith Gitau's recollections highlight not only the perverse distinctions made by a racist culture but a lingering ambivalence between African students and African Americans that persists. This was the case even though Martin Luther King Jr. stressed the inextricable link between colonialism and segregation in his correspondence with Tom Mboya, who approached him about underwriting a Kenyan student in Tuskegee. In King's view, "[t]hey are both based on a contempt for life and a tragic doctrine of white supremacy" (Shachtman 2009, p. 78).

Maathai's destination was the all-girls Mount St. Scholastica College, in Atchison, Kansas, which she later noted with pride was the birthplace of Amelia Earhart, America's pioneering female aviator. Maathai was so engaged in college life that she didn't recall "ever being homesick or lonely" (Maathai 2006, p. 79). The Kenyan students were caught up in the country's election fever during the Nixon–Kennedy presidential campaign, with Maathai and her compatriots supporting the Catholic Senator Kennedy, celebrating his win, and notifying friends and family back home about it. Her classes were challenging, but welcome. In one of her letters to her brother Nderitu, Maathai wrote about the classes (zoology, psychology, scripture, English composition, modern European history, and sports): "It's a bit of work, enough to keep my little brain busy" (p. 80).

Maathai's new life in America was adventurous, especially when compared to her Kenyan high school's puritanical aversion to romance. Her Catholic orthodoxy was tested; she began to question traditional Catholic beliefs and practices such as the prohibitions against eating meat on Friday and the celebration of mass in English rather than in Latin, especially when the Church relinquished these practices following the Second Vatican Council (1962–1965). Her Catholic missionary sisters in high school had led Maathai to believe that the Church's precepts were unchanging and supreme. Still, the experience of querying long-held religious tenets triggered much soul-searching in her.

Boarding protected the Kenyan students in the virtually all-White school from the racism of the environs around them, though they also went out dancing in what Maathai recalled were segregated neighborhoods. The Kenyan boys at nearby St. Benedict's College chided the conservatism of Maathai and her friends before they adopted American lifestyles and fashions. Though removed from the rest of the Airlift Kenyans, those in the Midwest managed to attend some meetings of the East African Students' Associations at other schools. Maathai acknowledged the irony of learning more about Kenya from exposure overseas than she had at home.

The changing of the seasons and winter snowstorms seemed like miracles to the Kenyans, who longed for the moderate year-round temperatures of the Kenyan highlands. Maathai's friends remembered her delight in the "novelty of falling leaves and snowstorms" (Stone 2005). A friend named Florence (Conrad) Salisbury hosted them at her family's house during Christmas, Thanksgiving, and Easter holidays; this would become a second home. At an International Day celebration, Maathai and other classmates from China, India, and Japan showcased their cultural songs and dances, events that she felt gave them a sense of belonging. Years later, in 2005, Maathai traveled to Japan at the invitation of Mainichi Newspapers and was pleasantly surprised to meet her Japanese "fellow Mounties [alumnae] Shoko Komaya, Grace Mahr, Suzanne Tamura, Sonoko Takada, and Tuneko Shibuya, after a gap of more than forty years" (2006, p. 85).

Maathai had fond memories of Mount St. Scholastica's teachers, students, and their families. The college dean, Sr. John Marie, as well as her academic advisor and mentor in biological science, Sr. Imogene, were welcoming. Sr. Marcella, who taught home economics, helped Maathai and Wangeci make "the most beautiful new dresses" (2006, p. 79) at Christmas, while Sr. Gonzaga enlisted the pair in preparing care packages for schools in the Philippines. A Texan classmate never tired of giving the Kenyan pair presents embellished with the Lone Star. The Catholic nuns at the college helped her and her compatriots acquire summer jobs. Courtesy of Sr. John Marie, Maathai worked one summer as an intern at a tissue-processing laboratory in St. Joseph's Hospital in Kansas City.

Despite a demanding workload and some difficulty in understanding accents, Maathai made the dean's list several times. But not unlike traumatized victims who block out the experience, she fails to acknowledge the racism directed toward the foreign students. In her recounting, Maathai didn't observe the similarities between White racial privilege in her host country and that in her country of birth, Kenya. Nonetheless, as Cora Weiss recalled during our interview, the Southern colleges gave the African Airlift students menial tasks like cleaning toilets to supplement their scholarships. On campus, African students were cushioned from racism because they were an exotic minority; however, off-campus, indistinguishable from African Americans, they were forced to confront it. Maathai's classmate Edith Gitau spoke of being denied service at restaurants and sitting alone in church pews as the demeaned Other and recalled being dismissed racially in Kansas, "until people discovered I was not a Negro" (Shachtman 2009, p. 79).

Maathai's (2006) experiences at Mount St. Scholastica, particularly an encounter with Islamic radicals, triggered a critical re-examination of learned Christian principles and race relations. One time, a Black laboratory technician at the college invited her to a Nation of Islam meeting. The group claimed that Jesus was Black and had attended the University of Alexandria in Egypt (Maathai 2006). Maathai spoke out to correct the fallacy and was dismissed as another indoctrinated African sister. Subsequent to this event, she learned to be critical of religious teachings and felt more tolerant of other faiths.

Nonetheless, Maathai remained deeply immersed in her Catholic cultural education for the rest of her life. In a 2007 episode of PBS's *Religion and Ethics Newsweekly* television show, Maathai is shown speaking to a school on Chicago's struggling West Side, where students had named a garden in her honor, as well as to students at Trinity United Church of Christ in Chicago. At the church she cites Psalm 23 ("The Lord Is My Shepherd") and sings "Amazing Grace" in Kikuyu and English to an audience that included Sr. Thomasita Homan from her alma mater. Sr. Thomasita speaks of Maathai's profound commitment to the world community: "She has listened to people. She has heard their pain. She has listened to the planet and heard the planet's pain. And she has carried that Benedictine value of listening to a point that's worldwide. She's said yes, by my actions the world is my community" (Valente 2007).

In January 2007, Maathai returned to Mount St. Scholastica College, which had merged with St. Benedict's College in 1971 to become Benedictine College. In the mid-1980s, Maathai had missed the ceremony presenting her with the Offeramus Medal, the highest award given by the college, because she was in hiding from the Kenyan state machinery. Sr. Thomasita Homan, who was instrumental in bringing Maathai to the college in 2007, recalls former classmates describing her "as a serious student who knew how to have fun, a forward-looking person who was bright and dedicated" and a former instructor predicting "Mary Jo will go far" (Myers 2006). During her visit, "[w]ith many of her classmates from her graduating class in attendance, Dr. Maathai praised the community and college for introducing her to three of the most important words she lived by: 'commitment, persistence and patience'" (Myers 2007).

I find it interesting that although she lived in the United States in the 1960s, Maathai wasn't engaged in protests against the Vietnam War nor active in the civil rights movement. She had little contact with African Americans in general and admitted having limited interactions with the two African American students at Mount St. Scholastica. In contrast, one of the Black support staff, a Mrs. Collins, reached out to the Kenyan students and even invited them to visit a Black neighborhood.

Tavis Smiley asked about Maathai's experience with racial bias in the United States in an interview in 2009 (Smiley 2009). She recalled with gratitude how she and other Kenyan students had been received upon their arrival in Atchison. In her words, the predominantly White student body turned out to welcome them; yet in the 1960s, people who looked like her were, as Smiley put it in the interview, "catching hell." Maathai acknowledged having lived under a milder form of apartheid in Kenya, although she had been too young to understand the rationale.

Maathai appeared to deflect the issue of racism around White audiences, particularly when she traveled overseas. Focusing on the positive, she recognized the empowering role of education and also urged countries to promote foreign exchange programs to expose students to other cultures.

Graduate School

Before her graduation from Mount St. Scholastica in 1964, the Catholic missionary sisters signed Maathai up for a six-month leadership course at the University of Pittsburgh. She wrote a paper on "helping women in rural areas work together and promote development efforts" (Maathai 2006, p. 92), a strategy she later employed to initiate the Green Belt Movement. Even at this early stage in her life, she was making connections among the environment, women, and development. Subsequently she earned a scholarship from the Africa-America Institute to study at the University of Pittsburgh, earning an M.Sc. there in 1965 (Maathai 2006) and thus becoming the first Kenyan woman to earn a master's degree (Orlale 2011).

In *Unbowed*, Maathai recalled the support of Professor Charles Ralph, who drew her to scientific experiments; first a study of cockroaches, which she despised, and later to a study of the pineal gland in Japanese quails. The examining board judged her thesis, entitled "Developmental and Cytological Study of the Pineal Body of *Coturnix coturnix japonica*," excellent. Pittsburgh at the time was almost a poster-city for environmental pollution, yet it planted the seeds of the Green Belt Movement (Conway 2012). Maathai (2006) acknowledged that the skills of embryology, microanatomy, processing tissues, and microscopy learned at Pittsburgh were pivotal to her later work in Kenya. Awarding Maathai's honorary doctoral degree from the University of Pittsburgh 41 years later, Chancellor Mark A. Nordenberg took pride in the university's role in nurturing the "intellect and curiosity of a very bright young biologist," and having educated her "well and wisely" (Nordenberg 2006).

At Pittsburgh, Maathai perfected a tissue-processing technique unfamiliar to her Kenyan-educated colleagues, which earned her a research assistantship in zoology at the University of Nairobi. Maathai recounts her excitement at returning to Kenya after six years. Emotional as she beheld the country she'd left behind, she found it difficult to identify her siblings and other relatives; everybody had "grown grayer, taller, or thinner" (2006, p. 98). She rented a room at the high-class Stanley Hotel in downtown Nairobi, a place Blacks wouldn't have patronized before independence. But bias, as Maathai found out, went beyond racial differences. Maathai even recalls the date she reported to her boss, a professor of zoology—Monday, January 10, 1966: "To my dismay, without blinking an eye, he had the audacity to inform me that the job had been offered to someone else . . . and that that person was someone from his own ethnic community. To add insult to injury, that person was still in Canada" (2006, pp. 100–101). It was, perhaps, the first personal instance for Maathai of the ethnic and gender bias and corruption in Kenya that she would wrestle with for most of the rest of her life.

Fortunately, Maathai soon got another position with Professor R. R. Hofmann from the University of Giessen in the Department of Veterinary Medicine (Graham 1993; Maathai 2004) under the Nairobi-Giessen Partnership Program. She met her future husband, Mwangi Mathai, who had also studied in America. In 1967, Professor Hofmann recommended Maathai for doctoral studies in electron microscopy at the University of Giessen in Germany under Professor Peter Walter from the University of Munich. Maathai took classes at the Goethe Institute to improve her facility in the language. The German she had learned in Mount St. Scholastica proved useful in working with colleagues and in her later research.

Maathai returned to Kenya in 1969 to complete her studies at what the following year would become the University of Nairobi, which until then had been a constituent college of the University of East Africa at Makerere in Uganda, thus fulfilling her high-school ambition to attend Makerere. She began work as an assistant lecturer under Dr. Nderitu

Mathenge (a brother-in-law to Elizabeth Mathenge, a fellow graduate of Loreto Limuru), the first African dean of the Faculty of Veterinary Medicine. Maathai also lived with the family prior to her residence in university flats where she was a warden for the women's hall (Maathai 2006). That year, she and Mwangi Mathai got married, and a year later she was writing her dissertation entitled "Early Development in the Male Bovine Gonad," while pregnant with her first child. In 1971, six years after beginning her graduate studies in the United States, Maathai earned her Ph.D.

With the support of networks she acquired overseas, Maathai secured a post in the Department of Veterinary Anatomy in 1974 and served as chair two years later, although she wasn't a veterinarian and despite the fact that her male colleagues doubted her skills (Graham 1993). She became an associate professor in 1977, and had visions of rising to a full professor and then vice-chancellor, but she was cautious about her ambitions, given her gender and her being a biologist rather than a veterinarian by training. In the 1970s, Maathai's aspiration to become a vice-chancellor was unthinkable, yet she was otherwise moving in elite circles. She belonged to a number of civic organizations, including the Nairobi branch of the Kenya Red Cross Society, rising to become a director in 1973. She was also a member of the Kenya Association of University Women.

8

ACHIEVEMENTS

Maathai's achievement in being the first East and Central African woman to receive a doctorate symbolizes just how important education is for the empowerment of African girls (Mungai 2011). Maathai herself understood the significance of her education, at the same time as she was aware of the cultural limitations:

> Anxious to be a good career woman and set a good example to fellow members of my gender, students and colleagues who had not worked with women professions before, I did what I thought mattered: I reported to work on time and was both industrious and productive. Upward mobility seemed assured if the university authority would respect what they had written in the letters of my appointment! But the inevitable happened: there was a hurdle which nobody could articulate. It was not an academic hurdle nevertheless. Mobility upwards was too slow. It was as if I did not matter as much as the others. There was something I did not have and I could not have. The hurdle had nothing to do with passing examinations, having certificates of being a good teacher. It had everything to do with my gender! What a discovery! (1994, p. 8).

Maathai's skepticism complicates, even potentially debunks, the pervasive faith held by many that education is the panacea for social ills. She lauded her teachers' service as surrogate parents and attributed her growth to experiences at the University of Pittsburgh that "'nurtured in me a willingness to listen, learn, to think critically and analytically, and to ask questions'—thought processes that had been damped down during her education in Kenya, but which she recognized as being central to what she would be able to achieve in life" (Shachtman 2009, pp. 130–131). She acknowledged the impact of overseas study on her perspectives about herself, others, and society (Maathai 2006, 2009) and noted that travel within the continent had a similar impact. Yet as she conceded (Maathai 1994, 2006), social norms limited her choices and aspirations. Marriage especially appears to have circumscribed Maathai's ambitions and lifestyle.

Most of the professional openings enabling Maathai's advance and achievements were as rooted in happenstance as they were in her resilience and educational achievements. Education radicalized her views of self and prevailing gender ideologies. With so many "firsts" to her name, her role as trailblazer came naturally. In addition to being unique in her earned doctorate, she was the first female senior lecturer, the first woman to hold an associate degree, and the first to chair a department at the University of Nairobi, all of which put her among very few Kenyans in the elite. However, the renown she would gain on the national and international stages didn't protect her from sexism, classism, and ethnic discrimination. She encountered skepticism from male colleagues disconcerted by her academic achievement, and some resistance from predominantly male students in a science department.

Forty years on, Maathai's educational achievements remain remarkable, given the slow growth of progress in educating women in Kenya. The low numbers of females in science, technology, engineering, and mathematics (STEM) reveal poor academic preparation, high drop-out rates, and traditional gender bias. Girls are still perceived as low achievers, and students, parents, and school authorities are justifiably concerned about incidents of sexual violence and harassment, since female students are often victimized by male students as well as teachers (see Siringi 2009). In July 1991, 71 girls were raped and 19 died following a male student assault at the St. Kizito mixed Catholic secondary school in the Meru District, eastern Kenya. Chege and Sifuna (2006) also argue that career training programs and university admission requirements favor students who specialize in STEM subjects, an exclusionary situation compounded by beliefs that women lack the ability to handle such subjects.

Low teacher expectations of students and the lack of laboratory facilities available to female students set girls up for early failure to gain access to university. Male dominance in science classrooms parallels a similar bias in textbooks, where women are portrayed as intruders in a man's world. Despite growing numbers of female students, some families have little motivation to educate girls, since men often avoid marrying highly educated females, whom they view as threats to the long-established patriarchy and their own culturally inherited roles. A review of performance in the Kenya Certificate of Secondary Education (KCSE) shows girls excelling at language subjects (English and Kiswahili), perhaps as a result of the systematic diversion of females into these subjects.

Despite the obvious achievements of Maathai and other female colleagues, women are significantly underrepresented in tertiary education, notwithstanding expansions in universities and colleges within Kenya. At the top end there have been five Kenyan female vice-chancellors (Prof. Rosalind Mutua, Prof. Monica Mweseli, Prof. Leah Marangu, Prof. Olive Mugenda, and Prof. Mabel Imbuga) and just one female chancellor (Prof. Florida Karani) in the seven public and eleven private universities currently existing in the country (Kenyan Women Professors 2010). The relatively low numbers of women administrators is due to lack of political access as well as barriers to their entrance to higher education in the first place.

The number of vice-chancellors indicates that the proportion of girls decreases by 10 percent as girls ascend to the next level of education (Kinyanjui 1978, cited in Chege and Sifuna 2006). More females are enrolled in private universities, which offer primarily liberal arts–based programs and have a predominantly untrained teaching force, but which will accept students who fail to qualify for government-funded universities. The high cost of a private education also works to limit the number of enrollees, and when funds are limited, families still give priority to sons, a situation unchanged from earlier decades.

Reflecting traditional gender roles, women are still overrepresented in Kenyatta University's Home Economics Department, from which they graduate with exceptionally high grades. The low levels of education and career access underscore the marginality of women in professional and managerial employment, though there has been a slight increase in the proportion of females in STEM subjects in recent years (Chege and Sifuna 2006).

Years after Maathai's renown became established, women in science remain an anomaly in Kenyan society. Maathai and Dr. Grace Murila, Director of Kenya Agricultural Research Institute's (KARI) Trypanosomiasis Research Center, have much in common as Kenyan female scientists, both assigning their academic success to good fortune. Like Maathai, Murila credits her expatriate headmistress, Mrs. McDonald, and a project funded by the Slovakian government for encouraging her perseverance, which would lead eventually to graduate studies at Glasgow University and a Ph.D. in veterinary pharmacology and technology.

Although the number of women scientists has risen over the years, most work in universities and not in private enterprise (Mboyah 2011), and many Kenyan women still prefer employment that they believe aligns with childcare—farming, nursing, and teaching, or street hawking. Still, the number of women teachers lags behind their male counterparts: "They constitute about 40 percent of primary and 35 percent of [the] secondary school teaching force" (Chege and Sifuna 2006, p. 131).

Maathai did not publish in her scientific field of study, which would have required analytical review by experts, or write widely in academic literature. Nonetheless, she was a committed and inspirational teacher. She drew upon her academic training as much as her primary experience in rural Kenya in her lessons. She taught anatomy, histology (her specialty), and embryology until 1982 (Maathai 2004). Her classes at the Department of Veterinary Anatomy were made up of predominantly male students and she faced skepticism but, as she noted, the students knew who was boss at grading time (Maathai 2006).

Former students now professors Matthew Mbaabu (1976–1977) and Charles Warui (1979–1980) appreciated learning with Maathai at the Chiromo Campus in the late 1970s. In an interview I conducted with him, Professor Mbaabu recalled an encounter with Maathai that still choked him up years after the fact. Maathai came upon him buried in books in a laboratory over the weekend and overwhelmed with apprehension over a forthcoming examination. She walked over to him and told him to go out and take a break, reassuring him that he would pass and that there was more to life than the test.

Kenya's ubiquitous "chalk-and-talk" approach to education appears to serve prestigious private schools like Maathai's high school well, since the method apparently produces high performers on national examinations. In addition to structural inequalities in teacher expertise and experience, crowded classrooms and resource access, there frequently exists an underside of parents, children, and teachers colluding in exam cheating. In 2013, the Education Minister Mutula Kilonzo announced the arrest of eighty-eight culprits in exam-related irregularities, up from fourteen the previous year. Parents who can afford the requisite KSh 350,000 shepherd their children to "teach-to-the-test" schools, which guarantee high grades and better higher education prospects (Wokabi 2012).

In contrast to chalk and talk, Maathai apparently evolved a participatory pedagogical style that she would employ within the Green Belt Movement. During our interview, Professor Mbaya recalled Maathai's passion for teaching both in and beyond the academy: "Wangari lectured to many who, currently, are senior academics and administrators in most of the universities of Eastern Africa. She displayed extraordinary patience [with] her students. There were a number of days when I stood in the door of the students' laboratory at the appointed tea time . . . with the hope that she would notice me and, perhaps, cut short her penchant for presenting further discussions with the aim of clarifying an issue to the class. Now, I recognize that it was the same quality of patience she employed to mobilize the least informed of the civil society." Professors Mbaabu and Warui recall her passion and kindness in contrast to many of her more intimidating colleagues, who distanced themselves from students. Warui remembers Professor Maathai inviting a student to touch her "mammary glands" when endless descriptions failed to explain a related concept to the bewildered male student. She was unique.

As befitting the affectionate and respectful title "Prof.," which she was given by GBM associates, Maathai continued teaching throughout her life. In 2002, as the Dorothy McCluskey Visiting Fellow for Conservation at Yale University, Maathai co-taught a course on sustainable development, in which she focused on the Green Belt Movement and brought students to Kenya for experiential knowledge. Chad Oliver of the Yale School of Forestry and Environmental Studies described Maathai as "delightful, ebullient, and dynamic" and "a keen thinker." "She is able to look at a cloud of information and cut right through to the core," he added (Vogel and Malakoff 2004, p. 391). Maathai's pedagogical approach in classrooms and, later, GBM's civic seminars, echoed the call from John Dewey, author of *The School and Society* and *The Child and the Curriculum*, to link theory with practice in order to make learning meaningful and relevant.

Maathai (2006) drew on her scientific background to forge her model of social transformation. As an adult she observed the destruction of the natural environment: in contrast to her childhood years, hills were eroded and bodies of water were becoming increasingly muddy. Maathai's (1994) professional assignment in the Department of Veterinary Medicine at the University of Nairobi imprinted on her the significant role that scientists could play in a developing country. In her speech at the Edinburgh Medal ceremony in 1994, she spoke of the linkages among peoples, the environment, and domestic animals in her research in the 1970s, which she argued drew her to veterinary studies. The local livestock industry was undergoing destruction because of a degraded environment rather than "imported exotic breeds and their progenies" (p. 8).

Even though Maathai excelled in the academy, she rejected the widely held notion that education was a "guaranteed ticket out of the perceived drudgery of subsistence farming or the cultivation of cash crops for little return" (Maathai 2006, p. 71)—mainly because she felt that the potential for social mobility that education allowed too often meant that elites denigrated rural farmers, many of whom may have been, as was the case with Maathai, their parents and relatives. Of Kenya's current population of forty-three million, 40 percent are unemployed (2011 figures); 50 percent of the population lives below the poverty line (see Central Intelligence Agency); and about 90 percent of the rural population is poor (Maathai 2010). Of those who are working, 75 percent are engaged in agriculture and 20 percent in industry and services. The large percentage of Kenyans who are farm workers hasn't reduced its stigma as a second-rate career choice, particularly among African elites (Maathai 2010).

Maathai's (2006) entrepreneurship during her university tenure was as pragmatic as it was visionary. Aware of the low salaries and limited employment options available, she rented a general store in Nairobi to provide employment for her sisters Monica and Beatrice. When Maathai and Professor Mbaya won their case against gender pay inequality at the university in 1975, she bought a house that later served as her refuge and the office for the Green Belt Movement.

Maathai's experience in the academy is not untypical. There are thirty universities in Kenya, seven of which are public and twenty-three private. The seven public universities have a total of twelve constituent colleges. The University of Nairobi is the oldest university in Kenya, established in 1960. Kenyatta University College was established in 1970 and Moi University in 1984 (see Education in Kenya). A number of international schools cater to various educational systems, such as the American, British, French, German, Japanese, and Swedish.

In *Uncertain Safari: Kenyan Encounters and African Dreams,* Allan Winkler (2004) writes about his first-hand experience of life in Kenya's universities, on a Fulbright assignment. Moonlighting, he notes, is a regular practice among Kenyan professors at public universities, such as teaching part time at private universities like the United States International University, which can pay lecturers three to four times more than full professors earn in public institutions. Pressured to teach all day and most evenings, few have the time or resources to develop scholarship.

Richard Wafula, a lecturer at Kenyatta University for twenty-two years, knows about financial hardship firsthand. His initial monthly salary was KSh 5,750 ($68) in 1989, increasing to 17,000 ($200) in 2003. In 2006 and 2007, the government raised lecturers' monthly salaries to KSh 57,000 ($671) and to KSh 75,000 ($882) in 2008. Wafula's colleague James Mayaka reiterates the predicament professors face in Kenya. He has been a public university lecturer since 1992, having taught at Kenyatta University before he transferred to Laikipia University College. Despite his two-decade-long tenure, he has little to show for it. Professors train the country's experts but are reduced to living in substandard housing, selling personal property, and acquiring supplies from villages to make ends meet (Letiwa 2011).

Kenya has 352 professors teaching in its thirty universities with a student population of 200,000 (Muindi 2010). In late 2011, about 8,000 university professors brought the system to a standstill in a strike for an increase in salaries, which affected more than 170,000 students, many of whom were about to take their exams. Non-academic staff supported professors from the country's public universities. About half of the students were in government-funded programs while the rest were in self-sponsored programs.

Lecturers teaching general courses serve about 1,000 students, large class sizes that limit any teacher's ability to engage students. The number of lecturers rose from 7,000 to 8,000 within four years while student enrollment increased from 91,541 to 140,000. The industrial action of 2011 was the third time lecturers had gone on strike in twelve years. In October 2006, more than 3,500 walked out of the publicly funded universities, calling for substantial pay rises and better working conditions. Three years earlier, a work stoppage lasted for two months, and one in 1994 went on for nearly a year. University strikes have legitimized public demonstrations in a country that typically suppresses dissent (Mengo 2011).

To what may we attribute the neglect from scholars, journalists, and others about Maathai's sixteen-year tenure as a biological scientist at the University of Nairobi? Apart from her concentration on teaching as opposed to publishing, we can isolate two factors.

First, sexism. Minnich (2005) and Martin (2007) root inequalities in the historical context of education. Since history records "the public and political aspects of the past," the historical absence of women as authors and objects of study explains their omission and under-representation in a range of disciplines including literature, psychology, biology, and the fine arts (Martin 1985, p. 99). Secondly, those who write about Maathai (including herself) focus less on her academic achievements than on her social activism within the university, particularly the campaign for equal remuneration for female faculty members.

Maathai herself recognized the anomaly of her achievements in a patriarchal society. Leah Marangu of Embu, who won an Airlift scholarship a year after her husband in 1961 and earned a degree in home economics while he earned one in genetics, fended off "criticism from fellow Africans that [she] was pursuing degrees in an unseemly attempt to compete with her husband" (Shachtman 2009, p. 208). Maathai's husband, Mwangi Mathai, reportedly found his wife's independence, education, and success problematic (Maathai 2006), which led to their later marital problems. The regime also vilified Maathai for being too forthright, educated, and uncompromising. Seemingly, critical consciousness and autonomy remain male prerogatives.

As we've seen, Maathai (1994) herself questioned the links between education, a good job, adequate financial compensation, and a superior quality of life. In a patriarchal society, prevailing hierarchically justified cultural relations dictate much of the lives of particular members of a group (Okin 1994; Hirschmann 2008). Conversely, "deviations from prescribed or culturally sanctioned norms or, in this particular case, gender roles and expectations, threaten to undermine the unity and justice of society" (Okin 1994, p. 30). Nel Noddings (1989) admits that women who defy "traditional custom pay dearly in public ridicule and indignation" (p. 80). Western literature reinforces a similar caution. Ogunyemi (1985) notes how the Black female in conventional novels in English has difficulty finding a mate or pays a high price for her visibility. For women, the gender ideology in communities and folktales create a caste-like system that maintains a systematic disadvantage in social status including the "privatized, undervalued, and unpaid or underpaid" nature of their labor (Okin 1994, p. 42; Hirschmann 2008).

Another reason why Maathai's educational accomplishments have been downplayed is her notoriety. In the late 1960s, Maathai lobbied for gender parity in pay and benefits such as housing, health insurance, and pensions for academics. Only single women and widows on the professional staff qualified for housing benefits; the University denied these and health benefits to married women, presuming their husbands would take care of them.

Maathai, along with Professor Mbaya, appealed to staff and the university Academic Staff Association, but they failed to breach class and cultural lines. Junior staff and professors' wives worried about their partners' opposition and distanced themselves from her. Maathai achieved partial success, at best: only she and Professor Mbaya received their accumulated dues, to the exclusion of the other women academics. Both women were treated as "honorary male professors," and African women still remain underrepresented, decades later, in academia. Maathai expressed surprise at the sexism she encountered, although she was making a "substantial contribution to society" (2006, p. 117). She credited her vision and fortitude to education.

In discussing how early feminists traded political ideals for career mobility and self-interest, Verta Taylor et al. (2009) help explain tensions in the campaigns for women's rights. Differences in women's experiences and goals display the diversity of strategies used to resist gender inequality. The urban women who were skeptical of Maathai enjoyed privileges, some of which they owed to benevolent partners and employers.

Overall, gender consciousness increases with women's access to education. Maathai herself embraced prevailing gender roles in her youth and the early part of her married life, only later challenging them. More educated women like Maathai "use men as a reference group when assessing their access to societal rewards" (Taylor *et al.* 2009, p. 557). Chege and Sifuna (2006) decry the shift in focus toward the marginality of women in public employment but not within families. They argue for an inextricable link between gender inequality in public and domestic spheres, and that an exclusivity in focus can be divisive.

The diversity in women's experiences arises from differences in class, ethnicity, religion, and age (Yuval-Davis 1997). Some Kenyan women have power over men and other women (Chimbi 2012; Ombara 2009; Simiyu 2012; Wambugu 2012). Women are positioned differently in relation to women in other societies and to fellow citizens. The female household help (the maid, or *ayah*, in Kenya) faces inordinate challenges even in the homesteads of feminist scholars. In Western countries, female *au pairs*, nannies, and housekeepers are no less marginalized (Yuval-Davis 1997). Overall, societies view women as biological reproducers of nations but their role as cultural reproducers of citizens and nations is sidelined (*ibid.*). Maathai addressed the issue of poor rural women in an abstracted fashion, as though they were victims of exploitation by the regime, thereby absolving by omission women's exploitation by abusive husbands and wealthy women of her class and status.

Maathai's accomplishments are distinctive because they can be attributed to both her formal *and* informal education, what she terms her "dual identities" of Western and African cultures. As Jane Roland Martin (2007) has said, "education is so powerful that it can transform not merely what an individual knows but who that person is" (p. 6).

We can see this trope in fictional works like George Bernard Shaw's *Pygmalion*, as well as nonfiction like *The Autobiography of Malcolm X*, *The Wild Boy of Aveyron* by Harlan Lane, *Paper Daughter* by M. Elaine Mar, *Kaffir Boy* by Mark Mathabane, and *Hunger of Memory* by Richard Rodriguez. In his book, Rodriguez acknowledges the alienation he experienced from his Mexican roots, language, and familial interactions. Mathabane writes of being torn between his tribal roots and the calls of a cosmopolitan, celebrity lifestyle that his friends envy but also vilify. Although unacknowledged, education has always been more than a cognitive experience; it changes lives, sometimes tearing people away from their own identities, as well as the ones they have within their families, histories, and cultures. Malcolm X underwent four major identity transformations, from the model schoolboy to "the Harlem hoodlum, thief, pimp and drug addict," who emerged as a Muslim separatist leader in prison and then a "citizen of the world" prior to his death (Martin 2007, p. 48).

Maathai's education massively altered her worldview. Education inducted her into new activities and practices, shaping what she felt, thought, and how she acted. Her vision for social change built on the ideas and values embraced through her interactions with family, friends, and colleagues. Also present in her academic career was the same penchant toward activism, which undergirded the Green Belt Movement. The academic and social segments of her life, simply put, complemented and enhanced each other, enabling the achievements for which she is known.

III

THE ENVIRONMENTALIST

9

THE GREEN BELT MOVEMENT

Looking back near the end of her life, Wangari Maathai (2010) realized that the achievement for which she is known—the creation and development of the Green Belt Movement (GBM)—was driven by more than passion and vision. In *Replenishing the Earth*, she identifies four core values that undergirded her organization—a) love for the environment; b) gratitude and respect for Earth's resources; c) self-empowerment and self-betterment; and d) the spirit of service and volunteerism—although she acknowledged that such beliefs were not unique to GBM. She also recognized that these values were not necessarily religious, drawing from secular elements (people's experience and climatic changes) as much as spiritual (transcendent) ones. In a similarly syncretic manner, Maathai's concept of the divine drew upon Abrahamic traditions (Christianity, Judaism, and Islam) and what she defined as the "Source" (a place of knowledge and awareness), as well as her traditional Kikuyu philosophies.

Maathai (2007) stated that her vision for social transformation was inspired by the day-to-day occurrences within her community of birth, which created awareness of the importance of tree planting. Maathai's (2006) father planted trees on his ancestral farm in Nyeri and also on the Nakuru farm bequeathed him by D. N. Neylan. Her mother loved the beauty of nature. Maathai attributed her affinity for trees to these formative influences. Traditionally, Africans hold a mystical link to the land and feel an obligation to it and its produce. Among most Bantu groups, the solemn and inscrutable forests were an ancestral abode.

For instance, Maathai's Kikuyu communities worshiped and offered sacrifices under the sacred *Mugumo* and *Mokoyo* trees. Maathai's critique and vision for social transformation also drew upon her primary ethnic traditions, which fostered the values of community, care of the soil, and interdependence between the human and nonhuman world.

Christian missionaries condemned these beliefs and outdoor worship practices. While Maathai lauded the practice of keeping animals in houses, priests like Frs. Bouman and Grimshaw saw it as heathen compared to Christian homesteads, with their religious relics and partitioned houses. Fr. Grimshaw believed that Africans didn't have the natural law written in their hearts like his fellow Europeans (Burgman 1990). Linking the earth, poverty, and care for non-human species, Maathai reiterated the connection between human welfare and environmental sustainability—drawing upon her educational background and her religious beliefs. She worked to raise consciousness that humans were stewards of the Earth, a value that appears in most religious and philosophical traditions.

The concept of a tree as a link between earth and heaven is also central to these traditions. Both the Hebrew and Christian traditions call humanity to practice responsible living and environmental stewardship (Maathai 2010). Creation is good; indeed, very good: "Poetry of the prophets promises both man and land restored, and mythical trees stand tall at the beginning of the Bible in Eden and in the final revelation of the New Jerusalem" (Pierson 2011, p. 156).

Maathai's interest in trees reflected a range of traditions including her own primary culture, although her focus on trees was also pragmatic. Despite crediting Catholic religious sisters for modeling altruistic service, Maathai (2010) discounted the centrality of religion or faith in her creation of the Green Belt Movement. Her motivation, she claimed, arose from a literal and practical approach to immediate problems. In the seminars and workshops she attended, and through her interactions with rural women, Maathai saw their need for drinking water, adequate and nutritious food, income, and energy for cooking, and, in response, initiated ways of digging holes, planting trees, and mobilizing communities to sustain the environment. The forest could also act as a windbreak and reduce the pervasive swirling dust caused by erosion through the roots holding the soil in the ground. Humans and animals could rest in the shade of leaves.

Maathai was not unique in advocating tree planting, although her rationale was. Local communities prepared nurseries that supplied tree seedlings to the rest of the community—as they do to this day. Local representatives monitored activities on the land and paid families for trees that survived. Nor was the use of women unusual. Rural women dominate Kenya's subsistence agriculture: they experience "most directly the fallout from an environmental violence that is slow in immediate drama but high in long-term consequences" (Nixon 2006, p. 18). They are familiar with the growth patterns, as well as uses, of indigenous species and grasses.

The Green Belt Movement's symbolic use of a tree—for instance, to represent a culture of peace during the 1990s ethnic conflicts in Kenya (Nixon 2006)—also had its origins in the past. Maathai recalled how trees symbolized peace within her own Kikuyu ethnic group (Nagel 2005). Maathai planted trees in solidarity with the mothers of detained prisoners who held a hunger strike in Uhuru Park's Freedom Corner in Nairobi in 1992. Eight years later, she opposed the *shamba* system that allocated forests to be turned into cultivated lands—a system that candidates for political office promoted in order to garner votes. However, communities cultivated the land around Kenya's five forested areas prior to colonization in the 1900s (Maathai 2010), while maintaining forest reserves that housed populations of wild animals like leopards, elephants, and buffaloes.

Maathai's ecological vision was holistic. She saw that social transformation linked the planting of trees to planting hope, democracy, and peace. The former became an entry point for a larger social, economic, and environmental agenda (Climate Progress 2011 and Maathai 2011b), for men and women otherwise "powerless in the face of autocratic husbands, village chiefs, and a ruthless president," as Anna and Frances Moore Lappé put it (2004). Maathai's other genius was in connecting agricultural policies promoting cash crops in Kenya to colonial and post-colonial demands on Kenya from imperial and later international institutions to access the country's natural resources. The women's reforestation efforts took on the regime's deforestation at the national level (Nixon 2006).

Maathai saw the Green Belt Movement as serving a vital role in raising the consciousnesses of the people. After years of corrupt governments and the fear of reprisal, Kenyan communities lacked self-confidence and self-knowledge. They also lacked agency. Few Kenyans distinguish the secular from religious in outlook, believing always that "God will provide," or something will occur "God willing," or if it is done "in God's name." Kenyans tend to pray for a solution rather than take on an institution to transform an existing social structure or solve a problem. In a similar vein, faced with blocked waterways and soil erosion, Kenyans look to politicians, religious leaders, aid agencies, and foreign governments for solutions to local problems, a trait Maathai (2009) blames upon the vestiges of colonialism.

Meanwhile, churches focus on *sadaka* (offerings) that leave poor families without much-needed foodstuffs (which have been given to the priests and others), and looking forward to the world after this one and heaven at the expense of the immediate environment. Maathai (2009) decried the Easter ritual of making crosses insofar as it led to more felled trees. In her address to the 2007 Eighteenth General Assembly of Caritas Internationalis in the Vatican, Maathai urged delegates to make environmental sustainability a priority (*Catholic Review*, 2007).

Maathai bemoaned the deficit in the values that animated the Green Belt Movement, noting that governments could be both indifferent and often outright hostile to their citizens. Additionally, she recognized that the public often appeared skeptical about working for the common good. Pollution, waste, and the destruction of natural resources—landfills, smoggy cities, polluted and dried-out rivers, dead fish, soil erosion, global warming, overconsumption and waste, and deforestation—required redress, as did the plight of endangered species, loss of livestock, and infectious diseases. In her mind, local and national concerns were inseparable, and the alienation of self from others and the environment compounded crises that spread around the world (Maathai 2010).

ORIGINS

As is typical of cultural histories, versions of the Green Belt Movement's beginnings and its achievements vary with when that history was written and the source of that record. Maathai became professionally interested in environmental issues following the 1972 United Nations conference in Stockholm, Sweden, when she and her friends (including Dr. Julia Ojiambo) successfully lobbied for the United Nations Environment Programme (UNEP) to establish its offices in Kenya instead of in the United States, Mexico, Japan, or the Congo.

Dr. Ojiambo, who was serving as the Housing and Social Services assistant minister at the time, recruited the Kenyan president's daughter, Margaret Kenyatta—then Mayor of Nairobi—and Andrew Ligale, permanent secretary in the Kenyatta administration, to the cause (Maathai 2006; Obonyo 2011a). UNEP moved to Nairobi the following year under the directorship of Maurice Strong (Maathai 2006, p. 129) and his deputy Mustafa Tolba. Strong enlisted Maathai in the recently established Environmental Liaison Centre International (ELCI), a non-governmental organization set up to work with and monitor UNEP. Although it was initially run by officials from Europe, Asia, and North America, ELCI gradually recruited local talent like Maathai. That year, friends like Huey Johnson, Richard Sandbrook, Oscar Mann, Gary Gallon, and the late Anil Aggarwal involved Maathai in their environmental efforts.

In my interview, Vertistine Mbaya told me that she and Maathai associated themselves with a number of environmental organizations. Maathai and Mbaya met in the late 1960s when Maathai was a postgraduate student. Mbaya was a dormitory warden and Maathai was a junior faculty member. She, too, later served as a warden for the women's hall. Maathai walked up to her and introduced herself, one illustration of her forthrightness. Mbaya was the acting chair of the biochemistry department that was at the time supported by USAID (U.S. Agency for International Development).

Maathai and Mbaya joined a number of civic organizations before Maathai became a political agitator. They were members of Kenya Academy of Arts and Science's executive committee, which served to promote a science congress for secondary schools at the national level. They also belonged to the Kenya Association of Professional Women (KAPW). At the time, the club was exclusively for European women. At the invitation of Mary Kimani, then the chairperson of the Kenya Association of University Women, Maathai and Mbaya joined the KAPW and recruited more Kenyan women. Mbaya chaired the committee before serving as the treasurer when Maathai was chair.

Both also belonged to the Zonte Club, a charitable foundation supporting underprivileged girls. At one point, they staffed a stall at a five-day show in Nairobi to raise funds for the Mama Fatuma Children's Home, where eight children lived in ramshackle accommodation. As their first philanthropic venture, they set up shop with fifty packs of hot dogs, courtesy of Sr. John of the Kenya Meat Commission, Mbaya explained during one of our interviews. Founded in 1966 by the Kenyan Woman's Organization as an education and training facility for the physically handicapped in Eastleigh, Nairobi, the Mama Fatuma Goodwill Children's Home still exists. Mama Fatuma's son took over as manager after her death in 1997. Currently, it is run by a board of directors and serves about eighty-five orphans and vulnerable children (see Mama Fatuma Goodwill Children's Home).

By 1976, Maathai's work had begun to gain public attention, leading to an invitation to join the Environmental Committee of the National Council of Women of Kenya (NCWK), which promoted tree planting. The NCWK was founded in 1964 and supports women's issues, education, and skills on environmental management (see NCWK; Boddy-Evans, n.d.). Later, Maathai would use her expertise at building human capital as the national chairperson of NCWK. She eventually won the annual election to the organization's leadership, a position she held until 1987, at which point GBM became independent.

Another body that Maathai worked with in the mid-1970s was Men of the Trees, an environmental group established in the early 1920s by colonial chief Josiah Njonjo and the Englishman Richard St. Barbe Baker. Although the organization never flourished in Kenya, it still exists in Britain and Australia. Under the auspices of NCWK, Maathai had greater success establishing "Save the Land Harambee," which changed its name to the Green Belt Movement on June 5, 1977. As Professor Mbaya tells it, a friend invited them to a tree-felling ceremony to make way for the building of apartments at Westlands, a neighborhood in Nairobi. Maathai invited along George Githii, then managing director of the *Nation* newspaper group, who later became personal secretary to President Jomo Kenyatta, to cover the event. The owner of the property called the police to evict Maathai and her friends with little success, and the result was the first of Maathai's stands against corporate interests. A famous photograph of Maathai hugging an old tree in protest was taken. Although the tree was felled after the media furor died down, the incident drew sponsors and well-wishers to Maathai's cause.

Soon after, Maathai and her colleagues received their first grant from Mobil Kenya, which the group used to acquire office premises for NCWK next to the National Library and the old Survey of Kenya office on Moi Avenue in Nairobi. The group also bought a nursery plot of 50,000–70,000 seedlings near Kenyatta Hospital that for years was used as a demonstration site until relations with an officer of the nearby Public Service Club soured. There were other seedling nurseries in Nairobi: at the Nairobi Primary School, in the Mathare Valley, and in the Kilimani and Lang'ata suburbs.

School and church nursery sites were much easier to establish because they were on public property. In the community development of Maasailand Kajiado, GBM had one of their biggest nurseries at the Kanyari Anglican Catholic Church that neighbored a primary school. The site in Kiambu District also had a pilot cooking stove and kitchen garden at which the future U.S. vice-president Al Gore was photographed planting a tree in the early 1990s. There, GBM had a self-sustaining food-security project in which the community grew what was cooked and consumed by students at the school.

These urban nurseries galvanized public support and gave Maathai visibility. GBM's move from the urban to the rural environment arose from a need to expand as much as from deteriorating relations with city officials. It wasn't any easier becoming established in rural areas because of the difficulty of getting people to donate land for Green Belt developments. To avoid a shortage of nursery sites the group encouraged participants to use a percentage of their farmland to set up nurseries, while plowing the rest for subsistence crops. GBM relied on volunteers until funds from the Danish Forestry Department, Austria's CARE organization, and the Canadian as well as the Norwegian governments allowed it to establish more tree nurseries and to pay workers a small stipend for surviving trees.

Initially, Maathai received donations from individuals who sponsored one or a few trees, such as the United Kingdom–based Tudor Trust and U.S. philanthropist Joshua Mailman, as well as Steven and Barbara Rockefeller, who underwrote the purchase of the main GBM office on Kilimani Lane near Adams Arcade in Nairobi. Maathai (2004) received additional aid from a number of countries including Kenya, the U.S., Japan, Germany, and the U.K. In the early 1980s, a grant from the Norwegian Forestry Society as well as the Norwegian Agency for Development Cooperation (NORAD) allowed Maathai to hire personnel to mobilize thousands of women and expand her nurseries to plant millions of seedlings at the extremely successful Murang'a project (Maathai 2006).

Cyril Ritchie (2011) recalled his first meeting with Maathai in Nairobi in 1975 when he was the Chair of ELCI, a position that Maathai succeeded him at in the 1970s and 1980s. Ritchie recalled the pride with which Maathai took him around to meet the people she worked with and showed the implementation of her Green Belt vision:

> She took me to her very first tree nursery, carved out of the land on which a police station stood, already illustrating her immense powers of persuasion. Later I went out with her more than once, with a dozen or more women in a rickety minivan, to support her and to learn from her, as she spread the tree-planting revolution that became the Green Belt Movement. I have never forgotten her contagious enthusiasm, nor her calming stoicism as the minivan negotiated Kenya's rural roads that in that period occasionally resembled a riverbed!

The actual number of trees planted by GBM and the amount of people involved over the years remains contested. Odhiambo Orlale (2012) estimated 3,000 tree nurseries in 1977 and the involvement of about 100,000 rural women, a number that Maathai allowed was bolstered primarily by the growing women's movement across the globe. Judith Graham (1993) estimated a thousand GBM nurseries with the number of trees planted at ten million. Today, GBM's tally of trees grown ranges from thirty to fifty million. One source claims GBM planted over thirty million trees and benefited over 80,000 people in Kenya alone (*Social Education*, 2006). Remembering Maathai after her death, Kerry Kennedy, founder of the Robert F. Kennedy Center for Human Rights, praised her for reaching out to farmers in a predominantly agricultural nation, noting that Maathai and GBM had planted thirty million trees and helped about 900,000 women (Maathai 2011b). Even the location of GBM's first nursery is uncertain: *Unbowed* locates it near a government nursery at Karura Forest, courtesy of the forester Kimathi wa Murage. *The Challenge for Africa* (2009) identifies Lang'ata as its first location.

Peg Snyder helped to engineer the first big grant to GBM—$122,700 in the late 1970s—through UNIFEM (United Nations Development

Fund for Women), which she had helped establish. As she recalled years later:

> UNIFEM (then called the Voluntary Fund for the UN Decade for women) got an unusual, innovative request in 1980: to assist village women to plant thousands of trees. It came from the Green Belt Movement, an offshoot of the Kenya National Council of Women. We sent the proposal for review by UN foresters. Their reply was shocking: "Foresters, not village women, should plant trees." They said, "We propose that you not fund this request." What to do? We put the request before our selection committee, together with the pro and con recommendations, noting Kenya women's exceptional organizational skills.
>
> Professor Wangari Maathai, leader of the GBM, was astonished to receive more than $100,000 for tree planting, to be dispersed in small amounts by the UN office in Nairobi. Thanks to UNIFEM, the women no longer had to go around begging for a few shillings to plant trees. I had not met her at the time, but Wangari told us later that the foresters in Kenya had raised the same obstacles as our UN foresters.

Maathai (2006) refers to Snyder and the co-donors as "truly midwives to the Green Belt Movement's birth" (p. 169).

FORESTERS WITHOUT DIPLOMAS

Taking Root: The Vision of Wangari Maathai, a 2008 documentary film by Alan Dater and Lisa Merton, depicts Maathai's early activism as a consistent process of trying to deepen her sense of wonder and knowledge about the natural world. She built on a tradition of pre-colonial freedom fighters and contemporary activists, and White as well as Black patrons. Maathai's vision for social transformation demonstrated how change begins with people in the places they inhabit: "She did this by challenging political, economic, or gendered power systems while simultaneously teaching people to recognize and stand up for their rights" (Kushner 2009, p. 18). GBM began with rural women in their material environment but its impact extended to their spouses, children, lifestyles, and ultimately their advocacy in the public sphere.

Breaking with tradition, Maathai urged local women, whom she labeled "foresters without diplomas," to draw upon their lived experiences in selecting, planting, and maintaining nurseries and developing green belts around villages. This change in approach to creating nurseries did not sit well with the trained foresters, but for GBM the rest was history.

Maathai (2003, 2006, 2009) initially bought trees from the Department of Forests. She approached the government's chief conservator of forests, Onesimus Mburu, to acquire 15 million seedlings to prevent soil erosion and to provide fuel for poor rural women. Underestimating the venture's viability, Mburu offered to accommodate this request until it exceeded his supply of seedlings. At that point, he asked for a small fee, fearing existing supplies would be depleted. Maathai gradually turned to the women's resourcefulness for the supply and maintenance of seedlings. To diversify trees and, perhaps, to avoid the alienation she'd experienced while sitting in literature classes in the United States, Maathai urged women to draw upon everyday insights to identify indigenous seeds, plant, and nurture trees.

Though predominantly a rural women's group, GBM has always involved sons and husbands in its operations. It also trains "youth in income generation, job skills, and entrepreneurship" (Kushner 2009, p. 74). Males have greater mobility and access to public forums, particularly in rural areas. The young male nursery attendants also have the advantage of speaking local languages as well as English. In a patriarchal community, male representatives give credibility to GBM. Maathai's insistence on local language fluency for operations was revolutionary in an era that privileged the official languages of English and Kiswahili.

By engaging sons and husbands in the movement, Maathai circumvented patriarchal barriers that pitted genders against each other (Michaelson 1994). In "The Women's Rights Movement and Democratization in Kenya," Mumbi Ngugi (2001) emphasizes the importance of empowering men as much as women, although men have traditionally benefited from the patriarchal system. She argues that men need to be educated to acknowledge and promote women's empowerment in homes and the public sphere.

. Maathai's endearing qualities—her intelligence, articulateness, enthusiasm, and energy—elicited early support from key stakeholders, such as women's groups, institutional funders, and (in the early years) the government. The positive reception of Maathai's venture showed the practical need to alleviate poverty. She resisted a critique of tree-felling, a ubiquitous practice in African communities where wood is used as cooking fuel. To that end, GBM, at least initially, mirrored governmental policy. By aligning with the government's rhetoric of development and practical reforestation efforts, GBM chose a "consensus approach to environmental and social transformation" (Michaelson 1994, p. 547). Because GBM focused on women, rural areas, and the domestic sphere, issues that society associates with females—women parent children, work farms, and labor alongside other women—the regime tolerated Maathai and her organization.

March Michaelson (1994) distinguishes between traditional, overly confrontational approaches and consensus movements to solving social problems. In choosing reforestation and education to transform society, GBM judiciously avoided traditional political arenas and therefore the outright pitting of civil society against the state. Maathai herself conceded that GBM "reaffirms accepted roles for African women as mothers, wives, housekeepers, income earners, and community organizers . . . [and any] who wish to be involved can also be comfortable doing so, since agriculture is both a female and a male domain" (Boyer-Rechlin 2010, pp. 70–71).

Consensus-building social movements like NGOs and self-help projects simultaneously improve material conditions and empower participants. Michaelson attributes the prevalence of self-help movements in developing countries to: a) inadequacy in government social services and the paucity of formal institutions; b) repressive regimes that suppress activists viewed as dangerous and seditious; and c) the regular use of these movements for delivery of humanitarian aid from international institutions. The Green Belt Movement falls within these parameters, given the national scope of its operations and impact on society, as well as its mobilization of large groups of peoples in an activist agenda that created political consciousness and democratic transformation (Nixon 2006).

Michaelson (1994) notes that, since its inception, GBM has had a "core bureaucracy of paid office staff, while at the grassroots, members are mobilized in small decentralized groups. Linking these two levels is a large corps of field workers" (p. 549). Michaelson notes how GBM's "field staff carry the dual responsibilities of teaching new groups and monitoring local level activities. Grassroots-level work is facilitated, processed, and monitored by a combination of record keeping and site visits. . . . Essentially, the bureaucracy serves both to facilitate the movement's work and maintain accountability. . . . These activities have been effective because they are simple, visible, and replicable" (p. 550).

The immediate material benefits of GBM—wood products and income—make the movement attractive to typically marginalized groups. GBM's ties to the global community also make possible expansion as more parties, local and international, join up and promote ecological sustainability. Even though GBM was founded before climate change became widely discussed, GBM's viability as a means of mitigating global warming through planting trees shows the prescience and importance of Maathai's vision of ecological sustainability.

Taking Root provides several examples of how GBM grew by word of mouth in Kenya's oral culture. A segment of the *Strides in Development* series, called "Wangari Maathai & the Green Belt Movement" (WEDO 2010), features volunteer Lydia Gathii's work with the Tumutumu Nursery in Nyeri, growing and transplanting seedlings. The group's income-generating activities include constructing beehives and raising a

German breed of goats that is disease-resistant and produces much more milk than other species. The group also sells timber worth KSh 100,000 ($1,300) and constructs pipes for water. Gathii speaks Kikuyu and is portrayed comfortably working and singing alongside local women. Gathii explains that singing at work creates a collective consciousness, makes work less monotonous, and focuses the mind. Maathai enjoins support staff to have passion and patience. She acknowledges the challenges of working in rural areas but understands the importance of local ownership and the success of projects.

In *The Green Belt Movement*, Maathai identified the following objectives for GBM: 1) to help community members establish a sustainable source of wood fuel; 2) to generate income for rural women; 3) to protect environmental consciousness among the youth; 4) to empower people at the grass roots; 5) to demonstrate the capacity of women in development; 6) to curb soil erosion; and 7) to disseminate information on environmental conservation. GBM has focused on food security and water harvesting to address recurring famine and rampant poverty. To ensure food security, GBM encourages sustainable farming methods and educates communities on food production and nutrition. GBM promotes sustainable, organic farming and crop rotation, trains communities on proper agricultural techniques, and supports food production on the household level. Maathai's (2009) efforts outside Kenya focused on combating consumerism, the waste of resources, and climate change, which has both global and local effects. Nancy G. Wright (2011) highlights how climate change threatens the cleanliness of food and water and impacts the immune and reproductive system.

However laudable GBM's achievements in transforming lives, communities, and the landscape, not all of Kenya has benefited. Obstacles to grassroots movements range from a lack of resources and education, interethnic suspicions, and the tendency to avoid responsibility for one's actions, as well as the government's inadequacies and occasional malice toward such movements (Nixon 2006). Much is made of Maathai's mobilization of women through GBM, yet her intervention was limited, both ethnically and regionally. Because of a shared language, GBM has networks in the central highlands and the Rift Valley, primarily Kikuyu districts like Naivasha, Nakuru, and Nyeri; Kiharu in the Murang'a District; and Kanyariri Secondary School in the Kiambu District. Despite reaching out to the Kikuyu, Kamba, Kisii, Luhya, Meru, Embu, Samburu, Taita, and Maasai communities, Maathai and GBM were dogged with charges of regionalism (Maathai 2009). GBM was trivialized as a Kikuyu organization, an accusation Maathai quickly dismissed (Nagel 2005).

GBM's concentration in east and central Kenya may have benefited these areas, but nomadic peoples such as the Maasai and Turkana remain marginalized. Located in primarily semi-arid and arid lands with poor soils and limited rainfall, these pastoralists traverse the region in search of water for themselves and their livestock. GBM has not reached Nyanza near Lake Victoria in the Kisumu District; the Kakamega District; Ukambani in the Machakos District; the Kitui District; and the Isinya Kajiado District to the south of Nairobi (Maathai 2006). In Maasailand, an early project failed because of a lack of personnel as much as cultural habits. Maathai offered the community two donkeys to carry water to the trees but the locals rejected the idea of donkeys taking on women's traditional role of ferrying water. Overall, although the imposition of English and Kiswahili as official languages fosters cohesiveness among ethnic groups, Kenya's linguistic divide can limit the spread of ideas.

To a certain extent, as Bethany Boyer-Rechlin (2010) acknowledges, cultural initiatives—no matter how broadly intentioned—will always contain inherent bias. If a movement relies on member "participation," not all individuals or groups will have equal access. Further, in multiethnic groups, traditionally dominant groups will show the bias. Boyer-Rechlin also recognizes that GBM's reliance on private property excludes the landless and urban residents. This limitation is particularly poignant in communities that restrict women's access to resources and their managerial expertise, both of which constrain their participation in the labor market because of conflicting demands on time for household chores and their absence in decision-making forums.

Ever the scientist, Maathai worked out the logistics of GBM efforts in advance but adapted plans to existing realities. *The Green Belt Movement* presents the history, objectives, organizational structure, source of funding, achievements, plans, and the implementation status as well as the vision for the organization. With each endeavor, Maathai urged organizers to conduct a needs assessment and use the information to establish projects and their linkages as well as priorities. By harnessing consensus among participants, GBM facilitators would motivate communities to excel through ongoing expert advice and some financial support.

In an agriculturally dependent economy like Kenya, environmental degradation is both the cause and symptom of poverty. Maathai designed a ten-step procedure for initiating a tree-planting campaign. The execution of these plans built on this foundation and identified development approaches that the communities found practical and acceptable. The plundering of forests disclosed just how demoralized and disempowered Kenyans felt at changing policy. Maathai understood the "bond between a beleaguered environment and a beleaguered polity" (Nixon 2006, p. 22).

In spite of the limitations enumerated above, the Green Belt Movement has achieved a great deal. Its success can be attributed to a range of factors. Although GBM has employed men, Maathai placed women front and center in efforts to transform society because they are at the bottom of the social pyramids around the world and experience firsthand the impact of degraded environments. It is women who spend days in search of food for the family and are the last to eat in many homes. They walk further in search of water when nearby wells dry up. They know firsthand what sacrifice for the other on a daily basis involves.

As Maathai noted in her address to Caritas Internationalis, women are central to sustaining the environment: "They reproduce nations and cultures as well as giving 'many of us our values and can help us change our values' to those that respect the environment, reduce waste and live life in moderation" (*Catholic Review* 2007). Maathai reached out to the underprivileged that the country's progress depended on—in this case, the agricultural sector—and honored local wisdom and women's roles in sustaining community, a role that had been denigrated since colonial times.

Here, too, Maathai was building on foundations that had been laid. GBM was partly the cause for growing numbers of women participating in civil society in Kenya and beyond, but the empowerment of women was already recognized as vital for human social progress. The United Nations first acknowledged the importance of women in its Decade for Women (1976–1985). A further effort was made at the Fourth World Conference on Women in Beijing in 1995. These forums created a global awareness of women's plight and fostered visions for development. In 1985, Maathai led a cadre of rural women at the women's conference in Nairobi to promote GBM and its participatory methods rather than have communities rely on government technocrats who lacked the requisite political will. She advocated a similar, open-minded, adventurous approach to her workers.

Another cause of GBM's success was its roots in Maathai's pedagogical approach. Jennifer Lara Simka Kushner's (2009) dissertation *Righteous Commitment: Renewing, Repairing, and Restoring the World—Wangari Maathai and the Green Belt Movement* presents Maathai's GBM as a model of adult education. Maathai used rural women's lived experience as a starting point for understanding "interlocking systems of oppression" (p. 25). A primary aim of adult education is giving members agency. In GBM, women pooled resources and challenged each other to make responsible progress. Maathai further empowered rural women by drawing on what she termed "woman sense." Learning experiences were accessible and inclusive, in contrast to formal schooling, which privileges a few in a country that lacks free and universal education. Maathai promoted people's engagement in governance, human rights, and advocacy as well as environmental conservation and reforestation (Kushner 2009). Yet she distinguished GBM from the adult education programs offered by the Ministry of Education, which impart skills rather than an ethos of compassion for humans and the environment (Maathai 1993).

Maathai bridged the gap between Kenya's rural and urban populace (Nixon 2006). In developing her infrastructure of office staff, decentralized grassroots groups, and field workers, she avoided the ivory-tower intimidation typical of government development projects. No longer did rural women rely on predominantly male government foresters or the academician Maathai to direct operations. They used traditional tools, skills, and common-sense knowledge to grow trees and sustain forests (Nagel 2005).

A third reason for GBM's success was that, although Maathai (1994) decried disempowering social structures that privileged a minority, hers was not a lone voice. She was in a long line of women, mostly unknown and unacknowledged, who knew they were worth more than the social definitions imposed on them. She also built on a history of Kikuyu women who were part of the nationalistic movement working alongside Mau Mau freedom fighters (House-Midamba 1996; Mutiso 1975), such as *Mbai sya Eitu* (Kamba's "Clans of the Girls") and *Nyakenyua Mabati* ("Acquiring Corrugated Iron Sheets") (see pp. 140–141 for more details). In 1913, the female warrior Mekatilili wa Menza from the Giriama people along the coast led a rebellion against the colonial administration's policies.

GBM's success can also be attributed to the balance between scientific methodology, rural development, and a womancentric consciousness. In relying primarily on illiterate rural women to establish GBM, Maathai transcended traditional gender expectations to envision a world of equality and rational decision-making. She experimented with new approaches to tree-growing and trained rural women in management and supervisory skills. In her writings, Maathai attributed her realism to her education, as well as to her time in America. The choice of working with rural women to address environmental issues was always pragmatic (Shachtman 2009). Aili M. Tripp (2003a) underscores the role of women's organizations in building rural–urban linkages and bridging gaps between professional women and local women's groups. Maathai trained her GBM associates, empowering them beyond prevailing gender ideologies to transform social structures, beginning with personal independence.

This, as James Baldwin (1988) understood, was the very purpose of education:

The paradox of education is precisely this—that as one begins to become conscious one begins to examine the society in which he [sic] is being educated. The purpose of education, finally, is to create in a person the ability to look at the world for himself, to make his own decisions, to say to himself this is black or this is white, to decide for himself whether there is a god in heaven or not. To ask questions of the universe, and then to learn to live with those questions, is the way he achieves his own identity. But no society is really anxious to have that kind of person around. What societies really, ideally, want is a citizenry which will simply obey the rules of society. If a society succeeds in this, that society is about to perish. The obligation of anyone who thinks of himself as responsible is to examine society and try to change it and to fight it—at no matter what risk. This is the only hope society has. This is the only way societies change. (pp. 3–4)

GBM confronted endemic social ills—poverty as well as rural women's marginalization—to alleviate them.

Schools have for long operated like distinct entities unsullied by the complexities of life. Textbooks promote a similar view of definitive processes and end products. Maathai's formal studies had involved an examination of the natural world in classroom settings, which has been the traditional approach of testing and defining universally applicable concepts, whether it be of how humans function or reality and appearances. The dangers in this approach are evident: Who selects what is culturally worth coding and transmitting? Minnich (2005) cautions against the circular reasoning that avoids reassessing prevailing social norms: "When tools of analysis, methods, concepts based on unquestioned assumptions are claimed to be neutral, we yield too much power to those who developed them. If we care about truth, meaning, and justice, we cannot afford to yield such power to an exclusive past and its major beneficiaries" (p. 162).

Typical of traditional scientific processes, knowledge is constructed in laboratories using well-defined experimental procedures that can be replicated for validity. Knowledge is thereby the end product of problems that are compartmentalized, described, and categorized with scant attention paid to the context or its relation to other things and places. In classrooms, students learn pre-ordained scientific concepts devoid of life's complexities. Maathai understood how science might devalue the subjects of that research and experiential knowledge, and her environmental intervention contrasted with typical commercialized and technical agroforestry in that it emphasized the interconnectedness of the environment and people's lived reality (Gorsevski 2012).

Maathai's approach to rural development corresponded to the process depicted by the late Brazilian educator Paulo Freire, whose book *Pedagogy of the Oppressed* (2000) emphasizes partnership between teachers and students to upend the notion of a relationship where the professor holds all the knowledge and the power. By contrast, no matter their age, students arrive in classrooms with some prior knowledge and aspirations that influence their receptivity to official knowledge. Echoing Freire's approach, Maathai (2003, 2006, 2010) designed seminars to create awareness of local resource devastation and develop intervention strategies that both empowered and helped feed families, often in the absence of male support, and to construct tools for self-exploration and environmental conservation.

After years where the government had acted with impunity in Kenya, Maathai began to stress the importance of self-perception as a means to transform the society. She spoke of shocking people out of their passivity to know themselves and understand their situations. Eventually, Maathai's mobilization of rural women and the disenfranchised drew the regime's ire. Through the civic and environmental education seminars she organized, Maathai engaged rural women, encouraging them first to identify social problems, develop strategies for addressing pressing issues, and make decisions about how to improve their material conditions. Her transformative approach lay in empowering individuals to be critical and self-determining. Kenyans' growing opposition to autocratic leadership during this time reflected just such changes in attitudes among the populace.

GBM's success was also predicated on a symbol that was rooted and literalized in resistance, flexibility, and growth: the tree. GBM created a belt of trees around landscapes to protect them, foreshadowing the work of Maathai's later years, when she modeled and helped create structures of accountability in Kenyan society. Maathai (2006) understood the centrality of trees materially and symbolically in a country dependent on the environment and whose political system had been stunted by imperial and autocratic agendas:

Trees have been an essential part of my life and have provided me with many lessons. Trees are living symbols of peace and hope. A tree has roots in the soil yet reaches to the sky. It tells us that in order to aspire we need to be grounded, and that no matter how high we go it is from our roots that we draw sustenance. It is a reminder to all of us who have had success that we cannot forget where we came from. It signifies that no matter how powerful we become in government or how many awards we receive, our power and strength and our ability to reach our goals *depend on the people,* those whose work remains unseen, who are the soil out of which we grow, the shoulders on which we stand. (p. 293)

GRASSROOTS REVOLUTION

The truly radical nature of the Green Belt Movement is found in a female-driven cooperation that undermined patriarchal dominance in public policy and its implementation. The consequence, as we will see, is exemplified in that GBM went from being a tree-planting organization broadly supported by the government to a forceful opponent of the

Kenyan political regime. Despite harassment from the state machinery, Maathai's teach-ins raised grassroots consciousness, criticized the status quo, and unleashed energies and capacities in formerly marginalized groups who began the process of self-knowledge. Overall, her activism awakened people's yearning for democratic space and the claims that the state was making on natural resources (Maathai 2006).

Here, too, Maathai drew upon a pre-existing Kenyan tradition: the Mau Mau oppositional ideology of conserving trees and fighting government corruption. Seeking to eliminate hypocrisy among the powerful, Maathai evoked the imprisonment of Kikuyu elders during the Mau Mau confrontation with state-sponsored vigilantes in Karura Forest. Ngugi wa Thiong'o's *A Grain of Wheat* and other Kenyan writings depict the forest as the "geographical and symbolic nexus of a peasant insurrection" (Nixon 2006, p. 23). Maathai and scholars like Ngugi, Mukaru Ng'ang'a, and Maina Kinyatti viewed the Mau Mau as the ultimate symbol of ordinary people's bravery and resolve to wrest power from the colonialists, with the ultimate aim of political self-determination.

Jomo Kenyatta and the writer Sam Kahiga were among those who downplayed and disassociated themselves from the Mau Mau (Mwangi 2010). Partisan interpretations of political activism also played out in the period after independence. Despite government suppression, the protestors against land grabbing, among them Maathai and GBM, won insofar as the government eventually stopped allocating public land to political cronies (Nixon 2006). Similar to previous interventions by Maathai, a disillusioned public resisted governmental abuses as Davids fighting Goliaths . . . and eventually won the day.

Always aware of the opportunity to educate, Maathai used everyday events to protest government detentions. She would exploit an event to expose government impunity by contextualizing an immediate crisis and linking it to previous patterns of injustice. To Maathai, moments of crisis provided forums for civic education. She consistently urged the audience to understand the root cause of a phenomenon and the pattern behind seemingly isolated incidents of government graft.

Registering standard gender roles and expectations, albeit in an uncoordinated manner, the media constructed Maathai's public image to highlight her activism, particularly with respect to the domestic and agricultural spheres dominated by women. To this end, the mass media framed what was being discussed in the public sphere in its selective portrayals of events and persons, legitimizing and sometimes dismissing issues by omission or through stereotypical coverage. The focus on gender avoided the complexity of factors that affected women's identity, such as age, class, religion, and ethnicity.

Nancy Worthington (2003) has critiqued the African media's focus on group identity and nationalism at the expense of the individual and subcultures, a choice that marginalizes women's voices in the public arena. In the case of Maathai's deforestation campaigns and their consequences, Rob Nixon points to the irony of forests as a bastion of so-called "warrior masculinity" becoming the locus for political resistance to neo-colonialism by unarmed female "foresters without diplomas." Muthoni Likimani's *Passbook Number F.47927* exposes another inaccuracy in national narratives. Her memoir "gives graphic details about women's heroism and suffering at the hands of the colonial state" (cited in Mwangi 2010, p. 105). Works by Kenyan women like Likimani and Maathai show how overlooked women's concerns and historical contributions have been in and to the body politic. The absence of women's voices, resilience, and self-assertion illustrates the partiality in those cultural histories and within social mores.

Another facet of GBM's success lay in its championing of the ordinary work, wisdom, and realities of women farmers in an age when urbanization and industrialization trivialized or ignored their expertise and experience. Walter Rodney's influential 1972 book *How Europe Underdeveloped Africa* attributes Africa's weakness to European exploitation. By contrast, Maathai blamed Africa's demise partly on the industrial world's erasure of traditional knowledge. Western education focused on White people's cultural wisdom, their religions, geography, history, and language and dismissed local insight. Maathai carefully avoided taking on mainstream science in its focus on observable, systematic, replicable, laboratory-type, constructed knowledge, and credited her transformation to the ideas and values she found in Western education. To this end, the "Western" mirror served its purpose in Maathai's life and work. Yet Maathai's analysis of Christianity's erasure of traditional knowledge captures her critical (re)evaluation of mainstream definitions. Although she accepted that her appreciation of local cultures was long in coming, it was her overseas experience that provided a turning point in bringing her literally and metaphorically back home to them.

Maathai's commitment to environmentalism complemented the challenges for local women raising children and managing homesteads in the absence of husbands (Maathai 2009; Tripp 2000). Her motivation was as personal as it was political. Throughout Africa, women like Maathai's mother are responsible for child rearing and domestic chores (Tripp 2000; *Social Education* 2006). As across the African continent, rural women in Maathai's (2010) primary surroundings relied on subsistence farming and natural resources—water, trees, fruits, soil, etc.—and continue to do so. Maathai was also concerned about the deforestation of her once-lush homeland, its richness inextricably tied to people's welfare. Her book *Replenishing the Earth* links human alienation and degradation to environmental degradation (Campbell 2011). Yet, not all citizens, specifically women, are equally marginalized or similarly disposed.

Marginalized people disassociate from a public that doesn't consider their contributions significant. They leave politics to the politicians. Their lack of civic engagement empowers self-serving kleptocrats. Yet, as the breadbasket of developing nations, rural areas and the agricultural sectors employ and feed a majority of the populace. In empowering poor rural women, Maathai combatted the inertia and self-destructive activities marginalized people engage in as they look to local and foreign governments to improve their standard of living. Although altruism is generally associated with believers, prophets, and saints of religious traditions, Maathai demonstrated that the spirit of service and volunteerism could ensure that countries were built on shared values and enhanced the common good. She insisted that shared reality could guarantee cohabitation among humans and nonhumans. The local, for her, was global. Humans had much to value in the environment and wasting resources depleted a nation's productivity and increased poverty.

10

UHURU PARK

Throughout the 1980s, buttressed by Cold War politics, the one-party state of Daniel arap Moi kept a stranglehold on any stirrings of opposition. Yet, even as the political landscape changed between 1989–1991, with demands for a multiparty system and an end to political suppression, the government clamped down on dissent and the political opposition: "[I]nstead of ending detention, the government arrested leaders who then were charged under section 5(10)(d) of the Public Security Act. The Act states that 'any person who prints, publishes, displays, distributes or circulates notice of, or in any other manner advertises or publicizes, a public meeting or public procession which has not been licensed under this section, shall be guilty of an offense'" (Adar and Munyae 2001). The Act prohibited public gatherings, particularly of opposition parties, without a state license. GBM was affected, as its civic education and environmental seminars addressed issues of governance, culture and spirituality, Africa's development crisis, and human and environmental rights (Maathai 2003). The opposition coalition known as Forum for Restoration of Democracy (FORD) galvanized various parties to repeal this act. It is in this context that Maathai's campaign for Uhuru Park can be seen. It was the first and most visible of her run-ins with the government.

Uhuru Park sits at the hub of Nairobi's city center and contains an artificial lake that offers boat rides for patrons. Its grounds generate cooling shade and act as a location for entertainment and occasional political and religious gatherings. The benches are packed throughout the week with Kenyans who want to trade the city's pressures, heavy car and human traffic, and dusty streets for fresh air, greenery, and a view of the Nairobi skyline. The park's walkways offer venues for skaters and lawns provide intimate spots for lovers. There are always photographers taking pictures for clients for whom a camera is a rare possession.

More significantly, Uhuru Park is the only recreation site for Nairobi's poor, in contrast to Kenya's elite who have backyards, private clubs, and golf courses: "The expansive lawns, shade trees, and well tended gardens in Uhuru Park make this one of the most attractive green spaces in the city, drawing throngs of city residents on weekends and public holidays. This in turn has made it a favorite with charismatic preachers looking to bag a few souls, and make a living from tending to their spiritual needs" (see Uhuru Park).

In the fall of 1989, the government revealed plans to build the Kenya Times Media Trust (KTMT) business complex. The construction was controversial because it would take up land in Uhuru Park. If erected, the proposed complex would "encroach on the park and diminish its usefulness as a public recreation area" (Worthington 2003, p. 143).

March Michaelson (1994) believes that Maathai's entry into the political arena was inevitable because of her local and international visibility during the founding of GBM. When the Kenya government announced plans to "build a $200 million 60–storey skyscraper with a 30-foot statue of President Moi . . . [s]he quickly became the leading opponent of the project and was joined by Public Law Institute Director Dr. Oki Ooko Ombaka, scientists and researchers at the National Museums of Kenya, and the Architectural Association of Kenya" (*ibid.*, p. 552). Meanwhile, an informal group of women, including Peg Snyder, Bella Abzug, and Carol Coonrod of The Hunger Project lobbied U.S. senators on the Committee on Africa, such as Al Gore and Edward M. Kennedy, to pressure the Kenyan government not to construct the complex.

On November 8, 1989, Kenya's National Assembly devoted forty-five minutes to vilifying Maathai and accusing her of appealing to Kenya's colonial masters. Both the government and Maathai claimed to represent the voice of the people. President Moi ignored the dissent and held a small ground-breaking ceremony on November 15. Maathai then wrote to Robert Maxwell, the managing director of KTMT, urging him to consider the consequences of the project on Kenyan citizens. Maathai also appealed to the representative of the United Nations Development Programme (UNDP).

Although Nancy Worthington acknowledges that "the African press under-represents, trivializes, and stereotypes women" (2001, p. 169), she also argues that media coverage of Maathai's confrontation with the president demonstrated their own vulnerability in a precarious political system. At the time, Kenya was beginning its tumultuous shift to multiparty politics after years of autocratic rule with tremendous power invested in the ruling president. The *Weekly Review*, a magazine that provided primary coverage of the prolonged contest, shifted loyalties between the regime and Maathai to reveal the political climate.

As in the colonial era, the regime monopolized and controlled national radio and television networks. It banned those congregating without a license, a tactic reminiscent of the pre-independence clampdown on freedom fighters like the Mau Mau. Robert Maxwell, a naturalized Englishman, owned 40 percent of KTMT's *Kenya Times*, the *Review*'s rival, and was seen as representing foreign interests, reminiscent of colonial leverage on local affairs. Kenyan media have been predominantly foreign-owned and therefore enjoyed more freedom to cover the news. In contrast, the locally funded *Review* struggled financially until the ruling party took over its assets and liabilities in 1981.

Worthington (2003) identifies three key phases in the *Weekly Review*'s coverage of the Media Trust complex protest: 1) nationalism and class conflict; 2) more questions than answers; and 3) Wangari Maathai as transgressor of African traditions, frustrated divorcée, and Kikuyu chauvinist. Worthington reminds readers that Maathai held the helm at the National Council of Women of Kenya before establishing herself as the guru of the Green Belt Movement. She had come through a humiliating public divorce in 1979, well before the Media Trust complex protest's publicity. She had been involved in multiparty discussions despite her inability to enter presidential politics in 1982. Her views were not unique and she did not fear controversy. Meanwhile, President Moi had dismissed the opposition's call for political pluralism, arguing that it would fuel the prevailing ethnocentric rhetoric. The media played a key role in legitimizing each party's position, presenting one and then the other as the voice of reason.

In the first two months of the controversy, the *Weekly Review* depicted Maathai as a champion of the underclass against self-promoting elite politicians. Worthington (2003) notes: "The two early frames were supported by journalistic techniques that privileged Maathai's arguments and discredited those of the KTMT and party officials" (p. 149). The *Review* emphasized Maathai's credentials, accomplishments, international connections, and awards. Her comments appeared in the "neutral third party perspective." An op-ed piece in the *Review* by a representative of the Public Law Institute stressed the class divide between the majority and a minority. It paraphrased the positions of party officials and placed them against those of poor, average citizens.

On November 24, 1989, Maathai filed a suit with the High Court seeking a permanent injunction against the Times Media Complex project's construction, but the court dismissed her, claiming she didn't represent the public. She turned to the Attorney General, but he declined to support the injunction. The government's backlash was swift and vicious, and Maathai was labeled as misguided, emotional, unhinged, unattached; a madwoman, an unprecedented monstrosity who lacked a husband to rein her in. At the height of Maathai's opposition to President Moi's "ego-driven 60-storey" complex he scolded her kind as people who had "*dudus* (insects) in their heads" (Warigi 2011, p. 3).

Meanwhile the party's women's organization, Maendeleo Ya Wanawake (a Kikuyu-dominated group at the time), criticized Maathai. Shortly thereafter, "GBM was given 24 hours to vacate the government-owned offices it had occupied for the past 10 years" (Michaelson 1994, p. 553). Mungai (2011) roots Kenya's vilification of Maathai in patriarchal insecurity and a fear of women who transcend their culturally sanctioned roles of "subordination, dependency and timidity."

In my interview with Professor Mbaya, she recalled how Maathai had not considered the consequences of how her campaign might affect whether her organization could continue to operate out of government premises. "She was totally oblivious of the implications," Mbaya added with a chuckle. The president wondered why women hadn't restrained their wayward member and found it "un-African and unimaginable for a woman to challenge or oppose men." Mbaya's observation illustrates how Kenya's patriarchal opposition to Maathai's achievements and assertiveness drew on traditional gender roles and expectations, further sidelining women's issues—something that Minnich (2005) and Martin (2007) critique as the insidious devaluation of tasks and activities as well as the traits and dispositions that society associates with females.

The NCWK chided Maathai for belittling the president and the regime (Maathai 2006) and her sociopolitical critique of Moi's regime was "sacrificed at the altar of male chauvinism" (Nasong'o and Ayot 2007, p. 183). The Green Belt Movement was portrayed as subversive (Graham 1993). One of the fallouts of Maathai's opposition was the National Assembly's denouncement of the international networks that she'd built, especially those in former colonial powers. She recalled a local MP "located around Mount Elgon near the border with Uganda, because of [her] supposed disrespect for the president," barring her from his constituency (Maathai 2006, p. 197).

In the *Weekly Review*'s second phase, the newspaper "described KTMT plans as legal or policy violations while source reporting and mentions of Maathai diminished" (Worthington 2003, p. 153). Robert Maxwell carried the brunt of the *Review*'s probe. He announced the launch of a second TV channel when the information minister was out of the country. Although the paper acknowledged the benefits of increased competition for audiences, the *Review* questioned KTMT's control over Kenya News Agency, a situation that undermined the Ministry of Information. The president's role in the matter was sidelined, exonerating him in absentia. During the same period, the president indicated his approval of the Uhuru Park project and applauded its "scenic beauty." KANU, the leading political party, claimed it would underwrite the Media Trust complex. Despite the confusion as to who owned and would finance the complex, the public appeared to have resigned itself to the situation.

In the *Weekly Review*'s third phase, Maathai re-emerged in the spotlight, but as the vilified opponent. The *Review* focused on her gender, ethnic identity, her status as a divorcée, and behavior that the newspaper considered disturbing. Maathai was portrayed as obstinate, desperate, wayward, disrespectful of authority, and stubborn. Even Maathai's appeal to the Attorney General was genderized and parochialized, given her rationale for opposing a sitting president: "On my behalf and on behalf of my children, my unborn grandchildren, relatives and friends" (Worthington 2003, p. 156). The *Review* avoided linking charges of Maathai's tribalism to the privileging of Kikuyu interests by the previous regime (the Kikuyu president Jomo Kenyatta, for whom the downtown center was named).

In response to the regime's disparagement and dismissal of her opposition to the Media Trust complex, Maathai turned to her international political alliances. Maathai built up opposition against the regime by appealing to various ministries— including the director of the National Museums of Kenya; UNESCO; the British High Commissioner in Nairobi, Sir John Johnson; UNDP; professional organizations in Kenya; and the general public. It was a strategy she utilized in later confrontations with the government. On the national level, Maathai discovered chinks in the regime's political armor that she and the opposition party later exploited to create a multiparty system in 1992.

On January 29, 1990, following local and international pressure, the government finally shelved the project: "Maathai's long and lonely crusade had finally ended in victory" (Michaelson 1994, p. 553). Overall, both Maathai and the media's confrontation of the sitting president demonstrated the transient nature of political power. Maathai took on the establishment and won (Bartoo 2011; Warigi 2011). She made the unthinkable thinkable.

But the action had not been without cost. Maathai lost her connections to the government machinery. The backlash shook GBM to its foundation: "Some members left the Movement, fearing association with Maathai's GBM would be perceived as racial and seditious" (ibid., p. 554). Clearly to punish her, the Registrar General, Joseph King'arua, required Maathai (2006) to submit GBM's financial reports for the past five years. Maathai supplied financial statements for the previous ten and sassily challenged KANU to disclose one year of its financial statements, to which she received no response.

In subsequent months, Maathai shrewdly tried to re-establish links with the government, aligning GBM's efforts with the administration's rhetoric of improving the environment. Nonetheless, she gained fame as well as notoriety for her opposition to the skyscraper in Uhuru Park. Amutabi (2007) includes her among Kenya's homegrown activist intellectuals who are married to a cause and "constitute the political martyrs" (p. 202), whose popularity with and championing of marginalized groups pits them against an oppressive status quo: "Their actions and concerns range from human rights, public land, political grievances and education for the marginalized to environmental issues, and include in their agenda anything that requires intervention on the side of the masses" (p. 203).

11

ANTI-DEFORESTATION CAMPAIGNS

In 1998, Maathai opposed the government's deforestation of the Ngong Hills, the southwestern part of Mau Forest, Karura Forest, Mt. Kenya National Park, and Kabiruini Forest. Her appeals to the administration went unanswered. As a consequence, she mobilized allies to protest the construction of buildings in the forest, frequently visiting the areas to plant trees. In line with previous protests, Maathai retained supporters and international observers as well as the Kenyan press with her. She regularly invited the media to her events, exposing government abuses that fostered public ire against the regime.

The biggest protest involved the government's proposed sale and construction of private properties in Karura Forest, an expanse near Nairobi of about 2,500 acres with a catchment area for four rivers, and a national landmark. The government appropriated parts of it and resold it to certain cabinet ministers and other presidential cronies for the building of golf courses, hotels, and gated communities. Supporting Maathai's campaign, on October 27, 1998, Klaus Toepfer, executive director of the United Nations Environment Programme (UNEP), named Karura Forest a unique cultural heritage.

National indignation over the regime's appropriation of Karura Forest drew in university students and other disaffected constituencies in Nairobi. President Moi acted surprised that citizens opposed the "luxury developments" in Karura Forest. "After all," he said, "much of Nairobi had been built out of forest land, and this was just another example of the city striding forward into the future" (Maathai 2006, p.

270). Yet the proposed golf course and gated communities provided a stark contrast with Kenya's congested neighborhoods, of the rich and the poor, something true even today: "Despite a much-lauded average five percent growth during President Mwai Kibaki's five-year term, almost half of Kenya's thirty-six million people survive on $1,200 per annum or less, while cabinet ministers annually take home on average around $155,000" (Nyambura-Mwaura, cited in Nixon 2006, p. 30). The difference in space available to the wealthy and the destitute was, and is, also extreme: "In the city's Kibera slum, some areas have 80,000 inhabitants per square kilometer, while in the glossy suburb of Karen only 360 inhabitants live in a comparable area" (Vasagar, 6, cited in Nixon 2006, p. 31).

The regime manhandled Maathai and her fellow protestors when they came to Karura Forest, and many were arrested and imprisoned. Maathai (2006) herself was hit on the head and only survived fatal injury with the help of her good friends John Makanga and Lillian Muchungi, who grabbed her and ran with her to escape. Maathai went to the police station and signed the police report in her own blood. The Kenyan regime faced another barrage of international outrage from United Nations Secretary General Kofi Annan and other world leaders, who spoke out against the assault on Maathai.

GBM's anti-deforestation efforts weren't confined to Karura, but spread to other parts of Kenya, including Kahuro in Murang'a, Kitale, Embu, Meru, and Nyandarua. On August 16, 1999, the government conceded to demands to stop the allocation of public land in Karura Forest.

Maathai was jailed once more in March 2001 when she joined GBM in Wang'uru Village to protest another land-grabbing scheme. The state police hijacked her Land Rover and later locked her up. Once again, pressure from the international community compelled the government to release her without charges.

Maathai discovered early on the international community's leverage in Kenyan governance, and employed it shrewdly. By the time she became *persona non grata* to the Kenyan government in the late 1980s, she was already known through the international funding networks that sustained the Green Belt Movement. Maathai had a complicated relationship with this source of funds. Despite Maathai's criticism of how foreign governments dispensed aid, NGOs like GBM rely heavily on international resources to create and maintain grassroots' projects. Maathai also appreciated the global image of her promoted by the mass media—both local and international—because it guaranteed her welfare and credibility, and gave her organization a donor base. But as was to be seen in her campaigns (e.g. in her efforts to save Karura Forest), the media could be a hybrid dragon every bit as dangerous as Konyeki.

As an environmental scientist, Maathai understood not merely the instrumental value of forested land, but its larger role—and, increasingly, as climate change moved onto the international agenda, the biosystemic and mitigatory value of healthy, diverse forests became part of her call to action. The United Nations requires nations to set aside at least 10 percent of its land for forests, yet Kenya lost 90 percent of its forested land between 1950 and 2000 leaving only 2 percent forest cover. Maathai lamented that the government planted exotic species of trees for the timber industry, calling the commercial plantations biological deserts (Maathai 2008).

As a further ecological threat, a government-proposed *shamba* program allowed people to grow crops in forested areas, where the soil was fertile. Farmers ideally would have rotated their crops and replanted wooded areas after use, but such responsible practices were rarely pursued. Maathai dismissed government claims that the *shamba* system eased demand for agricultural land, maintaining that it was an expedient policy perk for politicians seeking votes.

Maathai's tree-planting ventures were a "seditious act of civil disobedience" (Nixon 2006, p. 20), but they had lasting value beyond the political arena. Even for Monica Wangu Wamwere, a mother who protested the incarceration of her son as a political prisoner in 1992, Maathai's greatest achievement was not political but in conserving forests: "Dundori forest was destroyed and water was becoming scarce but when she intervened the destruction was halted" (Mureithi 2011, p. 10). Wamwere's appreciation of Maathai's achievements was echoed in private and communal as well as international forums.

12

GLOBAL INFLUENCE

In her appeals to international bodies, Maathai drew upon industrialized countries' sense of the importance of proper stewardship of natural resources. She emphasized the interdependency of nations and called for cooperation to combat ecological disaster. The linkage between poverty and environmental degradation, which she was one of the first to make, remains strong:

> According to the World Health Organization, a quarter of all diseases affecting mankind are attributable to environmental risks. More than 4.7 million children under 5 die each year from environmentally related illnesses, the WHO said. The 30-acre Dandora Dump in Nairobi takes in garbage that includes industrial and medical waste like used syringes. The UN study found high levels of lead, mercury, and cadmium at the site and surrounding slums in eastern Nairobi. . . . The study found that half of 328 children tested had lead concentrations in their blood exceeding the internationally accepted level. Most of them . . . suffer respiratory problems." (See MSNBC.com)

The most populous city in East Africa, Nairobi has an estimated urban population of between three and four million (see OSFEA). About 60 percent of the city's population resides in slums or "informal settlements," and most of the residents earn less than US$7 a week.

Nairobi's largest slum, Kibera, is the second largest in Africa (after Khayelitsha, on the borders of Cape Town, South Africa).

The Kenya Slum Upgrading Project (KENSUP) estimates about half of Nairobi's population resides in a hundred dense and insecure settlements with little or inadequate access to safe water and sanitation. It is not a new phenomenon: "Between 1971 and 1995, the number of slums within the Nairobi divisional boundaries rose from 50 to 134, while the estimated total population of these settlements increased from 167,000 to some 1,886,000 individuals. Today, both natural growth and rural-to-urban migration continue to contribute to the growth of Nairobi's informal settlements" (see KENSUP). Although residents hail from different ethnic groups, slum dwellings are for the most part divided along ethnic lines.

The fragility of Kenya's human and natural ecosystems is reflected in other parts of the continent, as Paul E. Rosenfeld and Lydia G. H. Feng document in *Risks of Hazardous Wastes* (2011). In Maathai's address at the fifth Edinburgh Medal ceremony (1994), she linked the happiness and fulfillment of individuals to the survival of the rest of humanity and the global environment. Identifying herself with grassroots women, men, and children of all races and religions at the bottom of the social pyramid, Maathai underscored our shared humanity and our custodial responsibility for the environment, an aspiration that may have endeared her later to the Nobel Peace Prize committee.

Globally, as developing countries like Kenya grapple with endemic poverty and urban blight, industrialized countries face the challenge of integrating a marginalized urban populace. In late 2005, France witnessed riots involving North African immigrants that led to the arrest of suspected jihadists, although there appeared to be no direct link to any group (see International Crisis Group 2006). Similarly, London had a spate of race- and class-related mass riots in August 2011 (see The Voice of Russia 2011).

Maathai attributed these and similar incidents of social discontent to a disconnection from one another and from the environment. How embedded ecological disaster is in other social problems can be seen in the spread of diseases, financial meltdowns, global terrorism, and the Arab Spring of the last few years. The cause can be as simple as ash from Iceland's Eyjafjallajökull volcano disrupting the airspace over Europe for more than a month in 2010 and thereby causing Kenya's international flower industry to lose about $3.8 million *each day* in revenue from unshipped product. Global interdependence is a reality and one country's plight or success affects other nations. Maathai understood that an ecological campaign inherently crossed national borders and cultures.

Today, nations grapple with the excess and refuse of our consumerist electronic age. Developing countries also contend with the pressure from industrialized nations seeking offshore locations in which to dump their waste. Europe sends most of its used paper, plastic, and metals to China, while electronic waste tends to go to African countries, in particular Ghana, Egypt, and Nigeria (Rosenthal 2009). In 2010, *Science Daily* magazine reported on the surge of hazardous material that had been sent to developing countries, including old desk and laptop computers, printers, mobile phones, pagers, digital photo and music devices, refrigerators, toys, and televisions. The report reviewed current policies, skills, waste collection networks, and informal recycling in eleven representative developing economies in Asia, Africa, and the Americas. It also outlined options for sustainable e-waste management in those countries.

Such efforts, while laudable, appear inadequate given the magnitude of the problem. Kenya's waste alone is estimated at "11,400 tonnes from refrigerators, 2,800 tonnes from TVs, 2,500 tonnes from personal computers, 500 tonnes from printers, 150 tonnes from mobile phones" (*Science Daily* 2010). Countries like Kenya face further threats from a polluted environment and poor public health. Maathai's concern about the ecological danger of plastic bags pales in comparison to the growing e-waste hazard (*ibid.*).

In June 1992, Maathai (2006) addressed the UN Conference on Environment and Development (UNCED) during the Earth Summit in Rio de Janeiro. In spite of criticisms levelled by the Moi regime against

Maathai, UNCED honored her by selecting her as a chief spokesperson for the NGOs in attendance. Throughout her life, Maathai participated in the major environmental sustainability and climate change world conferences, including the Kyoto Convention on Climate Change in 1997 and the Copenhagen Climate Change Summit in 2009. In October 2009, she attended the UN General Assembly meeting and the Clinton Global Initiative, where she called for U.S. leadership to save the world's disappearing rainforests.

Maathai visited the U.S. Green Party's offices in Washington, D.C.; North Carolina; Maine; Rhode Island; and Virginia. In May 2006, she spoke at the invitation of Canopy, a Palo Alto–based environmental organization that had received a $142,000 grant from the California Department of Forestry and Fire Protection to purchase, plant, and care for more than 600 trees in East Palo Alto (McPherson 2006). Canopy was just one of the various organizations that recognized Maathai for her inspiration (Kushner 2009).

At Oxford University, Maathai joined a campaign sponsored by UNEP to plant a billion trees worldwide, beginning at Exeter College on February 10, 2007. She challenged participants to take action by planting a tree themselves. The launch was preceded by a seminar entitled "Keeping Our Promises to the Earth," with speakers from the college, the World Conservation Union, and the Centre for International Sustainable Development Law (CISDL) in Montreal, Canada: "The seminar marked the formal launch in Britain of the Earth Charter, an internationally agreed document on environmental sustainability and human rights. The CISDL also announced the start of an annual lecture series on environmental law at Exeter College" (see University of Oxford).

George Oloo, a Kenyan student who attended the seminar, recalled Maathai's approachability in contrast to the power-wielding and often remote politicians in Kenya. In my interview with him, he said:

This was the first time I had met Wangari in person. The larger-than-life figure which I had built up in my mind melted as she stretched her hand in greeting. She was just about 5 feet 5 inches tall, a little smaller than I had expected, wearing a long African print dress and her trademark matching head scarf. She had a very warm, convincing smile as she greeted me in Kiswahili, as she had been told I was Kenyan: *Habari Yako?* The chitchat that followed lasted just about five minutes. It was almost what you would get between a nephew and auntie, including down-to-earth comparisons of cultural differences between life in Oxford and Nairobi, and of course the weather. I tried some clever talk and managed to blurt out how proud she had made us with the Green Belt Movement and her fight for justice. She was not having any of that, and encouraged me to continue with the work on protecting the environment, as it was now up to the younger generation.

I was lucky to take a photograph with Wangari, which I cherish to this day. At the end of the session, she gave me a hug and wished me well, and asked me to visit the Green Belt Movement offices in Nairobi when I was next in Kenya. I managed to wish her an enjoyable stay in the U.K. and asked her to pass my greetings on to brothers and sisters in Nairobi. As I was walking away, I looked back and marveled at how respectful other delegates to the seminar were in taking turns to talk to her. I still could not believe that I had met the great Wangari, and that the five minutes had passed so quickly. . . .

Wangari strikes you as the tough African mom who took on the might of an authoritarian government like Moi's. Yet, when you meet her, she can almost pass as an average citizen of the world: humble, with a rich smile, gentle speech, and never hurried in communication. She made communication very simple, an obvious contrast to the character of the fighter that I had grown to know of her. . . . When a BBC survey was launched to nominate the global personality of the century, you can guess whose name I put forward: Wangari, of course!

Although Maathai's ecological outreach extended to the industrialized world, her work on the African continent is more illustrative of her Green Belt Movement vision for social transformation. Her activism was unique insofar as she went beyond abstract critiques to establish alternative structures. Within Kenya, she initiated the Green Belt Safaris (GBS) to "offer community-based and other eco-tourism packages through which environmental conservation and community development can be promoted" (Maathai 2003, p. 53) and to involve clients in "field activities (seed collection, nursery participation, tree planting, food security/processing and civic education), community projects, harvesting, and meal preparation" (Kushner 2009, p. 125).

Between 1989 and 1994, GBM engaged in efforts to export its operational model to other African countries, establishing the Pan-African Green Belt Movement (PAGBM) on August 8, 1992 (Michaelson 1994). Internationally, Maathai focused on environmental conservation in industrialized or rapidly industrializing economies like Norway, Japan, India, Mexico, Puerto Rico, Philippines, France, Spain, Sweden, the United Kingdom, and the United States. She presented at special sessions of the General Assembly on environmental issues and served on the Commission for Global Governance as well as the Commission on the Future (Maathai 2006).

The scholarships and awards Maathai received from many organizations and institutions across the world testify to the effectiveness of GBM and her vision of social transformation (see the "biography" page of the Green Belt Movement website). Having built GBM into a global entity, in 2011 Maathai engineered her transition by "approving a new [GBM] constitution expanding the new membership of the board and set in motion the process of bringing in a new chairperson" (Menya 2012, p. 2).

On April 1, 2011, GBM organized a surprise party for Maathai's seventy-first birthday. Fifty people, comprising a few family members, well wishers, and GBM associates attended—such as biocarbon project manager Benjamin Kimani and GBM Nairobi Executive Secretary Lucy Wanjohi, both of whom organized the event. Kimani likened Maathai's passion to the stature of the sturdy and tall *Muthengera* (Podocarpus) tree. This was only a few days after Maathai had returned from New York, where she'd been undergoing treatment for ovarian cancer, and she joked about having been in hospital only on two other occasions in her life: when she was giving birth and after a beating by President Moi's regime. The venue for the birthday party at GBM's office was surrounded by trees, each a memory of some event, one of which was planted when Maathai won the Nobel Prize. Maathai planted her last sapling, a Meru oak tree, at the site.

IV

THE POLITICIAN

13

POLITICAL BEGINNINGS

When Wangari Maathai was asked by television personality Tavis Smiley about Africa's poor record on leadership, she attributed much of Africa's woes to corruption (Smiley 2009). The Kenyan government directly "oversees the destruction of forests and grabbing of public lands," she said, which threatens Earth as the very support of human life. Kenya, she noted, had made little progress, four decades after independence, to increase access to education for its youth. She blamed African leaders, skirting around the issue of whether or not the problem was uniquely African.

Attaining political independence symbolized African's promise, she said, despite the legacy of colonialism and cultural denigration, as well as ongoing negative portrayals in the media. Although these factors were real, she acknowledged the danger of using them as excuses for Africa's failure to make progress, for violating human rights, and for tolerating corruption and financial irresponsibility. Unlike many African countries, she observed, nations in Southeast Asia, some of which had been colonized for longer periods of time than Kenya, had nonetheless managed to make significant economic and social progress.

Maathai maintained that the lack of accountability shown by African leaders who were the recipients of foreign aid raised the question of just how valuable that aid was. In an op-ed in the *Los Angeles Times* on March 16, 2009, Maathai argued that President Barack Obama had no financial or emotional obligation towards Africans because of his paternal lineage. Yet, in the same piece, she admitted Africa's need for technology, capital, and advice, similar to developed countries like the United States, which borrows considerable amounts of money from China. Even if African presidents (such as then Kenyan president Mwai Kibaki) relinquished personal assets—like private cars and planes—the revenue would not compensate for the loss in foreign aid, she said.

Maathai relentlessly criticized African leadership in *The Challenge for Africa*, insisting on the necessity of holding leaders accountable. Her promotion of civic education for a predominantly uneducated populace was intended to raise awareness of the danger of relying on and supporting leaders along ethnic lines and exchanging votes for bribes. Citizens could not, she said, afford to be passive observers (Smiley 2009).

Despite Maathai's role as female trailblazer and singular voice, her journey is replete with men and communities that endorsed her choices and provided her with help, and with men and communities who dismissed her. Sometimes they were one and the same. In 2002, Maathai was elected to Kenya's parliament with 98 percent of the vote for the constituency of Tetu, where she'd been born and raised, only for her to be snubbed five years later because of her opposition to the political agenda of Mwai Kibaki, a "favorite son" from the same ethnic group. In reinforcing patriarchal structures based on tradition and the colonial period, the Kenyan legislature both sanctioned male identity and males' primacy in social construction (Nasong'o and Ayot 2007).

Certainly, Maathai and other women faced daunting obstacles in Kenyan politics. Omwa Ombara (2011) considers Kenya after independence to have been "a man's club," where women confronted hostility and contempt within a chauvinistic environment. Men acquired land title deeds, paid taxes, and were the first to become paid laborers, all of which legitimized male dominance in the public arena. Writing more generally, Kata Fustos (2012, p. 18) attributes male privilege to a community's acceptance of gendered norms. Sexism is "normalized either through socialization or as a defense strategy" (Kanga 2004, p. 35). Although Ruth Nasimiyu (1997) and Simiyu Wandibba (1997) associate gender socialization among the Bukusu and Kikuyu to a "pre-modern" era, Shadrack Nasong'o and Theodora Ayot (2007) root the patriarchal ideology firmly in the colonial legacy, which they contrast with a pre-colonial sexism that was ameliorated by complementarity between the genders. Across the country, scholars argue, customary practices and legislation continue to reinforce women's oppression (Ikonya 2008; Mucai-Kattambo and Kabeberi-Macharia 1995). The state determines the national agenda, electoral protocol, budget allocations, and legislation—essentially maintaining tight control over both the public and domestic sphere.

Maathai's achievements in education, activism, and politics placed her among the elite in Kenya and, ultimately, made her a global celebrity. Nonetheless, she stood with the ordinary folk and utilized grassroots pedagogies rather than professorial lectures in order to promote civic and democratic education: "She was found in villages, wearing ordinary *kitenges* [African dress and matching garb] and braids, planting trees with ordinary women" (Warigi 2011, p. 3). Maathai defied most parameters—including the feminist, elitist, and political—which Gitau Warigi associates with designer outfits, clipped English accents, and the hypocritical moral pretensions typical of Kenyan politicians (2011, p. 3).

But perceptions of the political nature of what Maathai represented are not uniform—although they sometimes express themselves in uniforms. Some critics have pointed out her privilege as an educated woman, which Maathai herself acknowledged. Maathai's cosmopolitanism expressed itself initially in her preference for Western clothing; she got married in a long white wedding gown with a veil and even carried a bouquet of white flowers. She recalled strolling through Nairobi city-center shops and cafes in the late 1960s, patronizing dance clubs with fellow students who studied overseas. Her husband's run for office provided a reality check for the young, fashionable, and Western-oriented Maathai:

It became important for me not to wear clothing that might put me in a compromising situation because it was too tight-fitting or short. Therefore, long dresses and skirts became practical as well as comfortable and stylish. I gradually abandoned the short dresses (even my nice red one!), trousers, and high heels I had accumulated and loved to wear in America when I was single and independent. (Maathai 2006, p. 111)

Once she was divorced, Maathai acquired a different persona. She was now without the support of her husband, a Kenyan male protector in a patriarchal society, and many Kenyan women distanced themselves from her for overstepping cultural boundaries in opposing President Moi and in her subsequent challenges of human rights abuses by the regime. As we have seen, Kenya's largest and oldest women's organization, Maendeleo Ya Wanawake, ostracized Maathai for her opposition to the Media Trust complex in Uhuru Park, though other Kenyans felt empowered by witnessing a successful challenge to a dictatorship that many referred to as the "wall of fear" (Bartoo 2011, Warigi 2011). Comments made at the time by Maina Kiai, the Executive Director of the Kenya Human Rights Commission, are insightful:

Kenya's human rights record has been dismal. Political assassinations, deaths in police custody, detentions without trial and police brutality have been prevalent in Kenya since the reign of Kenya's first president, Jomo Kenyatta . . . (and when Daniel Moi assumed the presidency in 1978), government critics were harassed and intimidated through brief arrests and interrogations. By 1980, however, the regime had severely circumscribed freedom of expression and a culture of silence and fear began to permeate society. (Cited in Michaelson 1994, p. 546)

It wasn't solely her gender or her association with the poor (as opposed to glad-handing among the elite) that impeded Maathai in politics. In some ways, Maathai was a metapolitical force, navigating the choppy waters where civil society, moral authority, and party political activity meet. The Green Belt Movement was inherently political in the broadest sense of the meaning, in that it reflected, engaged with, and transformed the polity. To call Wangari "a politician" and mean only her time as an elected representative is to fail to account for her importance in, and contribution to, all facets of the Kenyan state.

Maathai spoke truth to power when it was taboo to do so, and her courage was a turning point in Kenya's silencing of political dissent. In defying sexist dismissals of women as "divorcées" or "unmarried," she blazed a trail for women torn between careers and motherhood. Following her divorce and jail sentence, she ingeniously added an "a" to her husband's last name (changing Mathai to Maathai) to differentiate herself from him. She promoted political consciousness among marginalized groups.

Maathai's Green Belt Movement propelled her into Kenya's political arena. Although she only served in parliament for five years, from 2002 to 2007, for thirty years her interest in civil society never wavered. Her visibility in local and international forums boosted the transformation of Kenya's political landscape, particularly in critiquing male dominance of the national discourse. Her personal and public achievements compelled Kenyans to appreciate women in classrooms and in high places (Mungai 2011). She spoke of learning from her mistakes (Maathai 2006) and was always ready to adopt new strategies.

In her first attempt at running for public office in 1982, her application was disqualified, and she lost tenure at the University of Nairobi within a week. Compelled to vacate university housing, she moved to a house she bought from accumulated pay following her campaign at the university for gender parity in the early 1970s. She secured a job with UNDP through Robert Kitchen, the then permanent representative of the United States to the United Nations, who had also been involved in the Kenya Airlift. Kitchen helped her get a consultancy assignment to assess the teaching of veterinary education across the world, an assignment that involved a station in Zambia and six months of overseas travel. Maathai left her three children at their father's residence without informing him of how long she would be away, and he took over childcare responsibilities well beyond the projected six months. The arrangement was unique in Kenya's patriarchal family structure, yet she makes no more mention of Mwangi in *Unbowed* or in later writings.

Against all odds, Maathai refused to back down despite pressure from colleagues and other women who distanced themselves from her at the behest of their husbands. Her education in a patriarchal communal culture and overseas transformed her on a personal level as much as her vision for society. She became more confident in honoring individual voices sidelined by Kenyan society.

* * *

We should be careful to remember that the image of poor, illiterate, and disempowered women in rural Kenya is partial—just as we should recognize that the Green Belt Movement's organization of women wasn't an unheard-of phenomenon. In a brief account, Mutiso (1975) relates the story of two women-initiated groups, *Mbai sya Eitu* (Kamba's "Clans of the Girls") from the Machakos District and the *Nyakenyua Mabati* ("Acquiring Corrugated Iron Sheets") from the Nyeri District, who were non-*asomi* (non-educated and unaffiliated with missionary groups). In modern terms, members would fall under the category of "single women," demonstrating beyond doubt that "women's groups are the most significant political group since they seem to be structurally more continuous and innovative than any other organizations in the rural areas" (Mutiso 1975, p. 249).

Between 1961 and 1963, the *Mbai sya Eitu* model was comprised of twenty patrifocal clans with obligatory commitments among members. In the 1950s, these clans raised funds to educate their sons in England, South Africa, and other overseas universities. Women (sixteen–twenty years of age) rose in prominence as *mwethya* (village) group leaders, long-time and consistent workers in developing and maintaining communal terracing practices, in contrast to the men, most of whom sought employment in urban centers. Akamba veterans from Burma after World War II returned disgruntled and "agitated for better working conditions and against discrimination" (Mutiso 1975, p. 259), and joined the predominantly women-run communal work and terracing *mwethyas* rather than support the colonial regime's structures. The men took over the leadership of the organizations. In later years, *mwethya* leaders, now in their mid-fifties and older, engaged in tasks ranging from "making bricks to whitewashing completed classrooms" (*ibid.*, p. 277). Mutiso attributes their solidarity to an oath taken by initiates, which in typical male fashion downplayed rural women's civic engagement and agency.

Similar to the *Mbai sya Eitu*, the Nyeri-based *Nyakinyua Mabati* emerged in response to the everyday pressures of motherhood a decade earlier. According to Mutiso, these women's groups were caught up in the Mau Mau insurgency, and participated directly or lost family members. As cultural producers and transmitters, they "sang political songs and did traditional dances" (1975, p. 280). Building on their customary role as thatchers of roofs, they found ways to improve homes and, in an emerging cash economy, they bought "iron sheets (*mabati*) for roofing their houses" (*ibid.*). Fifty-member family groups would raise KSh 330 each in two or three weeks to roof a member's house.

Such numbers indicate impressive mobilization and success: "Between 1966 to 1970, 578 groups were registered. These [groups] had a total membership by June 1971 of 48,685. The membership represents about a seventh of the total district population which in the 1969 census was 360,845" (*ibid.*, p. 281). *Mbai sya Eitu* diversified their activities, raising funds for better roofs and for "water-tank building[s], buying of grade cows and poultry-keeping. . . . Politically these groups have forced the politicians and civil servants to pay attention to their demands," achieving a comprehensive rural development approach that had perpetually eluded the federal government since independence (*ibid.*, p. 283). By 1970, *Nyakinyua Mabati* had over 176,000 members. Yet today, the group is known for its commercialized cultural entertainment on national holidays rather than its political activism.

Thus, Maathai's GBM education seminars and the Green Belt Movement built on years of rural women's initiative in community development. Surprisingly, she makes no mention of these legendary women's groups in the region of her birth, which could mean she gave it no thought or didn't make the link, either of which demonstrates her complexity as a human with familiar flaws. Not even the media connected the activism of the predominantly rural Kikuyu women who took to the streets in 1991 calling for the release of detained sons and husbands to their historic role during the struggle for independence. The Kenyan regime and media portrayed them as merely a front for male counterparts—the political opposition and church officials—and at one point blamed Maathai for inciting the rural women to revolt.

Henrietta Moore (1986) notes how gender hierarchies mirror social practices: "In the normal course of events women are rarely consulted formally and their ability to influence major community decisions [is] restricted to their ability to influence individual men" (p. 164). Women avoid organizing against patriarchal oppression through revolution. Instead, especially in rural areas, they sidestep ideology by ostensibly adhering to men's rule while transforming the posture into informal power through "back-door-decisions" that influence local and national events and processes (Abwunza 1997, p. 27). Both Judith Abwunza and Aili Tripp (2000) attribute the back door–decisions approach to expediency.

Maathai's Green Belt Movement offered a similar approach to social transformation in her civic involvement prior to her becoming a parliamentarian. Maathai worked with existing civic organizations, such as Men of the Trees, the Red Cross, and women's professional associations to promote women's issues. Maathai also employed male associates for door-to-door canvassing in communities that would be wary of such mobility in women. Women have traditionally downplayed their engagement in political activity by stressing the economic and social aspects of their work to avoid threatening a political caucus dominated by men, as Maathai appeared to have done in the early stages of GBM. Egara Stanley Kibaji (2005) surmises that the portrayal of women as powerless deliberately avoids threatening patriarchal systems. We have seen how Maathai sidestepped confronting the government and criticizing the public for cutting down forests whether for public buildings or to provide fuel for homesteads. It was years later and once she was acknowledged as an environmentalist that she publicly opposed government use of lands and forests for personal interests.

Women's organizations on the African continent have dramatically increased in number, stemming as much from increased female literacy as from a deepening economic crisis that compels women to earn money for daily survival. In most rural areas, these organizations are primarily intended for generating income, in which women pool together to raise funds for projects none could afford separately. Some raise money for children's education; others engage in small businesses like hairdressing, roadside vending of foodstuffs, running fruit and vegetable stalls, selling local brew in rural communities, managing kiosks, and hawking household items (Tripp 2003a).

Some groups emerged as Christian communities that gradually undertook income-producing projects. These movements propelled women into the public sphere and made many aware of their overall capabilities (Yuval-Davis 1997). In "Women's Bank Leaves Them Financially Stronger," Florence Sipalla (2011) highlights how these assemblies have empowered women and families. The 215 networks of the Kenya Women Finance Trust (KWFT) are known to serve about 600,000 rural urban women, promoting green energy, maternal health, and measures to combat domestic violence. Instead of requiring assets to secure loans, KWFT networks rely on a debtor's character references from other women. Mainstream Kenyan banks have tools that target a similar clientele, such as Cooperative Bank's Msamaria Women's Loan and Standard Chartered Bank's Diva Account. KWFT has invested KSh 16.5 billion ($20 million) in women, with loans being on average about KSh 40,000 ($470) each. At the grassroots level, women and men belong to *chamas* (merry-go-round groups) where they pool resources for tuition, weddings, and funerals, or large-item purchases.

The cliché "capacity building" is endemic to many of these movements and, as a result, women are represented on national commissions and quasi-governmental boards. Of concern is that women still shy away from positions of national leadership and, in some cases, elect men to executive positions even though the group consists mainly of women (Arndt 2000). Although women gained visibility with the political openings of the 1990s, these opportunities have been limited and precariously held when taken (Tripp 2003a).

In neighboring Uganda, women's associations have assumed leadership roles and brought women's issues to the national agenda. Women are vocal on issues of sexual harassment, rape, wife beating, and child abuse, and they have helped draw up a domestic law bill that gives women in cases of divorce or marriage more rights, and assists them in other discriminatory customary practices around inheritance and property rights (Tripp 2003a). In 1991, Uganda lowered admissions standards for underrepresented university women students and initiated the formation of a women's studies program. They introduced sex education into the curriculum to curtail the AIDS epidemic. In many African communities, women's groups have fostered community across gender, class, religious, ethnic, and party lines (Tripp 2003a and 2003b).

Tripp (2000, 2003a and 2003b) and Mary M. Kolawole (2002) credit the impetus of women's mobilization across the continent to the 1985 and 1995 UN Women's conferences in Nairobi and Beijing, in both of which Maathai was active. These forums placed women's experiences beyond mainstream feminism and the men representing them (Kolawole 2002). Even so, organizations such as Kenya's International Federation of Women Lawyers (FIDA) avoid confronting the male-dominant state on matters pertaining to the equality of gender and representation.

At their best, women's organizations have pressed for legislative changes and conducted civic education. GBM and FIDA are such examples. They have forged alliances across "ethnic, religious, clan, racial, rural–urban, generational and other divides" (Tripp 2003b, p. 253). Maathai (2004) saw government-registered groups as crucial to rural development. These localized groups mobilize to raise capital for a common cause, as well as to strengthen ties among families and friends. Tripp also underscores the role of informal patronage in politics, with the state granting licenses and extending funds to NGOs. On the one hand, "throwing state power behind the promotion of individual autonomy can 'weaken or undermine' such groups" (Okin 2002, p. 225). On the other, financial and logistic support of local NGOs can provoke the "accusations, especially by local patriarchal groups opposed to their activities of these organizations, that they are nothing but traitors and offshoots of western imperialism" (Yuval-Davis 1997, p. 121).

Tripp and Kolawole also emphasize the role of informal patronage in politics with the state granting licenses and extending funds to African NGOs. First ladies (Nana Ageman Rawlings of Ghana, Dr. Maryam Babangida of Nigeria, Betty Kaunda and Vera Chiluba of Zambia, and Janet Museveni of Uganda) have played key roles in securing funds and overseeing nongovernmental operations. However, most regimes hijack the agendas and finances of women's movements, reducing them to government mouthpieces (Tripp 2003b).

Akosua A. Ampofo, Josephine Beoku-Betts, and Mary J. Osirim (2008) caution against the reliance on female political representatives to address gender inequality. Kiai (cited in Nasong'o and Ayot 2007, p. 182) recounts the physical and psychological trauma Edna Sang, a parliamentary candidate endured at a rally: "They blocked my exit . . . they attacked me and undressed me." This action demonstrates the silencing of assertive females as much as it limits their entry into a public sphere dominated by men. The year Sang ran for office in Kenya, only sixteen women were elected members of parliament yet over 200 women were on the ballot.

Sang's is not an isolated incident, as John Ndeta (2013) recounts. In 2013, only thirty women in Kenya received clearance to vie for seats at the national and county level. An aspirant in the Thika District relocated to a Nairobi hotel to avoid consistent electoral violence and intimidation. Her opponents distributed thousands of condoms on the eve of the nomination with her name as the supplier. Another female candidate from the Kisumu District was accused of running for office for personal gain. In Nyalenda within the Kisumu District, a woman candidate who lost to her male counterpart faced similar challenges: "My car was smashed by the youth in Nyalenda when I stopped to address them just before the nominations. The mob started demanding for money. I only escaped miraculously" (*ibid.*). Other women aspirants were cautioned against running for office at the risk of personal harm.

The harassment of female political candidates shadowed Maathai's and Charity Ngilu's runs for president in 1997. Kelvin's (2011) concern about a lingering "second in command paradigm" in female candidates ignores the price paid for these ventures. Women understand the price of political visibility besides money and power. Maathai herself asserted that a woman politician needed to have the skin of an elephant. Hers and Ngilu's aspiration to the presidency was in itself courageous and inspiring.

The integration of women into the discussion of how nations analyze themselves is a "recent and partial endeavor" (Yuval-Davis 1997, p. 3). Women's exclusion from mainstream narratives of nationalism means their historical significance and contributions are omitted. Simply put, were Maathai a Kenyan man, her story would have been eulogized in song and cultural histories as has been the case for male freedom fighters and political activists.

Yuval-Davis views the private/public dichotomy as ennobling men and their social roles. The main issue is where power to shape public policy lies. National heritages typically focus on men, war, and intellectuals. Kenya's heritage (finally) celebrates the Mau Mau movement, Kenya's legislature, political appointments, and members of parliament—all of which for the most part sideline the work of women and children. Unlike men, who dominate the public sphere, women are located in the private sphere—family, homes, the soil—which "is not seen as politically relevant" (Yuval-Davis 1993, p. 622). This trend undoubtedly made Maathai's efforts more complicated and difficult. As we saw, she was compelled to use male nursery attendants in GBM because of their mobility and access to communities; by contrast, women had less education and could not "go knocking on people's doors" (*ibid.*, p. 172). This is reminiscent of the Kenyan cliché "She is like a man," used to describe assertive women; one wonders if GBM male associates felt the same way about Maathai. They undoubtedly supported her activities for pay, yet it is questionable if they treated their own sisters and wives as equals thereafter.

Community representatives in traditional communities have been men, who naturally assumed leadership in the post-independence era. Social interactions and existing structural power relations normalize male privilege (Rogoff *et al.* 2003). What is left out of these national narratives is that women and old men managed domestic affairs and maintained the social fabric of the community when men flocked to urban areas and/or joined the army (Yuval-Davis 1997). Maathai's (2006) family structure indicates a similar pattern, as her father worked away from home.

As I've argued before, in rural communities, where the state often has limited penetration, "gender and social relations are determined by cultural and religious customs of the national collectivity" (Yuval-Davis 1993, p. 626). Community elders and councilors are mostly men. Despite the presumption of homogeneity in cultural groups, not all members of a cultural collectivity are equally committed to that culture (Yuval-Davis 1993). What passes for cultural norms represent the few who have access to and control the *polis,* and the national agenda reflects the authoritative voices of community representatives more often than the majority of actual members (Yuval-Davis 1993, 1997). John Armstrong refers to these cultural police as "border guards" (cited in Yuval-Davis 1993).

The control of women's mobility by men is not limited to Muslim communities, as some assert. Maathai's mother moved her family to Nakuru and back at her father's behest (Maathai 2006). It is improbable that she would have taken such important decisions in the home without his sanction. Maathai granted as much of her own marital relations with Mwangi.

President Moi's "misogynistic and myopic" regime dismissed GBM's members as a "bunch of divorcees" (Warah 2011), which was particularly hypocritical, considering President Moi's own marital separation. Kenyan columnist Salim Lone (2011) views Kenyan society during Maathai's lifetime as a police state that was highly male chauvinist and limiting of women's freedom and ability to speak as well as act. Okiya Omtatah Okoiti (2011) elaborates on how, at its apex, Moi's regime conducted an "outright scandalous" abuse of state power: "They killed and maimed many, destroyed private property and looted national coffers with demonic abandon, while espousing platitudes about faith, God, family values, morality, love, justice, peace, unity and freedom for all" (p. 13). They rigged elections indiscriminately and "alternative thought was criminalized and ruthlessly silenced through murder, torture, detention, dispossession or exile" (*ibid.*). Yet, at a time when Kenyan society expected women to "sit back silent and demure," Maathai ran for political office and publicly challenged the ruling of the judge in her publicized and humiliating divorce trial (Gaitho 2011).

MARRIAGE AND DIVORCE

The personal is, of course, also political. From the start, Maathai's union with Mwangi Mathai was not easy. At the wedding at Our Lady of Queen of Peace Church in Nairobi, Bishop John Njenga from Maathai's Catholic Church and bishops from Mwangi's African Independent Church officiated. This ceremony, at which Maathai wore a Western-style wedding dress, was actually the second; the other rite was a traditional one on her father's farm in Nakuru. Although the couple was married in a Catholic church, both of them attended service at Nairobi Baptist church.

By 1979, Maathai and Mwangi were divorced. The failure of Maathai's marriage provides a classic example of unequal power and vulnerability in heterosexual unions. Maathai acknowledged her husband's privileges only after the divorce. His interests were a priority in the marriage. She kept the home and raised their three children—a son, Waweru, born in 1969; a daughter, Wanjira, born in 1971; and another son, Muta, born in 1973—setting aside her own interests, including a run for political office and greater visibility.

Yet Mwangi unceremoniously left his wife and children. Maathai's sense of guilt and insecurity that she writes about in *Unbowed* mirrors the self-doubt of many women who take responsibility for everything negative and little credit for the positive. Her own lack of hesitation at defying gender roles was evident when she left her children at their father's home for her job in Zambia. However, Maathai plays down any allegations of her husband's abuse of power in dealings with family in her writings. She talks about the plight of women and men, but makes few linkages to unequal gender relations. It is as though Maathai and her ex-husband's relationship, as independent and highly educated adults with career options, was a Kenyan norm. In marked contrast was Maathai's vocal and consistent criticism of the abuse of power in the public sphere (Maathai 2006).

Maathai and Mwangi's divorce was a complete surprise to Professor Mbaya because she'd seen no indication of problems between them. Mbaya, however, acknowledges disparities in the couple's political and religious ideologies. Mwangi initially worked for a number of corporations, and returned to this kind of work years later after his time in politics. He has married twice since his divorce from Maathai. Mwangi grew up in Joro in the Rift Valley before his parents relocated to Maathai's birthplace, Nyeri. But their interests were different (Maathai 2006).

The relationship may not have withstood the trials of a marital union, but the couple shared responsibilities in raising the children. Mwangi took care of the children when Maathai was out of the country and even came by the house when Maathai was arrested in the middle of the night during Moi's clampdown on advocates for the multiparty system. The children's choice to retain their father's name testifies to either his reliability or merely their decision to abide by African custom. At the least, both mother and children respected his parenting skills. Professor Mbaya lauds Mwangi for raising the children without fostering animosity toward Maathai despite the fact that he and their mother went on separate paths. Mwangi supported Maathai's run for political office and during her last days Mbaya recalls his question to those at her bedside, "How is it with her soul?"

Maathai (2006) recognized the toll their careers and cultural expectations took on the marriage. They were a young couple, trained in America and with demanding jobs: politician and university professor. She attributed her husband's sexist demands to cultural dictates, as such absolving him of responsibility. Rarely does society extend such rationalizations to explain women's choices or peccadilloes. Maathai lamented the wasted energy, time, and delay in fulfilling her potential caused by her married life (Maathai 1993). She refused to play the underling or downplay her God-given talents to accommodate an insecure partner (Maathai 2006). The devastating three-week divorce proceedings "fostered an inner strength and sense of personal empowerment that she could tap into later on" (Kushner 2009, p. 142).

Notwithstanding her obvious frustrations and sense of betrayal, Maathai's development as an independent and visionary person appears to have been gradual, as was her increasing knowledge of herself. For instance, Maathai's response to changes in religious expression (such as the mass being recited in English instead of Latin) and her tolerance of public displays of intimacy capture the cultural shift she, and others, went through. She surprised herself and the world in her academic and activist achievements and in how she became more critical of sociopolitical structures.

The nation state, of course, controls women in other ways, such as in determining their reproductive rights, or lack thereof. (See Kenya's woeful record on this at Center for Reproductive Rights 2007.) Policies that affect maternity leave and childcare facilities, the availability of contraceptives and fertility clinics, the legality of abortion, and sterilization determine the population and its growth rate (Yuval-Davis 1993, 1997). But portraying women as merely "losers" or "victims" runs the danger of them being represented "simply [as] passive recipients of social change rather than active participants" (Moore 1988, p. 79).

Women play an important role in controlling younger women and sometimes have power over some men. They also promote prevailing ideologies (Yuval-Davis 1997). Such was the case in October 2000, when Kenyan Muslim women demonstrated against the proposed affirmative action and gender equality bill. Talcott Parson's functionalism theory attributes these character contradictions to a "judicious complicity by internalizing prevailing norms" (Smith 2001, p. 27). Nigerian Professor Amina Mama recalls the community's pressure on her for being much more assertive and confident than her peers, although she came from a family of political activists and her mother was a schoolteacher (Salo and Mama 2001).

These contradictions in gender constructions underlie a range of issues. Is child rearing in the nuclear family subjugating and inhibitive of women's flourishing? Is women's altruism in opposition to women's self-actualization? Are professional prestige and earning potential the ultimate measures of individuation and accomplishment? What are the barriers to women's public life? Do women take refuge in the role of motherhood and absolve men of their responsibility, citing male unreliability in childcare and housekeeping? Must a woman choose between career and motherhood? How do women choose?

Maathai knew that sexism and tribalism cost her initial job offer upon her return to Kenya from overseas studies. At the University of Nairobi, male professors received higher salaries than their female counterparts. She was aware that the regime was intent on silencing her for opposing Moi. Over the years, she became cautious in her choices. She spoke out in the presence of the media and with the tacit or direct support of the international community. She (1994) expressed shock at her husband's abandonment, but she confessed to ongoing tensions in the marriage.

Yet, there is no mention of her confronting her husband over the unceremonious separation and divorce. In traditional African communities, relatives-in-law would have spoken for her or against her. But the divorce was settled in court rather than by cultural elders.

African culture considers the conspicuous omission of relatives and neighbors as suspicious. By way of contrast, the Nigerian historian Toyin Falola details in his memoir *A Mouth Sweeter Than Salt* how personal, family, historical, and communal stories overlap in village life, providing a multiform way of assessing rightness and wrongness.

The traditional role of women has undergone transformation, although within a consistent range. Urbanization, education, and social migration have restructured family structures, eroding the direct supremacy of men in homes. Within the onslaught of new ideas, values, and choices in the early Kenyan republic, women have assumed a more public role in maintaining the family in the husband's absence. Sometimes adult men and women report to non-kin members or younger men in workplaces. And increasingly, the wife's salary supplements a husband's income. Nonetheless, a gendered politics of labor persists in the domestic and public sphere in Kenya.

By her own admission, Maathai (2006) embraced the role of a politician's wife. She toned down her tastes to avoid jeopardizing her husband's public image (Chege 2011). She allowed that wearing the elegant, long, African gowns called *kitenges* was a judicious choice (Maathai 2006, p. 110). Kenyan society still scorns women thought to be excessively "modern"; however, she felt the focus on her clothing and how forcefully she spoke to be sexist. Society rarely dictates men's clothing and behavior or questions the duplicity of upholding "'Africanness' through their wives, both at home and in society" (*ibid.*, p. 111). While both men and women transmit culture, women embody it. President Moi questioned her Africanness and femininity, to which she replied, balancing the tongue-in-cheek and emollient with the pointed and direct, "These are the kind of issues that require the anatomy of whatever lies above the neck" (Maathai, 2000).

Tripp (2000) also notes the paradox of men upholding tradition through their womenfolk. Within Maathai's Kikuyu-dominated Central Province, vigilante Mungiki groups comprising dissatisfied youth boast an estimated million members. Since the late 1990s, Mungiki—in addition to advocating a Kirinyaga kingdom (a return to traditional practices including sacrificial offerings to Ngai wa Kirinyaga, God of Mount Kenya), polygamy, and female circumcision—has publicly encouraged female circumcision, terrorized women (chasing them along the streets for wearing revealing clothing, such as miniskirts and tight jeans), and stripping them naked in streets, although their own ancestors wore "miniscule [sic] pieces of animal skin or tree barks or beads" (Oriang 1999).

According to Fustos (2011), cultural beliefs and practices can add to the unequal power between genders. Much older men take on more than one wife in marriage and, in most cases, marry girls a lot younger. About 43 percent of women experience sexual and physical violence from partners (Chimbi 2012b). Maathai's class and age would have protected her from the street vigilantes. However, among my own Bukusu community, the late Elijah Masinde's followers harassed women in the marketplace for similar breaches in attire (Florence 2011).

Maathai's assimilation of Western lifestyles dovetailed with a quest for cultural allegiance to inherited values. In marriage, Maathai put her husband's interests first and only admitted to injustices after he abandoned her and filed for divorce. During one of her classes, as her former student Professor Mbaabu (1976–1977) recalled in his interview with me, Maathai raised the issue of gender relations and group-think. Her husband had alleged that she was in a "locked" room with a man. "Is it possible for a man and woman to be in a room together and not engage in sex?" she asked the class. The class laughed at the incongruity.

During her divorce proceedings, Maathai received a six-month jail sentence for contempt of court. Her braided, dreadlocked hair with beads, on which she had spent money and time, was cut before state police consigned her to a cell filled with inmates imprisoned for petty crimes. Maathai's long hair displayed her mood as much as her status as a university professor; few rural women could have devoted such time or resources to personal grooming. The physical plucking of her braids, although routine for prisoners following sentencing—the usual procedure utilizes scissors and razors—was publicly humiliating and an added punishment, particularly because of her status and political visibility (Maathai 2006). It was, in my assessment, a deliberate ploy to bring the educated and reputedly strong professor to heel.

Maathai acknowledged the injustice of cultural gender roles in her marriage only after the divorce. Where to draw the line of victimization? In her interview with me, Professor Mbaya vouched for Maathai's integrity:

Wangari enthusiastically supported her husband's own ambitions for a parliamentary seat and was considered an important contributor to that success. Subsequently, she employed some of the same methodology to attain a parliamentary seat for herself. However, in spite of achieving the political prize of parliamentarian, she resisted the invitation to secure her prominence through the practice of "tribal" politics. So she supported . . . or refused to support . . . individuals in accordance to her own conscience and perceptions. Consequently, she did not follow blindly "tribal" leaders, and her own constituency decided to punish her for that.

Maathai (2003) had longed for political office since she campaigned for her husband in 1974. At campaign rallies, when she appeared on her husband's behalf, voters urged her to stand for office herself. In contrast to self-promoting politicians, she took her promises to heart. She challenged her husband on the same after he won office. Along with a family friend, Mr. Murefu who had campaigned for her husband, she kept one of the promises made to the Lang'ata constituency: to establish a tree nursery in Karura Forest, during the forester Kimathi wa Murage's tenure. A young man, Charles Githogori, managed the small project and Maathai personally established Envirocare, Ltd., employing semi-literate women to clean up homesteads in Nairobi and plant trees where necessary.

In running for political office in 1982, Maathai (2006) recalled the comments she received in campaigning for her husband. Some supporters cited Maathai's initiatives and achievements through GBM as the reasons they voted for her. At the time, however, only two women were elected MPs, with the rest appointed by President Moi. Females had limited power in a male-dominated political assembly.

According to data from the World Bank (2013), women now constitute almost a fifth of Kenya's parliament. Yet politics remains a man's club, even in the United States: "Data compiled by Rutgers [University] shows women currently hold 16.6 percent of the 535 seats in state legislatures. There are [only] six female governors; of the 100 big-city mayors, eight are women. . . . [And the] women [who are fortunate enough to be] in Congress are still really in a situation where they have to prove themselves to their male colleagues and constituencies" (Stolberg 2011, p. 12). In her Edinburgh address, Maathai (1994) explicitly attributed lack of political and social progress to Kenyan society's sexism.

At the sixtieth anniversary celebration of Maendeleo Ya Wanawake in 2012, President Mwai Kibaki urged "women to seek for elective positions in the coming General Election instead of waiting for posts on a silver platter" (Barasa 2012). He implied that all it took was hard work; women should not wait for handouts (presumably as political appointees). Article 27 of the constitution prohibits the domination of any one gender in institutions. Kenya's situation is not even mirrored in East Africa, where parliamentarians who are women are "56.3 per cent in Rwanda, Uganda (35 per cent), Burundi (30.5 per cent) and Ethiopia (37.8 per cent)" (Barasa 2012). Further, the Maendeleo Ya Wanawake Organization has a network of four million members and 25,000 affiliate groups, making it a viable forum for advancing women's representation in Congress (ibid.).

The advent of Kenya's new constitution allowed women's representation in parliament to leap by ten percentage points. Yet efforts to entrench women's political presence have constantly been stymied. I have encountered within my own birthplace in the Bungoma District a weariness regarding efforts to enable women to advance socially and politically. Siblings complain about females inheriting property regardless of marital status. Married women have claims on both their husband's and parents' property. Some couples express concern about women taking liberties with legal protection: "You cannot touch them these days!" men and women say. Within corporations and educational institutions, quotas pit colleagues and classmates against each other, with charges of bias from either party. The response to many questions of historical patriarchal privilege too often remains a dismissive sigh.

14

THE MULTIPARTY SYSTEM

At independence in 1963, the Kenya African Democratic party (KADU), led by Ronald Ngala, was suppressed in favor of President Jomo Kenyatta's Kenya African National Union (KANU). After its early promise, the Kenyatta government was soon riddled with corruption. In the article "Why Kenyatta's Sunset Years Led to an Orgy of Official Graft," a serialization from his book *Kenya: A History Since Independence*, Charles Hornsby claims that friends, relatives, and political allies of the president engaged in rampart exploitation of natural resources. For instance, with regard to ivory exports, he writes:

> [R]eceipts in destinations such as Hong Kong suggested that at least 345 tonnes of ivory had been exported from Kenya in 1973, [and] indicated the death of at least 15,000 elephants in a year, three times the official number. . . . One problem was that the Kenyatta family itself was implicated in poaching and ivory exports. Margaret Kenyatta, Kenyatta's daughter, was chairman of the United African Company, one of at least ten companies exporting ivory despite the ban. Ivory could earn KSh 300 (US$36) per kilogramme, making one elephant worth thousands of dollars. (Hornsby 2012)

Hopes for a change following Kenyatta's death in 1978 and the accession of his vice-president, Daniel arap Moi, soon disappeared when the corruption intensified. Activists did have some institutions to which they could apply to redress human rights abuses, besides regular courts: the Law Society of Kenya was established by an Act of Parliament in 1949 and *Kituo Cha Sheria* (Legal Advice Centre) was founded in 1973. The Geneva-based International Commission of Jurists-Kenya Section (ICJ-Kenya) was registered in 1974.

Nonetheless, the history of Kenya since independence has been marked by clandestine, sporadic abuse of human rights—not only in violence around the time of elections but in the unsolved murders or "accidental" deaths of noteworthy individuals such as Tom Mboya, J. M. Kariuki, Bishop Alexander Muge, and Robert Ouko.

By 1990, Daniel arap Moi had been in power for more than a decade. Moi had lost his battle over the Media Trust complex and his regime had become more oppressive, with an extremely hardline attitude toward GBM. On July 7, 1990, pro-democracy advocates including Kenneth Matiba, Charles Rubia, and Raila Odinga (later prime minister and presidential candidate) organized a rally, memorialized as Saba Saba Day (also called 7/7), despite the government's ban on public gatherings. Maathai planted a tree to honor the event and met with pro-democracy proponents.

Meanwhile, in June,

the Roman Catholic Church, the Presbyterian Church of East Africa, the Methodist Church and the National Council of Churches backed the Anglican Church's [call] for reform [and] urged President Moi to dissolve parliament, convene a national constitutional conference and hold free and fair elections. Large-scale political demonstrations erupted in July, which prompted a government crackdown, with the government detaining its most vocal critics, charging them with sedition. . . . In response, Bishop Alexander Muge of Eldoret and his colleague, Bishop John Okullu of Maseno South, called for the president to step down and for fresh elections. On 12 Aug 1990, Labour Minister Peter Okondo warned Bishop Muge that if he and Bishop Okullu entered the Busia district "they will see fire and may not leave alive." (*The Church of England Newspaper*, 2012)

On August 14, 1990, Bishop Muge along with his staff were driving in a car bound for Busia in the Diocese of Eldoret when their vehicle collided with a truck and he died on impact. The truck driver died in prison. In Kenya, threats of assassinations should be taken seriously.

Robert Ouko, the popular former foreign minister tipped to succeed Moi, was murdered under mysterious circumstances and his death remains unsolved. Ouko's suspicious death intensified the opposition's charges of corruption, and Moi responded by imprisoning political opponents. Amnesty International accused Moi's regime of human rights abuses, and Moi lost credibility as the international community condemned his actions. Perhaps partly as a result of such pressures, Moi legalized political parties in December 1991 and agreed to multiparty elections thereafter.

The international donor community played a key role in Moi's concession, especially when that community operated in tandem with domestic pressures that "were clearly influenced by economic decline, increased government corruption, intimidation of the press, the proliferation of human rights abuses and tortures, and the increase in the number of pro-democracy movements in various regions of the world" (House-Midamba 1996, p. 291). One cannot underestimate how essential the decision in November 1991 by international donors gathered under the auspices of the World Bank to withhold $350 million of aid to the Moi government was to forcing economic and political reforms in Kenya.

Following the reintroduction of multipartism, efforts were made to form an effective opposition to contest the 1992 elections. But unseating the incumbent Moi proved difficult, with the opposition splitting the vote along ethnic lines. In response to state-sponsored human rights abuses against multiparty advocates and groups not aligned with Moi's Kalenjin ethnic group, masses of victimized citizens demanded protection and a right to self-determination. Thousands lost their lives and many more were displaced, and the issue of state violence became personal for families throughout the nation. President Moi instigated a political witchhunt that targeted pro-democracy advocates.

Maathai was a key figure in Kenya's multiparty movement that fought Moi and his abuse of human rights (Murunga and Nasong'o 2007). Maathai was herself targeted for assassination, exemplifying not only how sharp a thorn she'd become in the administration's side but how the administration treated the opposition. In 1992, after a three-day siege of her Nairobi residence, Maathai was arrested and jailed in Lang'ata Prison. She had no blanket in a cell that was filthy and wet, with lights on day and night. She was fifty-two years old and suffered from arthritis coupled with back pain. Again, the backlash from the international community was swift. International figures like Al Gore, Paul Wellstone, and six other U.S. senators intervened for her release (Kushner 2009).

Maathai worked to forge consensus among the opposition, which was fractured among Oginga Odinga (FORD-Kenya), Mwai Kibaki (the Democratic Party), and Kenneth Matiba (FORD-Asili). Maathai tried without success to unite the FORD ticket under the Middle Ground Group (MGG) to avoid splitting the votes. She was drawn to FORD-Asili to consolidate the Kikuyu vote with her compatriots Kibaki and Matiba. Nonetheless, in November 1992, amid charges of vote-rigging and other irregularities, Moi won the elections, a feat that shored up his credibility both domestically and internationally (Michaelson 1994).

Following the ethnic violence that marred the elections, the Green Belt Movement intervened to alleviate the sufferings of the wounded and displaced. Maathai initiated teach-ins through the MGG in downtown Nairobi to raise awareness about a range of issues pertaining to democratic rights (2006). A year later, the Kenya Anti-Rape Organization demanded a redress of violence against women, while the Kenya Human Rights Commission (KHRC) focused on human rights protection and monitoring (see Nwankwo n.d.).

FREEDOM CORNER HUNGER STRIKE

The work with the MGG was directly political; however, Maathai acted politically in a more indirect manner. In early 1992, a group of fifty rural Kikuyu mothers approached Attorney General Amos Wako about the detention and incarceration of their sons. The establishment of the multiparty system had invalidated the reason for the arrests of political activists by the regime. This had been understood since the multiparty campaign of October 1990, yet the regime had continued to make such arrests in the intervening two years.

The mothers received no help. Denied representation by the state legislature, on February 28 the group arrived in Nairobi to protest. They drew upon their traditional authority as concerned mothers—a portrayal that would resonate with the family-oriented Kenyan culture. Setting up a makeshift camp in a part of Uhuru Park they called Freedom Corner, the women went on hunger strike and were joined in solidarity by Kenyans of all ages, nations, professions, and religious orientations against government security forces (Amutabi 2007; Maathai 2009; Nasong'o and Ayot 2007; Tripp 2003b). They "set up microphones for anyone who wished to speak" (Tripp 2003b, p. 251). Some victims of police brutality spoke out. Four days into the strike, the police "descended on protesters with truncheons and tear gas" (Warah 2011, p. 19). In protest, three mothers stripped to reveal their breasts to the police, which represented the ultimate insult in African traditional cultures (Tripp 2003a). The women's curse (*guturamigra ng'ana*) was not lost on Kenyans, including the police, some of whom turned their faces or walked away.

Although Nancy Worthington (2001) links the women's actions to media reports at the time of South African protests against apartheid, the strategy of women baring themselves has long existed among African communities. Seventy years earlier, "[t]he colonial regime's abuse of female laborers was a central complaint articulated by [Harry] Thuku, and women vociferously protested his arrest.

Mary Muthoni Nyanjiru was catapulted into the political limelight of colonial Kenya on 16 March 1922 amid what came to be known as the Harry Thuku riot. In a split second, amid a political impasse, Nyanjiru stepped into the political vacuum and became etched into history forever. Even though she was killed by the colonial authorities on the same day, Nyanjiru's brief intervention in the riot rewrote the role and place of women in Kenya. (Ikonya 2008; see also Mary Muthoni Nyanjiru)

"Nyanjiru stripped to shame a passive crowd of 7,000 to 8,000 into rioting" (Worthington 2001, p. 180).

In Uganda, 1,500 women marched through the streets of Gulu to protest violence in April 1989. For five hours they processed in a dirge and, half-naked, lifted their breasts as a curse against wrongdoers (Tripp 2000). In the case of Freedom Corner, Worthington (2001) acknowledges the confusion over who the targets of the women's curse were: the police, the president, or the nation? The violence shocked the nation as much as it scapegoated the police force.

Throughout the hunger strike, and in the yearlong vigil that followed it, the widely read Weekly Review failed to acknowledge these rural Kikuyu women's political advocacy, and reduced their protest to familial concerns for the welfare of their sons (Worthington 2001). Their cause was absorbed into the political contest between Moi's regime and the opposition. The opposition used the women's protest to undermine the regime, while the regime portrayed the strike as a subversive threat to political stability. Hillary Ng'weno, former editor of the Weekly Review, accused both sides of playing to the foreign media to justify their position and garner international credibility (Worthington 2001). In a manner typical of Kenyan politics, Moi's regime decried what it claimed was German and American meddling.

Supporting Moi's stance and the police action against the women was Maendeleo Ya Wanawake, largely staffed by the regime's relatives and friends, in contrast to other women's groups like the NCWK and

Mothers in Action, which had fallen out of favor with the regime. During the protest, the release of four prisoners reinforced Moi's image as a conciliator, given the strained relations between his regime and the protestors. The incident also showed the continued primacy of social class in the confrontation, since in their appeal to Attorney General Amos Wako before the strike and Moi's release of four of the sons, the protestors were seen to be reliant on a powerful elite within the state machinery to settle the dispute. The Kenyan women's political advocacy was submerged in a masculine power contest.

Maathai rallied protesters, bellowing out the words of the American civil rights movement, "We shall overcome," echoing its preference for non-violence. The *Weekly Review* photographed her seated with the protesters in conversation with a dissident religious leader. The media captured the beating she received and her collapse on the strike's fourth day, and a picture was taken of her lying unconscious on a bed in Nairobi Hospital.

Once again, the international community spoke out in her defense. What then became a yearlong vigil ended in success in 1993 "when all but one of the fifty-two sons were released en masse" (Maathai 2006, p. 225). Typically, the *Weekly Review* lumped Maathai's intervention with Moi's regime, the opposition, and church leaders to delimit the rural women's campaign to release their detained sons as merely another political maneuver.

Maathai's solidarity with the women drew them into the public arena of what Worthington (2001) terms "combative motherhood" and its moral authority, in contrast to the conventional marginalization of women in politics and media representation. Yuval-Davis (1993, 1997) reiterates this element of motherhood and the role's political agency in highlighting the significance of women as mothers of nations. At one point, the media portrayed Maathai as the leader of the rural women's strike. Linking the rural women's protest to public figures like Maathai gave the powers-that-be the chance to portray both Maathai and the women as pawns of someone else's movement.

Worthington (2001) also notes that only one mother of an incarcerated son, Monica Wangu Wamwere, was named in the media. The media's selective and skewed coverage of the rural women's protest for their detained sons "obscured [the] link between motherhood and political legitimacy" (Worthington 2001, p. 180). To that end, the media both failed to challenge essentialist portrayals of women as marginalized, uneducated, and not politically savvy, and delegitimized them as players in, and key contributors to, the public arena. Not surprisingly, the media portrayed Maathai's activism and the workings of the Green Belt Movement as atypical.

The media also influenced how the public received Maathai as a mother, an intellectual, and an activist. Her joining the rural Kikuyu women to call for release of their sons catapulted the group to the top of Kenya's list of human rights abuses (Worthington 2001). The rural women of modest means were contrasted with educated, combative, and modern urbanized women, symbolized by Maathai—and their protest was described as unusual and anomalous. The rural women upended conventional portrayals of women as "ill equipped for the political arena . . . yet the movement's unmistakable tie to the moral authority of mothers and their links to the rural majority defied the possibility of direct criticism that would be culturally acceptable" (Worthington 2001, pp. 180–181). Maathai's presence among the mothers of political detainees was a double-edged sword. She gave their protest credibility and international visibility but she also risked the mothers' movement being minimized as merely another of her "plots" against the regime.

ETHNIC RHETORIC

To a large degree, regional divisions in Kenya mirror the compositions of the country's ethnic groups. The Luhya and Luo are concentrated in the west of the country and Kikuyus inhabit the Rift Valley and central highlands. Swahili-speaking groups (the Chagga, Kuria, Taita, and Mijikenda) mostly reside along the coast and on the borderlands between Kenya and Tanzania.

Historically, ethnic group clusters guaranteed distinct formal and informal communal interactions, facilitating the transmission of cultural norms through the generations and embedding ethnic and cultural homogeneity. Village sports, rites of passage, myths and folklores, and proverbs and sayings demonstrated indigenous history and culture. Interactions among ethnic group members led to a natural development of routine practices, shared expectations, beliefs, and a worldview.

As we have seen, however, the introduction of European-style formal schools, churches, and mass media inevitably created broader-based coalitions and undermined the existing conduits for culture. Maathai herself embodied (and acknowledged) the transformative impact of formal education on her notion of who she was and her vision for social transformation.

One result of formal education is literacy, which, overall, fosters a cultural reliance on a literary, rather than oral, tradition to transmit and reinforce community values. The Green Belt Movement capitalizes on literacy and its website to promote its vision and to showcase achievements. Although Maathai called herself a child of the soil, she spent a greater part of her life in cities. These overlaps in learning, settlement, and self-representation before, during, and after colonialism make it difficult to distinguish changes that arose solely after the introduction of foreign rule and Christianity from those that evolved from internal cultural developments.

In her writings, Maathai (2006, 2009) bewailed the impact of ethnic loyalties. She located Kenya's simmering ethnic rhetoric in divisions that existed before the arrival of colonialism. She argued that the 1885 Berlin Conference created nation-states in Africa that disregarded existing ethnic alliances and cross-cultural integration. To this day, she noted, Maasai groups live in Kenya and Tanzania, Tesos in Kenya and Uganda, and Somalis in Kenya, Ethiopia, and Somalia (Maathai 2010). In a similar manner, you can find a Bukusu family settled in Mombasa or a Kikuyu family in Bungoma, a primarily Bukusu/Teso territory, breaking with historical settlement patterns.

Although this is one rationale for ethnic divisions in Kenya, among my primary ethnic group, the Bukusu, historical accounts attribute interethnic locations and divisions to early migrations and rivalry for land and livestock (Florence 2011; Makila 1978). Even as the colonial administration helped integrate different groups on farms and in urban centers, these interactions were limited and efforts to formulate a national identity were stymied (Kanogo 1987). These ethnic linkages, however, developed as institutionalized cultural frameworks of identity and group mobilization to access natural resources. Kenya's ethnic rhetoric precedes independence, as Maathai's experience illustrates, and lingering tensions flare up every so often (Amutabi 2007), particularly around election time.

The British colonialists, administrators, and missionaries controlled Kenya by pitting one ethnic group against the other, a pattern that was entrenched by the continued dominance of the Kikuyu, Embu, and Meru groups that benefited most from the early penetration of colonial capitalism, missionary activities, and access to formal education (ibid., p. 47). Since independence, ethnicity has been the centerpiece of political competition instead of parties with defined policies and programs. Kenya's first president, Jomo Kenyatta, consolidated his position through his patronage of fellow Kikuyus, much like his successor Daniel arap Moi did with the Kalenjins. Subsequently, "access to political power is a conduit for the acquisition of educational resources, employment opportunities in the state bureaucracies and state contracts, among others, by the ethnic group in power" (Munene 2013, p. 48). The Kikuyu and Kalenjin groups who have produced the presidents have benefitted the most from state resources and services.

Kenyan intellectuals argue that the Kenyatta and Moi regimes exploited ethnic rhetoric. Jomo Kenyatta's administration consolidated the Gikuyu (Kikuyu), Embu, and Meru Association's (GEMA) political and economic prominence (Gecaga 2007), and non-Kikuyus such as Tom Mboya and Barack Obama, Sr. were slighted by a Kikuyu-dominant regime (Shachtman 2009). Moi, Kenyatta's successor, established his own hegemony by creating a clique of aides and supporters. He resisted a multiparty system of governance, claiming that it would "breed interethnic violence" (Gecaga 2007).

Instigated by the ruling KANU government, the 1992 ethnic clashes in the Rift Valley, Western Province, and parts of Nyanza Province caused deaths, spread terror, and led to many people being displaced. At the 1997 elections, party affiliations continued to reflect ethnic-regional patterns (Oloo 2007). In response to the displacement of Kikuyus in Laikipia and Nakuru, a counterinsurgency against state-sponsored violence resulted in the emergence of the Kikuyu-based Mungiki, which has since morphed into a cluster of vigilante groups (Gecaga 2007).

The state's adoption of neo-liberal economic policies in the mid-1990s, through the use of Structural Adjustment Programs (or SAPs) led to privatization, financial diversification, and a reduction in social services like education and health, all of which heightened political-economic disparities. According to Joseph Kipkemboi Rono:

Families and the vulnerable have been exposed to severe socioeconomic risks such as inflation and unemployment, which have worsened poverty and increased regional differentiation as well as the gap between the rich and the poor. The SAPs have been linked to the stagnation in real per capita income growth, which is mainly associated with increasing poverty and unemployment and is related to the upsurge of the "culture of violence" and the deviance and crime rates in Kenya, particularly of violent crimes. Furthermore, the declining economy has been associated with increasing rates of non-enrolment, grade repetition and dropout in educational institutions, especially at the primary level. Moreover, marginalization of the poor in terms of education and the decline in quality of education in Kenya is also linked to the SAPs. With the vigorous implementation of the SAPs in 1990s, the quantity and quality of medical and other services have deteriorated substantially. (Cited in Rono 2002, p. 97)

Ethnic balkanization remains a problem in tertiary education. The Kenyan press regularly reports the frustration shared by politicians, policy makers, and academics in attempting to make public and private universities more inclusive and to avoid the use of ethnocentric rhetoric and competition. Nonetheless, appointments within these institutions represent the prevailing political leadership and have a history tied directly to the state's quest for political legitimacy (Munene 2013, p. 44–45):

Although the Kikuyu, Luhya, Kalenjin, Luo and Kamba, make up 66 per cent of the country's population, they take up 93 per cent of the jobs at Masinde Muliro University, 89.8 per cent at Moi University, 87.3 per cent at Egerton University, 86 per cent at Jomo Kenyatta University, 82.3 per cent at the University of Nairobi and 81.7 per cent at Kenyatta University. Out of 15 institutions surveyed, 10 had the majority of their staff coming from the same ethnic community as the vice-chancellor or principal. (Mathenge 2012)

The first major institutions of tertiary education, Nairobi and Kenyatta universities, were deliberately and strategically placed in Nairobi, close to President Kenyatta's Kiambu home. The vice-chancellor of Kenyatta University from 1970 to 1979, Dr. Josephat Karanja, had no university experience for his position except for his links with President Kenyatta, nor did many of his management staff. Kenyatta's ethnocentric university leadership decidedly shaped its political agenda.

Established in 1985, Moi University reflects its sponsor's political agenda. It was located close to the president's home and dominated by Kalenjin, Maasai, Turkana, and Samburu ethnic alliance (KAMATUSA). Moi's constituents weren't provided with adequate high schools to prepare students for the A-level examinations that served as gateways to university education. So to further counteract what he perceived as Kikuyu dominance, Moi abolished the A-level gateway to university education. He changed the 7-4-2-3 education structure (seven years of primary school, four of secondary, two of high, and three of college) in favor of an 8-4-4 system, which allowed all secondary-school students to compete for university positions According to the Republic of Kenya *Economic Survey*, between 2000 and 2013, university attendance rose from 50,700 in four fully fledged universities and a university college; to 143,000 students in seven universities and nine university colleges (Munene 2013, p. 52).

Kenya's current expansion of university education continues to be driven by a regime's agenda of patronage, guaranteeing political support/votes, and ensuring state legitimacy—a distinction from earlier times, when a politically explosive "white elephant" project (such as the building of the Times Media complex) was favored (Munene 2013, p. 55).

Yet the ethnic separation continues: Chuka University was founded among the Meru people and is headed by a Meru vice-chancellor. Kenyatta University has a Kikuyu leadership as does Kimathi University College of Technology. A Luo chancellor heads Maseno University; Masinde Muliro University of Science & Technology is run by a Luhya vice-chancellor; and Pwani University College is led by a coastal vice-chancellor (Munene 2013, p. 56). To reinforce the university's identity, staff and students set up "home" associations within the institution.

Inequalities in educational and political representation spill over into regional economic disparities. The government invests in financial and academic infrastructure, and extends loans and grants to students across levels of education. Universities draw further investments from industry and commerce, as well as through the buildings they own and the services they offer. All these lure students and migrant workers alike.

For instance, the siting of Masinde Muliro University of Science and Technology in Kakamega has led to the development of an airport, and economic development there since 2007 has meant a growth in agricultural output, further educational institutions, financial services, and shopping centers in the region. The benefits have extended to Webuye, a town 200 miles away, with a satellite campus (Munene 2013, p. 58).

Although, as is the case with Masinde, such state initiatives benefit regions that historically have remained on the periphery of economic and social development, the multiplication of academic programs with increasingly few job prospects portends considerable risk in the long term. The prestige and the ownership of universities for an ethnic group continue to take precedence over larger goals of national cohesion and harmony. The duplication of personnel and resources also increases the costs of running these institutions, which in turn delegitimizes the state by highlighting waste, patronage, and the creation of sinecures for the well-connected.

Maathai was acutely aware of the real dangers of ethnic chauvinism. In 1993, she tried without success to organize a seminar on ethnic conflict in Nakuru, but police blocked her from entering: "The provincial commissioner accused her of tribal incitement, and KANU MP Paul Chepkok went so far as to threaten her with circumcision if she were to return to the Rift Valley Province again" (Michaelson 1994, p. 555). In response, Maathai filed an injunction with the High Court against the state's prohibition. Circumventing the system, she formed a resettlement volunteer service to handle the displacement of persons from ethnic clashes.

With the emergence of multiparty politics in Kenya, pro-democratic groups united under the MGG opposition group. Maathai's one-on-one pedagogical approach drew on local expertise and evolved into civic and environmental education forums. Reflecting Freire's practice of conscientization, the forums drew on participants' day-to-day challenges—such as poverty and fear of the political machinery (Maathai 2004). Education, Freire insisted, is always political; one either sanctions the status quo or undermines it with a new vision (Amutabi 2007; Okin 1994). Maathai held teach-ins with forty to fifty people in her own house despite state harassment.

In 1999, another governmental attack on the opposition, with which Maathai was affiliated, drew international outrage yet again. In July 2001, Maathai was incarcerated in Gigiri Police Station for participating in the ten-year commemoration of Kenya's multiparty system and eleventh Saba Saba demonstration. In December 2002, in the first free and fair elections in her country in a generation, Maathai was elected a member of parliament for Tetu, trouncing her opponent. Maathai joined President Mwai Kibaki's new government but remained marginalized. Despite her academic credentials and global renown, the cabinet slot for Nyeri County went to a newcomer, Mukurweini MP Mutahi Kagwe, and Maathai was compelled to toe the political line. Kibaki, a neighbor from her rural county, impeded her prospects (he had been vice-president during the Moi regime), although she played the cheerleader to avoid political isolation (Obonyo 2011b).

In January 2003, Kibaki appointed Maathai assistant minister in the Ministry for Environment and Natural Resources. She would be the deputy to the Hon. Stephen Kalonzo Musyoka, a lawyer by training, in the new National Alliance of Rainbow Coalition (NARC) era of President Kibaki (2002–2005). Two years later, a constitutional referendum in Kenya divided along ethnic lines. President Kibaki's pro-Constitution group, the Party of National Unity (PNU), was primarily from Kikuyu and Meru groups. The "No" vote led by the Prime Minister Raila Odinga's Orange Democratic Movement (ODM) had the support of the Luo and Kalenjins (Maathai 2010). At the swearing-in ceremony of a new cabinet in December 2005, following the referendum, Maathai was among only three ministers and nineteen deputies who declined to attend, pending consultations with opposition parties, while the other twenty-six ministers and twenty-eight assistants participated.

For all the talk of national identity, ethnic rhetoric remains ubiquitous in Kenyan political life: "Kenya has not surmounted its development challenges simply because she has never enjoyed a leadership that is non-ethnocentric in the mindset; a leadership that is visionary in economic, democratic and social development; a leadership that is committed to national progress and not bent on personal aggrandizement or on that of inner supporters in his ethnic community" (Gwengi 2011, p. 6).

In the last few years, some have feared the "re-Kikuyunisation of Kenyan bureaucracy" (Amutabi 2007, p. 208). Maathai believed that a good leader mobilized people to a common vision, as opposed to exploiting the rhetoric of ethnicity endemic in Kenya. She devoted most of her political activity to trying to change a corrupt and inept regime from within existing structures—whether government, political parties, or the opposition. Like many Kenyans, Professor George Naholi at East Tennessee State University heard about the "good lady" during Maathai's tenure at the University of Nairobi. As he related in my interview, most memorable for Professor Naholi was his meeting with Maathai during the Constitution of Kenya Review Commission "at the Bomas of Kenya. She came across as an unassuming, down-to-earth lady, sometimes on her own in thoughtful moods. She was extremely humble."

The cultural lore surrounding Maathai's confrontations with the regime has often focused on Moi's belonging to a different ethnic group. Yet in the wake of the heavily contested 2007 elections, Maathai questioned the fraudulent victory of Kibaki (a member of her own ethnic group), demanded a recount, and condemned both sides for the violence in which thousands lost their lives and many more were displaced. On April 1 2008, her birthday, Maathai took part in a protest in Nairobi against the government's plan to increase the number of ministers in the cabinet and was tear-gassed by police during the encounter. In the middle of the post-election violence of 2007–2008, Maathai's GBM staffers reached out to wounded and displaced victims. In response, Kibaki's government withdrew Maathai's bodyguards and accused her of fueling ethnic tensions (Ogutu 2008a). She discovered the price of breaking ranks with an ethnic group. Maathai (2009) acknowledged the pressure to support President Kibaki, as well as the fact that the Kikuyu, Embu, and Meru were pitted against the other forty Kenyan ethnic groups, a split that left Maathai at a political crossroad.

15

POLITICAL CAREER

On September 27, 2011, a few days after Maathai's death, the *Daily Nation* carried an op-ed that argued that her venture into electoral politics had been *the* misstep of her rich life. Oscar Obonyo (2011b) labeled Maathai a political dwarf, whose stature was never quite large enough to reach State House, and whose political activism had failed to change the tenor of Kenyan politics and its culture of impunity. Yet that failure might have been, ironically, because of those very strengths that enhanced her stature. As Emongor Ekisa wrote shortly after Maathai's death: "Sadly, the current crop of politicians do not have core beliefs they subscribe to beyond flip-flopping on good governance, raw thirst for power and ethnic bigotry" (Ekisa 2011, p. 16).

Maathai's relative ineffectuality in political office was substantially due to the fact that as assistant minister for Environmental and Natural Resources, under Stephen Kalonzo Musyoka, the ex-vice president of Kenya, she had almost no authority in the ministry and government (Warah 2011). Assistant ministers typically don't achieve much and few distinguish themselves in office. Their role is primarily limited to reading the minister's speeches and deputizing in a public function for the minister in his/her absence. They don't replace the minister when their boss is away; if the absence is extended, another full minister is appointed in an acting capacity. An assistant minister cannot make policy and doesn't even sit in the president's cabinet. In this regard, Maathai had little or no stamp on that ministry beyond GBM and her Tetu constituency. Stephen Kalonzo Musyoka joked about having a deputy who was more famous than her boss after Maathai won the Nobel Peace Prize in 2004.

The award of the Nobel at the age of sixty-four failed to improve Maathai's political prospects, and her Tetu constituency rejected her for re-election in 2007. Maathai lost in the primary election for President Kibaki's Party of National Unity (PNU), which forced her to campaign under the banner of the Mazingira Green Party. There, too, she lost her bid for office (Obonyo 2011b). The NARC government's decision to abolish the shamba system in 2002 was supported by environmentalists, including Maathai. The system was nonetheless popular in her constituency and the decision to end it was condemned by many MPs (Maathai 2009). Maathai opposed cash handouts during the political campaign, an all-too-common practice in Kenyan politics. She lost to Francis Nyammo, a situation she attributed to "the politics of ethnicity and personality cult" (Chege 2011). Maathai stated that the failure of the Mazingira Green Party at the polls was due to her being punished as an ethnic traitor. She also (2009) acknowledged Kenya's historical pattern of electoral irregularities and rigging to explain her loss in the 2007 campaign, noting that it was not uncommon for constituencies to report electoral votes significantly higher than their registered voters.

Although a member of the elite and belonging to the largest ethnic community in Kenya, Maathai's ethnicity and class status didn't necessarily work to her benefit. We have seen that colleagues in the NCWK shied away from her following her divorce and fallout with Moi's regime. She lost her first job at the university because she belonged to the "wrong" ethnic group. She had greater success lobbying poor rural women who benefited from GBM in predominantly Kikuyu regions than building consensus during her university tenure or political engagement among the more affluent and urban populace.

Although her international visibility protected her from even further isolation or harm during the Moi regime, her success in Kenya owed as much to local organizations as it did to her fame beyond the country's borders. In fact, the role of international organizations could be problematic. After all, both Kenyans and foreigners have enabled the corruption of Kenya's political culture. International organizations often underwrite local NGOs and opposition movements, although they provide limited supervision or audits of day-to-day operations—sometimes requiring as little as disbursement of funds and an annual report to satisfy their criteria for effectiveness. This means that some groups are not held properly accountable for the money they spend or the effectiveness of their work. International support for GBM was never seemingly predicated on its outreach across the country.

Such regional selectivity has been true throughout Kenya's history, especially among missionaries. Quakers settled in Kaimosi and Webuye; the Consolata Fathers were predominantly in the Meru, Embu, and Nyeri regions, including Tetu. Catholic missions dominated the western and southern regions while most Muslims were found along the Mombasa coast and in parts of the Kakamega District. Within those regions, rare were breaches of the 10-mile zone, a *cordon sanitaire* between mission stations of different denominations. The centralized government that preceded independence sought to coordinate regional efforts in education, health, and transportation to curb Kenya's growing regional disparities.

In 2003, President Kibaki's regime launched Constituency Development Funds (CDF) of KSh 100 million to underwrite projects in rural areas. During her tenure as an MP, Maathai (2009) used government-allocated CDF to empower her constituents by providing bursaries for poor students and improving health as well as education infrastructure. She collaborated with her voters to select local representatives who identified, evaluated, underwrote, and monitored selected community projects. The government pledged 2.5 percent of its tax collected to the 210 constituencies with at least 25 percent directed to areas of high poverty.

About 70 percent of constituencies were guilty of "gross mismanagement, theft and misappropriation of funds amounting to an estimated KSh 422 million in fiscal year 2008–2009. Members of Parliament (MP) appointed friends or political cronies and squandered government Constituency

Development Funds (CDF) allocations" (Mwenzwa 2011; Okungu n.d.; Leftie 2011). The CDF board's chief executive, Agnes Odhiambo, identified twenty-eight out of 210 constituents that misappropriated funds within the decade. Of the twenty-eight worst constituencies, Nairobi and Rift Valley had three each, while Western, Coast, Central, Nyanza, and Eastern Provinces had four each in March 2011. Of those successfully administered CDF allocations like Butere, Kaloleni, and Gatanga, Maathai's Tetu constituency provided 600 scholarships, invested in classroom renovations, and expanded health centers and dispensaries. The momentum of community development was lost when Maathai left office in 2007.

We've already seen how the focus on Maathai the female politician overlooks decades of women's activism in Nyeri, her birthplace. Similarly, Maathai's concern for the underprivileged extended beyond her Tetu constituency and the requirements of political office. Salim Lone (2011) contrasts Maathai's "consciousness raising" transformative approach with the populist focus on hot political issues that gripped the nation: Maathai "withstood the more insidious and personal ethnic pressures . . . that many other previously courageous Kenyans wilted under too readily" (Lone 2011, p. 13). Philip Ochieng, an Airlift beneficiary, saw Maathai as suited to Kenya's echelons of power: "She was acutely intelligent, extraordinarily knowledgeable and deeply committed and she had a highly educated moral consciousness" (Ochieng 2011, p. 3). As she told Judith Stone in 2005, she was certainly tough enough: "'People often ask what drives me,' she recounted. 'Perhaps the more difficult question would be: What would it take to stop me? I'm driven by opportunities to confront the problems before my eyes'" (Stone 2005).

Columnist Rasna Warah (2011) commended Maathai's integrity in her run for political office: "What made her stand out from the rest was her open defiance of out-dated, male chauvinistic, neo-colonial and repressive attitudes and traditions that hindered not just the progress of women, but of Kenyan society as a whole" (Warah 2011, p. 19).

Maathai (2004) condemned the endemic corruption in regimes, noting that it had become the norm in leadership. She understood the importance of good governance, believing that the effectiveness of a leader reflected an engagement of the populace. She disputed the mainstream belief that Africa's ills lay wholly in the legacies of colonialism, believing instead that it was the responsibility of all citizens to create democratic space and strengthen civil society.

In the wake of the politicized violence that occurred before, during, and after elections, Maathai could have acted expediently and exploited it for her own political gain. Yet following the 2007–2008 conflict, she called on the international community to hold politicians accountable for the violence, if the country's judicial system failed to do so (as it had several times in the past). She wrote: "Reports circulated that some politicians not only were stirring up people along ethnic lines to attack their opponents, but were also paying young people to kill or burn down people's houses" (Maathai 2009, p. 201).

On January 24, 2012, the International Court in The Hague charged four Kenyan leaders with crimes against humanity following the 2007 elections. Two culprits, Uhuru Kenyatta and William Ruto, who are the current president and vice-president of Kenya, were charged, as were Ex-Police Chief Hussein Ali and the head of Public Service Francis Muthauria (Moore 2012).

In May 2013, Kenya's Truth, Justice and Reconciliation Commission (TJRC) released a report about the communal violence with much reservation. The reservation emerged among "commissioners [who] are allegedly divided over a section on illegal land acquisitions that is said to name prominent individuals who could face prosecution." Sources revealed the TJRC vice chairperson Tecla Namachanja went into hiding following "'unspecified threats from unknown persons. . . .' Some commissioners want the report changed for fear of falling out with the current regime since it implicates some of its leaders" (Mutua and Olick 2013).

Maathai's independence in her personal and public stances reflected her exposure to alternative modes of being, feeling, and knowing— perhaps even a new way of being political. She understood the role of education in exposing the roots of social problems. Her teach-ins illustrated the centrality of civic and environmental education in the protection of personal and common interests. She saw the personal as political. Like the trees she labored to plant in love and compassion for people and the earth, she strongly believed that change begins with people and in small ways. Her work initiated a grassroots revolution in values and social consciousness.

16

POLITICAL INFLUENCE

Maathai's activism touched the lives of individuals, transformed communities, and challenged the world to make responsible choices. Her opposition to the Media Trust complex in Uhuru Park benefited average *wananchi*'s (citizens') recreational opportunities in Nairobi. The campaign for multiparty representation and her solidarity with the mothers of political prisoners broke the wall of fear that sanctioned a regime's impunity. Hers was a consciousness that fought against the disempowerment that allowed the exploitation of natural resources by those in power and accepted hierarchical structure as the norm.

WOMEN'S AGENCY

Maathai's considerable achievements, as well as women's access to economic power and education, and their exposure to more egalitarian models have weakened but not eradicated patriarchal structures: "When one looks around whether in politics (ministers and commissions), education (university chancellors for instance), and the private sector (CEOs of companies), the story is the same. We see women deputizing men and in a few instances being at the top" (Kelvin 2011, p. 9). That President Kibaki appointed Maathai only as an assistant minister despite her *bona fides* reflected her ethnicity, gender, and lack of political access. In contrast, Musyoka Kalonzo was a lawyer whose credentials were far removed from environmental issues.

In national politics, Kenyan women remain voters more than political representatives (Arndt 2000). Their voices are sidelined in the public sphere and in setting the national agenda (Abwunza 1997; Yuval-Davis 1993, 1997). Women worry about school fees, sanitation, water, sanitary towels, breast cancer, paraffin for lighting up homes, access to sugar, vegetables, maize, etc.—some of the very issues Maathai's Green Belt Movement addressed—and yet these issues are rarely discussed in the halls of power. Laws such as those that give women the right to separate from their husbands because of drunkenness, infidelity, drug addiction, or sexual abuse are ineffectual in patriarchal societies, in which males dominate the courts, security forces, and the corporate world (Mucai-Kattambo *et al.* 1995).

The underrepresentation of women in politics has been rooted in their secondary status in cultural histories as much as prevailing beliefs and practices in Kenyan society. In *Reclaiming a Conversation,* the philosopher Jane Roland Martin (1985) attributes the phenomenon to the absence of women in historical narratives and philosophical interpretations, which has led to imbalance in what passes for mainstream knowledge. Intellectual disciplines including literature, psychology, history, art, etc., she writes, "fall short of the ideal of epistemological equality for women: they exclude women from their subject matter, distort the female according to the male image of her, and deny value to characteristics the society considers feminine" (Martin 1985, p. 3).

Maathai acknowledged male privilege in the Kenyan economy when she established GBM—her "foresters without diplomas." Yet she failed to address patriarchal structures within her own family and community, and instead used the metaphor of a cracked mirror to explain the denigration of indigenous cultures, races, and philosophies from Western influences. She was not alone in this: the impact of Western education and material control over colonies continues to shape how locals view themselves. Both Maathai and Martin highlight the impact of the omission and denigration of a group's values and practices on self-perception and overall aspirations. It's understandable that women underestimate their ability to lead in a society that portrays them in domestic realms and subordinate roles, even (or especially) in the stories, myths, and fairy tales that societies transmit.

For their part, some African men are examining their own ideological positions and roles. Charles Kanjama (2011) questions Kenya's cliché of strong men: "We tend to equate strength with muscles, strong character and tough physique. Hence the historical prejudice by which woman was called the weaker sex, meaning 'fragile' or 'frail.'" Meanwhile, society expects women to model their strength on masculine traits of physical or muscular dominance. What about characteristics women exhibit like fortitude, courage, patience, perseverance, loyalty, and humility? Kenyan women—educated and upper-class women in Nairobi as well as less-educated rural women—mobilized to influence public policy, such as in Uhuru Park in 1992 for the release of their sons. Their activism built on a tradition of rural women activists (Mutiso 1975). Women like Maathai transform societies by "articulating visions and goals that promise to link the state more effectively to civil society" (House-Midamba 1996, p. 290).

Aili Tripp argues cogently for women's centrality in national development. Women are fundamental for securing peace in their protection of their children and families. They head households, produce most of the food, and are primarily responsible for childrearing. The former Ugandan member of parliament and leader of the Forum on Women in Development, Winnie Byanyima, considers the culture of corruption and personal appropriation of state resources the result of the absence of feminine qualities of care: "serving, building, reconciling, healing and sheer decency" (cited in Tripp 2003b, p. 250). Women's representation and involvement in bureaucratic state mechanisms foster political consciousness within a marginalized group and enhance political participation as well as accountability in the broader constituency.

To that end, women in NGOs like the Green Belt Movement offer forums for defining their needs, designing community improvement strategies, and initiating social change. From having a voice in the home, the political consciousness within women's groups has spiraled out to the election and monitoring of government officials. Women are now more represented at "government, legislative, party, NGO and other leadership positions previously the exclusive domain of men" (Tripp 2003b, p. 234). The result of campaigns by celebrities like Maathai and wives of high-level politicians, women's groups dominate Kenya's organized sector—in particular, human rights organizations and lay organizations in both Protestant and Catholic churches (Tripp 2003b).

Kenya's new constitution requires elective public bodies to provide women with a third of all the seats. Yet, across the world, the upper echelons of power have an obvious absence of women. Men earn higher salaries than their female colleagues. Women make up only 6 percent of corporate board positions in Italy, while in Germany it's 11 percent. Even egalitarian countries in Scandinavia pay male full-time workers over 10 percent more than their female counterparts, and in the United States, more than 90 percent of the top earners in the largest corporate companies are male (Branson 2012).

The conventional rationale for this situation, says Bindra, is that "women are too emotional to make hard business decisions; they have too many children and take too much time off; they create bitchy, gossipy office environments; they don't have the same drive and determination that men do to succeed." Bindra insists the rationale only serves patriarchal privilege in contrast to reality: "Seventy per cent of household purchasing decisions are made by women, according to the Boston Consulting Group. Those decisions are not just about grocery lists or kids' clothes—women also choose big-ticket items such as cars and vacations. . . . Women have, cleverly and with the subtlety that escapes most men, been exercising 'soft power' for a long, long time. All that has changed is that this influence can now be measured." Communities need to include women in decision-making because they "bring a whole new dimension to management and leadership: they are more naturally able to share, collaborate and find win-win solutions" (Bindra 2012).

The absence and underrepresentation of women in public affairs results in what Martin (1985, 1994, 2007) terms *epistemological inequalities* in the conceptualization of a country's civic, political, and social life. Their absence from discussions on issues relevant to the nation also means that established policies for group rights—land ownership, marriage, inheritance, health, education, political representation, etc.— may well harm them. In Kenya's case, patriarchal structures carried over from the colonial era marginalize women in property ownership, education, employment, and access to social services.

The women's movement has endured because of its central premise that everyone should count in an age when only a few people and countries control the world's resources. When a country values each individual, their creative and productive capacities are unleashed to the nation's benefit. Although debates on a country's national policy or norms are important, at the end of day, families need food, shelter, and clothing. Because women are the primary caretakers within the family, the issues that directly affect the home need to be given more of a priority. In turn, a flourishing democracy requires the intelligent participation of the *whole* population in shaping public policy. Maathai's Green Belt Movement trained women to network and share strategies to develop their communities, improve agricultural processes, acquire new skills, and shatter glass ceilings.

NATIONAL DEBT

The conversation over the growing national debt in Africa is inextricably linked to foreign policies as much as to practices in the recipient countries. Within Kenya, dependency on foreign loans and subsidies demonstrate contradictory policies toward social problems and misplaced priorities in budget allocations. The country's investments in social infrastructure have not kept pace with its increased numbers of dependents. Although its rural regions are the nation's breadbasket, its infrastructure is better developed in urban centers.

Similar to the rest of the African continent, Kenya remains mired in an economic crisis that can be attributed to imbalances in commodity and labor markets, coupled with internal and external disequilibria, inflationary pressures, and a debt financing ratio that stands at more than 300 percent of its exports. Meanwhile, international donors complain about government inefficiency and graft.

What exacerbates matters is the continent's dependency on foreign countries. African nations rely on manufactured imports from needles and matchsticks to expensive capital-intensive machinery. The industrialized Global North dictates the pace, content, and direction of international agreements. On the domestic scene, rampant poverty, dilapidated infrastructure, ailing public services, and growing inability to provide basic services especially health and education exacerbate Kenya's economic underperformance.

Kenya's population growth, although slowing, has nonetheless increased densities on high- and medium-potential land, leading to the declining sizes of smallholdings, landlessness, and excessive land fragmentation. Overpopulation also contributes to the unsustainable use of marginal agricultural lands, deforestation, soil depletion, and overgrazing, adversely impacting agricultural output. On a national level, increases in population size translate to a higher social service budget.

We've already argued that the underrepresentation of women in national discourses sidelines issues central to women's lives—the right to health, water, sanitation, education, self-definitions, and political representation. Yet society's scapegoating of women contradicts the group's marginal status. Somehow more is expected of a group that delivers most and receives the least from national budgets.

Maathai (2006) advocated for years to reduce economic dependency at a personal, local, and national level. The reliance of African nations since independence on the Soviet Union, China, Israel, the U.S., and Europe can be seen at its most pathological in the legal and illicit sales of weaponry: "The United Kingdom sold more than £125 million ($200 million) worth of weaponry to Africa in 2000. Between 1998 and 2005, the United States sold more than $157 million worth of arms to Africa, with China accounting for $600 million, Russia $700 million, and western European countries (excluding France) accounting for $1.2

billion. France's arms sales alone were worth $900 million" (Maathai 2009, p. 109).

Developing countries like Kenya are constrained by ironclad deals with the international community that further limit national sovereignty. Africa's external debt has multiplied tenfold from its position at independence. African states are caught in a spiral, whereby loans are required to pay off earlier loans, as the debt and interest payments mount. That industrialized countries continue extending loans points to a complicity between these nation states and the political elites of the recipient nations, because the choice impoverishes average citizens. African leaders are more accountable to international donors than local citizens who know little to nothing about the deals. To that end, foreign aid "continues to be a venue for imperialistic agendas as former colonial powers have tried to maintain dominance and control through postcolonial development agendas" (Kushner 2009, p. 25).

For all her disapproval of how local and international governments were complicit in maintaining the financial quagmires of African regimes because of the agendas of their own nation states and trading blocs, Maathai benefited from international finance and political pressure on Kenya. Nevertheless, these never compromised her criticism of the growing national debt under which poorer developing countries labored.

In *The Challenge for Africa*, Maathai (2009) recalled with nostalgia her childhood years and Kenya's semi-economic independence. Village cobblers made and repaired shoes. Individuals sewed and repaired socks. The tailor took measurements of and made dresses for clients. *Mitumba* (bundles) of secondhand clothing was not the household word it currently is. The easy life is not any cheaper and the country's dependence on imported goods has grown exponentially, with demand for hair products, cooking oil, bathing supplies, clothing, and footwear as well as buttons and needles being met through imports. Meanwhile, the textile industry has since taken a dive. In 2000, the U.S. passed the African Growth and Opportunity Act, which allowed Kenya and other African countries to sell cotton products on American markets. However,

African nations used American yarn, although cotton is grown in Kenya. The contractual deal effectively eliminated Kenyan competition with American cotton growers.

In 1998, Maathai became the co-chair of the Jubilee 2000 Africa Campaign. She called for the cancellation of the "unpayable foreign debt" of the Global South, and repeated the call during speeches at the 2005 Beijing Plus Ten Conference held in New York (Maathai 2009; Nagel 2005). She criticized the United States and other Western countries for their shortsighted investments in cash crops, large industries, and markets that devour scarce human and natural resources. She also decried the flow of funds to corrupt governments. In April 2000, Maathai (2006) led hundreds of marchers, including priests and nuns, to appeal for debt cancellation. The event ended in police assault and arrests.

Debt relief is always welcome for beholden nations. In 2008, developing countries received relief for $88 billion (Graham 1993; Maathai 2009). Since then, according to Mark Roland Thomas (2012), "African governments have borrowed responsibly. . . . In the 26 African countries that benefitted from HIPC/MDRI [Highly Indebted Poor Countries/Multilateral Debt Relief Initiative] nominal public debt fell from a GDP-weighted average of 104% of GDP before debt relief to 27% after irrevocable debt relief (in most cases around 2006); by 2011 the ratio had risen only to 34%."

INTERNATIONAL DIPLOMACY

In her interview with me, Professor Mbaya called Maathai "an esteemed 'activist' with advice for both members of government and royalty in the international community. She was particularly persuasive with the envoys of governments and, consequently, was chosen to serve as an ambassador throughout the world on behalf of the Economic, Social and Cultural Council (ECOSOCC) of the African Union and the Congo Basin. Female diplomats like Maathai often advocate for women in their interactions with heads of states and fellow foreign ministers, and they also bring women's perspectives to discussions about national issues.

The practice of diplomacy, the waging of war, and the attainment of high political office have long been considered men's domains—although this is changing. Although few women have shaped global public policy and not all were pacifists or feminists, the United States has had three women secretaries of state: Madeline Albright, Condoleezza Rice, and Hillary Clinton. Before them, prominent leaders like Indira Gandhi, Margaret Thatcher, and Jane Addams (the first American woman to win the Nobel Peace Prize, in 1931) served their countries. Whatever women's political alignment, a broader representation of women at various levels of decision-making ensures a more comprehensive public policy in health, security, education, politics, foreign affairs, etc.

The Honorable Beth Mugo, the minister for Public Health and Sanitation, made this clear during a speech I heard at the Meet the President Session for Kenyans in the United States Diaspora, held in New York on September 27, 2012—the anniversary of Maathai's death. Mugo was one of two women among a panel of male government representatives including President Mwai Kibaki; Deputy Prime Minister Musalia Mudavadi; Dr. Josephine Ojiambo and Macharia Kamau, the two ambassadors to the UN; Sam Ongeri, the minister for Foreign Affairs; Elkanah Odembo, the ambassador to the U.S.; and Wycliffe Oparanya, the minister for Planning and National Development. Mugo spoke of cervical and breast cancer clinics in local districts, and contrasted them with the cost of healthcare in government and private universities, all issues that women confront on a daily basis. Mugo further noted how Ambassador Kamau referred to his colleague Josephine Ojiambo using a male pronoun. Conventional language reflects gender privilege, she averred. The Kenyan security personnel at the event were all men.

Unlike Mugo's speech, those of her male counterparts focused on technology, transport infrastructure, entrepreneurship, combating wars, and cross-border financial credit. President Kibaki used the word "village" dozens of times as he urged Kenyans in the Diaspora to return home. Devoid of specifics, the president's use of the word began to sound like he was summoning a utopia rather than a lived reality. One had to wonder when he'd last spent any time in an actual Kenyan village, rather than a presidential compound (Mugo 2012).

Although women manage most aspects of the everyday, that doesn't mean they always do it well. Nonetheless, even here, context matters. Maathai attributed women's poor land management to underfunding, neglect, and the lack of development priorities and agricultural extension services among African states. As her Green Belt Movement discovered, these women hold the key to solving Africa's poverty, conflict, and corruption rather than the dehumanizing exploitation, reliance on foreign aid, and servicing of illegitimate debts (or, for that matter, the praying for miracles) that hamstring local communities and nation states.

Given that Africa is still reliant on agriculture, the promotion of proper land use—complemented by government subsidies, fertilizers, and mechanization—could improve productivity and alleviate poverty en masse. Farmer's cooperatives are central to rural development. Besides disseminating information on crops and weather, they offer seedlings and services at affordable rates. In contrast, bureaucratic leaders prioritize in their budgets cash-crop farming, expensive dams, and the construction of luxury hotels and executive flats, monuments, armies, and supermarkets rather than focusing on the supply of basic services to citizens.

Maathai's concern with leaders' misplaced priorities was not unwarranted. Andrew Moran (2012) notes that Kenya's 220 members of parliament are the highest paid on the African continent. At a salary of $168,000 per year, they earn more than their counterparts in Great Britain, Canada, and France, and only started paying taxes in 2010. The lavish expenditure doesn't stop there: "BBC News is reporting that the country's taxpayers were charged $3,000 for each of the 350 red chairs [in parliament], which were constructed by the prisons department. Originally, the chairs had a price tag of $5,000, but MPs were skeptical about the heavy price. Each of the 350 chairs weighs 50kg, is fireproof and comes with a 30-year guarantee. In total, the chairs accounted for more than $1 million of the entire $12 million renovation budget"

(Moran 2012). Speaker of the House Kenneth Marende maintained the renovations would have a positive impact on governance. Meanwhile, "Kenya currently maintains a national debt of more than $7.7 billion, it has a $17.7 billion budget deficit and Kenyan Finance Minister Robinson Githae raised government spending by 25 percent" (*ibid.* 2012).

Unlike the government, Maathai's Green Belt Movement understood clearly how inextricably connected people's welfare was to the environment and each other. Maathai wanted to improve the lives of men as well as women, aware that "these miserable women are married to miserable men!" (Michaelson 1994, p. 548). In her speech on behalf of the Commission on Global Governance on September 11, 1995, Maathai reiterated the need for unanimity among peoples and governments. Despite the diversity and distance that appeared to keep communities apart, a common plight that many people in many countries labor under meant that we lived in a global neighborhood that compelled international cooperation. In a borderless economy, she observed, each country's welfare affected the other (Maathai 1996).

These and other calls Maathai made emphasized her commitment to a cultural transformation that redefined the notion of wealth as being about well-being rather than simply material possessions. Maathai rooted the world's partnership and cooperation in shared values, like the respect for basic human rights, justice, equality and equity, nonviolence, caring, and integrity, and she put women at the center of social transformation. This is a very different vision of "globalization" than the one that Wright (2011) critiques: to those who believe in environmental justice, the current form of globalization is "often nothing less than eco-imperialism, which is profit- and fossil fuel–driven, energy intensive, polluting, unjust, and wasteful, destroying the freedom and sovereignty of the other—whether other communities, countries, or species, especially the most vulnerable" (p. 171).

The celebrity and travel that resulted from Maathai's recognition, valorization, and protection by the international community—both before and after the Nobel—lie in sharp contrast with her appeal (both direct and indirect) to a bucolic past. Just as the Kenyan government criticized Maathai for relying on international funding, institutions, and people for her activism, even though the regime was itself deeply dependent on foreign aid and support, so the dream of a historical homogenous reality (the "good old days") ignores the interethnic and interregional differences that existed before colonialism.

A wholesale return to the past (admittedly a vision never articulated by Maathai), however noble that history might be, finds few supporters, and summoning mythical days of yore also begs the question of just how far back the return to ancestral norms ought to be in education, religion, economics, or political organization. In reality, the embrace of cosmopolitan values through the media, education, and internal migration by rural residents and urbanites, whether literate or illiterate, has irrevocably transformed Kenyans and indigenous societies. In the absence of any established literary tradition, existing appeals to an imagined past are essentially speculative.

Toward the end of her life, Maathai framed her work using a fable of the hummingbird, which she learned in Japan and told on many occasions and in many contexts. The bird flies back and forth with water in its small beak, throwing it on a fire that is consuming the forest, as larger animals like the elephant stand by, resigned to the loss of their habitat. She used this metaphor as a testament to resilience and how anyone can make a difference. It was also an example of her populist pedagogy after the loss of her academic career—an activist teaching the masses in informal venues and emphasizing traditional knowledge. Maathai redefined herself and questioned established definitions of gender as much as she exhibited a transformative education beyond the confines of academic and mainstream knowledge.

V

THE LAUREATE AND HER LEGACY

17

THE NOBEL AND CONTROVERSY

In the article "The Prize Is Right," Mia MacDonald (2005) writes about being with Maathai the day she won the Nobel Peace Prize. On the morning of October 8, 2004, they were in a van on the way to Nyeri when Maathai received several calls that culminated in the Norwegian ambassador in Nairobi telling her the good news. In MacDonald's words, Maathai "closed the phone's lid and said, 'We won it.'" Maathai saw the prize as a collective achievement, and confessed to feeling completely overwhelmed, considering that the Nobel Committee had selected her out of 194 nominations. The international community recognized and underwrote her vision of social transformation.

How did Kenya's village girl become an international celebrity? Charles Onyango-Obbo (2011) is aware that the most difficult part of explaining why Maathai won the award is "making sense of what her life meant" (p. 12), since it is so full of contrasts. Kushner (2009) commends Maathai for retaining her cultural roots despite her embrace of modernity: "It is a testament not just to her character, but also to the power of her Kikuyu heritage" (p. 95). She strove to remain true to her rural beginnings but she never settled in the village, not even in death, and her elite status protected her: "When Maathai began to publicly criticize government actions in 1989, she was too internationally well known for them to persecute, and GBM was too well established to disband" (Michaelson 1994, p. 552).

Like the tale about Konyeki, in which the dragons are outwitted, Maathai was astute about which battles she took on and which she didn't.

During her skirmishes with the state, GBM operated independently as a development-focused organization, protected by an international network that supplied funds and pressure when necessary. Within Kenya, Maathai wanted to project the image of a respectable African woman and mother in contrast to the charges that had been leveled at her that she was "a white woman in black skin" (Maathai 2006, p. 110). In her political activism, she made sure that she had the support of allies and the protection of the international community.

Yet, though she won the Nobel in 2004, Maathai yearned for appreciation by her own people and her loss of political office three years later was a severe blow. The community sidelined her in the interests of a "favorite son," which helps explain Maathai's amazement at her achievements. It was as if Maathai knew her celebrity was fleeting, and without it she might not have been able to change entrenched realities in Kenya.

In *Unbowed*, Maathai wrote of her astonishment at being associated with kings, presidents, and global celebrities such as Oprah Winfrey (Warigi 2011, p. 3). (Winfrey was one of the emcees for the concert that followed the Nobel ceremony in Oslo, which she attended.) Uniquely, Maathai not only was awarded the Nobel, but had received the Right Livelihood Award—commonly known as the "People's Nobel"—a decade earlier. Maathai's Nobel Prize speech conveyed her pride in African women's resilience; her emphasis on justice, integrity, and trust; the contribution of tree-planting to promoting a culture of peace; and the need to preserve both local biodiversity and cultural diversity. She issued a clarion call to leaders "to expand democratic space and build fair and just societies that allow the creativity and energies of their citizens to flourish" (see Appendix 3).

Criticism of giving the award to Maathai came from a number of quarters. Some questioned the legitimacy of awarding the prize to an environmentalist when the world faced global threats, terrorism being the most immediate. Yet another group disputed whether the Nobel conferred any honor at all. Others wondered why the Committee awarded a prize to an African initiative when Europe and the United

States remain the key players in world peace. Carl I. Hagen, leader of Norway's Progress Party, questioned the choice of an environmental activist at a time of world unrest (Vidal 2004)—the Iraq and Afghanistan wars were underway as well as tumults in the Middle East, Congo, and Sudan (Nixon 2006)—and the fact that Maathai's work did not focus on disarmament. Others recalled with dismay how she reportedly characterized the origins of the HIV virus (Gibbs 2004; *Economist* 2011).

So, why was Maathai given the award? In my interview with Cora Weiss, one of the organizers of the Kenya Airlift that brought Maathai to study in the United States, she reiterated the importance of Maathai's defining characteristic as a peace activist to counter "the people who are on a campaign to oppose the Nobel from being awarded to people like Wangari, Shirin Ebadi [2003] and even the recent three women [Ellen Johnson Sirleaf, Leymah Gbowee, and Tawakkol Karman, 2011] . . . because they don't represent any of the five points of Alfred Nobel's will. . . . I think that sustainable environment (Wangari) and human rights (Shirin) are part of peace, and we need to demonstrate that peace is a holistic concept, a recipe with many ingredients."

In honoring women and women's initiatives—Aung San Suu Kyi (given the prize in 1991), Rigoberta Menchú Tum (1992), Shirin Ebadi (2003), and Wangari Maathai (2004)—the Nobel Committee struck a blow against women's marginalization and that of women-led movements. Maathai understood the link between environmental conservation and peace long before accolades poured in along with international recognition, and had long stressed that global crises originate in a scramble over scarce resources (Holmes 2007). She understood the plight of real people and the planet at the grassroots, whereas disarmament speaks of nation states and top–down approaches. She compared the loss of soil to losing territory to an invading enemy: "Once you start making these linkages, you can no longer do just tree planting. When you start working with the environment seriously, the whole arena comes: human rights, women's rights, environmental rights, children's rights . . . everybody's rights" (Ndegwa, cited in Nagel 2005, p. 4).

HIV/AIDS

The announcement of the award was shadowed by news that Maathai had only two months before reportedly evoked a conspiracy theory that a scientist created HIV for "biological warfare." Given Maathai's scientific background and national renown, her claim was strange. (In her Edinburgh address in 1994, Maathai had contrasted the empiricism of science with cultural myths, which, she said, fostered fear and ignorance.) It was also irresponsible, since people, especially a rural audience in a developing world, were persuaded because the message was "advanced by [a] credible, trustworthy and likeable source" (Bogart and Thorburn 2006, p. 1149).

The day before receiving the prize, Maathai tried to explain her characterization of "evil-minded scientists" in the developed world "intentionally [creating] AIDS to decimate the African population" (Gibbs 2004). The *East African Standard*, a daily newspaper in Nairobi, reported that Maathai had likened AIDS to a "biological weapon, a point she claimed was taken out of context" (Gettleman 2011). Amos Kareithi, the reporter for the *Standard*, insisted these were Maathai's words at the AIDS workshop on August 10, 2004, in her hometown of Nyeri. She contested the charge, calling it speculation and citing Kenyan indigenous beliefs that attribute the virus to a curse from God (Kareithi 2004).

Maathai's putative allegation of Western complicity in the spread of the AIDS virus wasn't an off-the-cuff remark. On October 9, "a day after the Norwegian Nobel Committee named Dr. Maathai the 2004 Peace Prize laureate for her part in planting an estimated 30 million trees and her activities on behalf of women's rights," the same newspaper quoted her as saying, "I may not be able to say who developed the virus, but it was meant to wipe out the black race" (Kareithi 2004).

According to Tisha Steyn, Maathai reiterated her August 2004 claim that the AIDS virus was a biological agent, although she did not name the actual source: "Some say that AIDS came from the monkeys, and I doubt that because we have been living with monkeys (since) time immemorial, others say it was a curse from God, but I say it cannot be. . . . Us black people are dying more than any other people on the planet" (Steyn 2004). Sidestepping the controversy, Maathai urged scientists to help dispel the rumor that the disease did not result from a laboratory mishap. The Committee chairman, Ole Danbolt Mjøs, denies having known in advance about Maathai's reported views on the causes of AIDS (Gibbs 2004).

Maathai issued a statement following the receipt of the Nobel, in which she addressed the issue, and which is available on the Green Belt Movement's website:

> Like many others I wonder about the theories on the origin, nature and behaviour of the virus. I understand that there is consensus among scientists and researchers internationally that the evolutionary origin most likely was in Africa even though there is no final evidence. I am sure that the scientists will continue their search for concluding evidence so that the view, which continues to be quite widespread, that the tragedy could have been caused by biological experiments that failed terribly in a laboratory somewhere, can be put to rest.
>
> My hope is that those who understand the virus better can work with those of us struggling to better understand and eliminate ignorance, fear and a sense of helplessness.

Nonetheless, Maathai's reported statements on the origins of HIV/AIDS affirmed her critics' skepticism about her eligibility for the Nobel. Book reviewer Rachel Holmes noted that "*Unbowed* . . . excises altogether any mention of a key controversy three years before its publication. To date, there is a conspicuous absence of critiques of Maathai" (Holmes 2007). (Maathai wrote about AIDS in an afterword to the paperback edition of *Unbowed*, published in 2007.)

Maathai's evasive handling of the AIDS conspiracy prior to the Prize exemplifies a pattern of shrewd choices when confronting controversy. As a political activist, Maathai avoided wrangling among academics, in particular in her field of science. Her engagement of grassroots groups, typical of the Green Belt Movement, involved less rigorous academic claims and more pragmatic day-to-day choices in forums where she was the authority.

Furthermore, conspiracy theories among marginalized groups can show lack of formal access to information networks for engaging public policy. In the United States, Louis Farrakhan, the charismatic leader of the Nation of Islam, echoed the "widespread belief in conspiracy theories about the U.S. government and health care system among blacks, such as beliefs related to HIV, birth control and genocide" (Bogart and Thorburn 2006, p. 1144). These conspiracy theories have been endorsed by African Americans from different generations, classes, and regions.

On the African continent, conspiracy theories disclose unequal colonial and neo-colonial relations as much as a lingering discomfort with the effects of European patronage on their countries. About 23.5 of the estimated 34 million people who are living with HIV/AIDS are from the African continent (Avert 2011). In early 2000, the South African president Thabo Mbeki and his health minister Manto Tshabalala-Msimang also alleged Western complicity in the AIDS crisis, which led to many ordinary people rejecting HIV treatment and prevention messages.

Maathai could not have anticipated the criticism of her AIDS claims, given that she made them at a forum in her hometown, Nyeri, in the developing world. Maathai knew better than to make a similar allegation on the origins of AIDS in front of a predominantly European audience, risking a loss of credibility as much as the loss of sponsorship. Yet she owed it to the world to speak out on the virus as a prominent African leader (Gibbs 2004). She partly rectified this omission by devoting several pages of *The Challenge to Africa* to describing her work on HIV/AIDS in her constituency.

IMPACT OF THE PRIZE

Though the Nobel Peace Prize Committee "seeks to change the world through its conferral" (Krebs 2009/2010), few awards have a significant or an enduring impact on international politics. In the case of the Fourteenth Dalai Lama, the recipient in 1989, "contrary to neoliberal expectations, [the prize] exacerbated conflict and prompted intensive state repression, generating dynamics and consequences that are the opposite of the Nobel Committee's purpose" (Krebs 2009/2010, p. 594). The prize mobilized Tibetans, which elicited more repression from the Chinese.

The 2003 and 2004 recipients, however, garnered significant media coverage: "Shirin Ebadi appeared in the headline and lead paragraphs of merely three articles of major world newspapers in the three years preceding her award, but nearly 400 times in the three years thereafter. For Wangari Maathai . . . the corresponding figures are 8 and 216" (Krebs 2009/2010, p. 607). The Nobel gained Maathai and GBM global credibility and publicity, and provided Aung San Suu Kyi and the Burmese opposition with greater worldwide media attention, boosting "her name and aura." In Guatemala, Rigoberta Menchú Tum's 1992 prize appeared irrelevant. Coming in the midst of a civil war, the award had little impact on the stalled peace negotiations. For the most part, the impact of the Nobel on recipients is difficult to gauge. Most already have "a well-established track record and funding base and further success cannot be attributed persuasively to the award" (ibid., p. 599).

Mirroring the proverbial tale of prophets rejected by their own homelands, Maathai was the prophetess and heroine celebrated by the world but derided by Moi's regime and begrudgingly tolerated by the Kibaki administration. She "fell afoul of proliferating 'uns'—unAfrican, unKenyan, unKikuyu, unpatriotic, ungovernable, unmarried, unbecoming of a woman" (Nixon 2006, p. 28). Her Nobel Prize received limited recognition from the Kenyan government (Warah 2011).

Since 2004, three more women, including two Africans, among them Liberian President Ellen Johnson Sirleaf and Liberian activist Leymah Gbowee, have shared the prize. In this light, Maathai's clarion call to acknowledge, empower, and engage women in public policy was not in vain.

18

THE LEGACY

The accolades subsequent to Wangari Maathai's death from ovarian cancer on September 25, 2011, praised her indelible spirit and vision. Kenyan TV networks aired clips on her life and legacy (Koinange 2009). The global outpouring of grief and tributes were a testament to her uniqueness as well as the unusualness of her local and global status. The range of descriptors is instructive: tireless advocate; emblematic and captivating figure; champion of democracy, human rights, and environmental conservation; environmental icon; African heroine; national hero; true friend; trailblazer; great, dedicated, and selfless patriot; real-time legend; teacher; leader; guardian; proud Kikuyu woman, etc. Maathai had champions across ethnic and class lines on both local and international levels. In their remembrances of her, her former student Dr. Kiama Gitahi, the Director of the Wangari Maathai Institute for Peace and Environmental Studies (WMI), and Philip Ochieng, a fellow Airlift beneficiary, both lauded her as "peerless."

Chris Tuite, the senior advisor for Conservation International's Carbon Fund and former director of GBM's United States office, remembered Maathai's contagious humor and goodwill. Besides being a visionary, he noted, "[s]he was truly a master communicator; as she stood alone on a stage, she could make a thousand people fall in love with her in five minutes and be captivated by her simple and powerful message" (see "Wangari Muta Maathai: Share Your Condolences").

Maathai's neighbor Epharus Wanjiru Mbau recalled her campaign to change the name of the Dairy Men's Cooperative in Ihururu to something more gender-inclusive. Maathai inspired Mary Wangari, who campaigns against drug and alcohol abuse in Tetu, to fearlessly voice her concerns (Ndung'u 2011). Monica Wangu Wamwere, one of the mothers of the political prisoners Maathai advocated for in 1992, saw her strengths first-hand: "Her heart was for the poor and oppressed and she denied herself a lot of earthly pleasures to fight for the poor despite her rich academic background" (Mureithi 2011, p. 10).

Okiya Omtatah Okoiti (2011) credits Maathai for making "courage fashionable, more so, because she was a lone woman victorious against a cabal of male chauvinists" (p. 13). Maathai's valor gave Okoiti the courage to "crawl out of the woodwork" and write *Voice of the People*, the 1991 winner of the Nairobi Theater Academy's original playwriting competition. After Maathai's death, Tanzanian President Jakaya Kikwete cited her inspiration to women across Africa through her "magnificent visionary and embodiment of courage" (Okoiti 2011).

Maathai's influence was not limited to women, and she herself acknowledged the inextricability of women's issues from those of their male counterparts. According to Professor Calestous Juma of Harvard University, "[s]he was a true role model for me at a critical moment when I needed a mentor of her caliber, tenacity of character and sense of purpose. The world will miss a formidable environmental warrior" (Menya 2011a and 2011b). In Nyeri, Maathai's nephew Peter Nderitu spoke of having lost a "kind motherly figure who was concerned about other members of the family irrespective of their social status" (Nzioka 2011, p. 20).

Following Maathai's death, the head teacher of Ihithe Primary School, where Maathai began her formal education, extolled her for introducing tree planting on the site, although the classrooms from her time had since been demolished (Nzioka 2011). At her funeral service, President Kibaki, her one-time rival, praised her for pursuing education in an age of limited access for females and noted that her mother had enrolled her in school against the advice of neighbors, teachers, and friends, all of whom saw little need to educate a girl child (Chege 2011). Ex-Vice President and Home Affairs Minister Stephen Kalonzo Musyoka, Maathai's boss as the minister of Environment and Natural Resources (2002–2007), wrote on his Facebook page, recognizing Maathai's significance as a role model because of the comprehensiveness of her work: "Today, thousands of daughters, mothers and sisters are walking in her footsteps and our nation is massively better off for it" (Musyoka 2011).

In death, Wangari Maathai received the tribute from the Kenyan government that eluded her for the greater part of her life. Kibaki declared September 29 and 30 days of mourning and accorded Maathai a state funeral, an honor only reserved for heads of states and people of national significance. In Kenya's history, the honor has only been extended to the founding president, Jomo Kenyatta, on August 31, 1978, and on September 6, 2003, for Vice President Michael Kijana Wamalwa. Maathai's casket was draped in the Kenyan flag and driven in a hearse through the streets of Nairobi.

For a woman who fearlessly opposed this and previous regimes, the government's attention at her death was a kind of *mea culpa*. Mourners included ministers, diplomats, civil society activists, religious leaders, and ordinary folk. Ironically, the administrative police that harassed Maathai during her lifetime escorted her hearse to her final destination (Ndegwa 2011), and some claiming to mourn Maathai were the kleptocrats she exposed in the Karura Forest fiasco (Gaitho 2011). A regime that vilified Maathai for her vision hailed her wisdom in her death. Maathai was lionized and eulogized as "Kenya's most loved child and leading export to the world" (Obonyo 2011b, p. 10).

Befitting the occasion, the Kenya Forestry Service officials served as pallbearers for a ceremony that was held at Freedom Corner in Uhuru Park, the site of her confrontations with the state over the Media Trust complex in 1989 and the political prisoners in 1992 (Mureithi 2011). In sharp contrast, a low-key service took place in Maathai's mother's home in Ihithe, at which Maathai's cousin, Zaweri Wangari Muta, attributed Maathai's wish for cremation to her independent spirit (Mwaniki 2011).

Maathai's funeral arrangements displayed that spirit, global renown, and, particularly, her passion for environmental sustainability. She chose to be cremated at the Kariokor Crematorium in Nairobi, using an electric kiln to avoid employing wood. Even here, she courted controversy: Sheikh Swalihu Mohamed at Jamia Mosque in Nairobi stridently opposed Maathai's choice of cremation, which he believed the Catholic Church should have overridden (Ng'etich 2011). Green to the end, Maathai rejected a wooden coffin to avoid felling more trees, a decision she made after winning her Nobel Prize. The Kisumu Innovation Center constructed a casket framed with bamboo and made with papyrus reeds and water hyacinth. A fern was placed on the coffin instead of a bouquet of roses.

At the funeral in Uhuru Park, officiated by Archbishop Wabukala and the Rev. Phyllis Byrd Ochilo. The Kenya Wildlife Service, Administrative Police, and the Kenya Police played the last post and reveille. Ten students from her alma mater, Loreto Limuru, held young trees for planting with a banner bidding her farewell. An African wild olive tree (*Mutamaiyu* in Kikuyu and *Kang'o* in Luo) was planted in her honor at Freedom Corner, symbolizing a commitment by others to take up the mantle of her conservation work.

The day after Maathai's funeral, Dr. Isaac P. Kalua, the chairperson and founder of the environmental group Green Africa Foundation, oversaw the planting of seventy-one trees at the Wangari Maathai Institute, the first of 71,000 trees slated to be planted there in Maathai's honor. The plan was to eventually plant 5.6 million trees across the country before the first anniversary of her death to symbolize the 5.6 million Kenyan households that depend on firewood daily for cooking: "Research done by Green Africa Foundation indicates that each household uses a minimum of 10 kilograms of firewood for preparation of breakfast, lunch and dinner. Ten kilograms of firewood is the average equivalent of a three-year-old fast-growing tree. Our country Kenya therefore depletes 5.6 million trees every day in one way or another through direct use of firewood. An additional 13.3% of Kenya's population depends on charcoal for cooking" (Martins 2011).

Memorial services were also held in New York City, including at the United Nations Church of the Holy Family and the Cathedral of St. John the Divine (see Appendix 4). Green Belt Movement board member Peg Snyder spoke passionately to me of Maathai's universal appeal, her simplicity and storytelling that resonated with audiences in and beyond Kenya. She recalled Maathai's affection for St. Patrick's Cathedral, where she was enthralled by the organ music and the large choir, and was enveloped by the majesty and sacred aura of the church. "Maathai," she said, "was one of the few truly exceptional people I have been privileged to know. Village women and school children, sharing her vision and energy, planted 30 million trees. She went to jail to save Nairobi's only public park. She advocated protection of the Congo Forest, the world's 2nd largest 'lung.' She articulated the relationships between peace, poverty, environment, democracy, and gender and for that became the first African woman to receive the Nobel Peace Prize, in 2004." UN Secretary General Ban Ki-moon said that "no-one who met Wangari Maathai could ever forget her."

At one of the memorial services, Cyril Ritchie, the first chair of the Environmental Liaison Center International (a post Maathai succeeded him at), captured Maathai's global impact:

I personally had multiple further opportunities to cooperate with Wangari and to bask in her sun: UN conferences and commissions; the African Union Economic, Social and Cultural Council (ECOSOCC) of which she was the first president; the Union of International Associations; the World Future Council and more. She was truly a universal beacon of light. Now that that light is extinguished, what better legacy could Wangari have than the universal redoubling of the commitment of all of us to the values that she so outstandingly incarnated?

Ritchie lauded Maathai's resilience and political will. Nothing deterred Maathai, he said, nothing discouraged her, except perhaps the slow pace of governmental awakening, and response, to the environmental and sustainability crises confronting the planet. For Maathai, such incomprehension and inaction compelled her to redouble her efforts and the mobilization of civil society and academia worldwide.

After Maathai's death, Jeff Koinange of Kenya Television News (KTN) noted that the blossoms of Karura Forest, where Maathai fought her fiercest battles with Moi's regime, stand as a "worthy epitaph of her first love, the environment." For a girl born of peasant parents in a tiny village in Kenya, whose life was "destined to be ordinary and uneventful," in a country with little prospect of political independence, Maathai, he said, emerged as one of Kenya's best and brightest, celebrated with the likes of Barack Obama, Sr., and human rights advocate Philip Ochieng in global renown—one of "the greatest exports of Kenya."

Koinange lauded Maathai for her altruism in working for the underprivileged without praise or credit, as exemplified by the hummingbird story she often recounted. He noted with irony that those who praised Maathai the loudest in her death, when she could not hear them, excluded those who would miss her most: Kenya's "poor, impoverished, helpless and voiceless."

Michael Mungai (2011), co-founder of Dagoretti 4 Kids, expressed the sentiments of most Kenyans on Maathai's impressive achievements: "In an overwhelmingly patriarchal society as my home country Kenya, it is very hard to imagine that a woman can rise to the stature of being mentioned in the same breath as humanitarian luminaries like Nelson Mandela and Archbishop Desmond Tutu. From a society that has been very adamant [sic] to invest in the education of girls, forcing the little women into marriages with men old enough to be their grandfathers, how could one of them become an icon of global leadership in a continent riddled with corrupt despots?"

WANGARI MAATHAI INSTITUTE
FOR PEACE AND ENVIRONMENTAL STUDIES

The most concrete legacy, beyond the Green Belt Movement, that Maathai left behind at her death was the establishment of the Wangari Maathai Institute at the University of Nairobi. The Institute's mission is: "To transfer knowledge and skills on sustainable use of natural resources from academic halls and laboratories to the citizenry in villages and rural communities throughout Africa and beyond. And, in doing so, encourage transformational leadership grounded and focused on improving people's livelihoods and sharing cultures of peace" (Maathai 2010, p. 192).

Reflecting her experiences in childhood, Maathai (2006, 2009) wanted children to understand and appreciate the environment's significance to daily life. She was a bridge between the rural and urban life, and her vision for the WMI mirrored this desire for an outreach university connected to its surroundings. In 2012–2013, the Institute enrolled four Ph.D. students, including one from the United States, with an interdisciplinary faculty from the departments of geography, sociology, law, biological sciences, and anatomy. It also offers M.Sc. degrees. The WMI website presents its history, mission, core values, and its strategic objectives (see Wangari Maathai Institute for Peace and Environmental Studies).

I interviewed Professor Kiama Gitahi in August 2013. He had first heard of Maathai during secondary school (Kenyatta High School, 1979–1982), never imagining their paths would cross. Professor Gitahi spoke lovingly and proudly of his mentor in the same breath as he did of WMI. He said that the Institute spearheaded holistic multidisciplinary training, research, outreach, and extension services in environmental and nature management, good governance, and cultures of peace.

Over the course of her life, Maathai received many honorary degrees: eight from the United States, one from Norway, and two from Kenya (Bassey 2011). In a marked allegiance to her country of birth, Maathai rejected offers from top foreign universities including those in South Africa, Australia, and Princeton and Yale in the U.S. to house her papers. In discussions with Professor Agnes Mwang'ombe, the principal of the

University of Nairobi's College of Agriculture and Veterinary Sciences, Maathai chose to store her papers at WMI (Menya and Wesangula 2011).

Vertistine Mbaya recalled Maathai's deathbed wish that GBM and WMI would survive her, and Edward Wageni, GBM's former deputy director in charge of programs, considered GBM's survival the ultimate legacy of Maathai's achievements. To honor her wishes, Professor Mbaya and other GBM associates are working with her family on ways to strengthen both institutions.

Wanjira Mathai has taken on her mother's mantle as Vice Chair of the Green Belt Movement and project leader of the Wangari Maathai Institute. Speaking in Durban, South Africa, at the United Nations Climate Change Summit in 2011, Mathai urged the United States to support rather than obstruct climate change policies. On January 31, 2013, she joined outgoing U.S. Secretary of State Hillary Rodham Clinton at a forum at the State Department highlighting the global impact of public–private partnerships (U.S. State Department 2013). Shortly thereafter, WMI joined the U.S. Department of State, USAID, the MacArthur Foundation, the Global Alliance for Clean Cookstoves, CARE International, Solar Sister, and Swayam Shikshan Prayog to launch the Partnership on Women's Entrepreneurship in Renewables ("wPOWER"). According to a release from the Green Belt Movement issued on its website on November 20, 2013: "wPOWER aims to empower more than 8,000 women clean energy entrepreneurs across East Africa, Nigeria and India who will deliver clean energy access to more than 3.5 million people over the next three years."

Maathai invested her life and hopes in the Green Belt Movement; indeed, Maurice Amutabi (2007) called her one of Kenya's political martyrs. Even conservatives in Kenya are lobbying the government to erect a stature of Maathai in Nairobi, in Uhuru Park's Freedom Corner. Others are calling for changing the city's Procession Way to Wangari Maathai Way. Given Kenya's dire need for good governance, Ekisa (2011) advocates "a leadership devoid of recklessness, dishonesty and greed" as the lasting tribute to Maathai (p. 16).

Role Model for the Future

In her dissertation on Wangari Maathai, Jennifer Lara Simka Kushner (2009) recalls being struck by Maathai's wisdom, vision, and courage at their meeting: "From one interview, I determined she had a message of relevance to the field of adult education, as well as others committed to a just and sustainable world" (p. 18). Maathai could not anticipate the impact of her life on others. She understood leadership as exposing people to alternative modes of being and helping them recognize they had the resources and ability to transform structures (Maathai 2006).

Kushner credits Maathai with a range of sociopolitical initiatives in Kenya. Kushner's account also includes other voices of people touched by Maathai:

> In the film *Taking Root: The Vision of Wangari Maathai*, a member of the Green Belt Movement shares the profound impact Maathai has had on her: "Wangari has given me the strength to know if I fight for something, I can make it happen. Two options: I do it or I die." An environmental and human rights activist who was active in the same fight credits Maathai for the collective transformation she fostered: "Because that was the turning point in this country, that no matter who you are, how small, you can make a difference." (Dater and Merton 2008, cited in Kushner, pp. 145–146)

Maathai inspired people around the world: "'Wangari Maathai is a unique presence on our planet,' wrote Mary Evelyn Tucker, cofounder of the Forum on Religion and Ecology at Yale University. 'She exudes love and joy in all she does. Her words and deeds manifest to us that Earth is a sacred community including humans, ecosystems, and all species. . . . She reminds us that there is no lasting peace until we have peace with the Earth itself'" (quoted in Lamb 2011).

"I hardly recognize a myth surrounding Wangari," said her friend Vertistine Mbaya to me, "because she was one of the least pretentious persons one could meet. There was no grasping of eminence and no loss of her sense that she was ordinary. So she remained so true to the image that friends knew her to be, that her personal status seemed to be some 'after-thought' by others rather than a new definition of the Wangari that we knew." Indeed, she was deeply appreciative of people who supported the establishment of the Green Belt Movement and helped keep it funded. On her last trip from New York, following a series of treatments for cancer, she asked Peg Snyder to host a luncheon for her close friends on February 27, 2011. They reminded Maathai of how they first met and shared some of their experiences together. These relationships sustained her during her difficult years in Kenya.

While the history of Maathai's influence remains to be written across the globe, stories continue to emerge. In 2012, twelve-year-old Stephen Njoroge, the next "Kenyan Maathai," was honored at the UN International Day of Peace for his three-year effort to create a sustainable future for Kenya. His classmates from Mariki School in Nairobi were present at the celebration. Njoroge has planted over 10,000 trees and has already made it into the history books. Crediting Maathai's legacy for his vision, Njoroge and his family officially established a "We Care Club" at an event attended by the Ministry of the Environment as well as Kenya Forestry officials. His aspirations include a trip to Indonesia as an ambassador for Kenya, visiting five continents, and, one day, running for the presidency. Turning the tables on gerontocracy, Njoroge takes on the mantle of role model: "I noticed that it's only older people who are inspiring children. Now I'm trying to make children inspire older people" (Mojtehedzadeh 2012).

On October 5, 2012, in Morningside Park in Harlem, the Wangari Maathai Award for Civic Participation in Sustainability was launched in front of the tree that had been planted earlier in Maathai's honor. Among the attendees were NYC Parks Commissioner Veronica White and the award's initiators and supporters from the New York Restoration Project, the Rockefeller Foundation, the Bette Midler Family Trust, and the Municipal Art Society. I and Nicole Haas were also in attendance.

Mia MacDonald, chair of the Green Belt Movement-U.S., spoke on behalf of GBM. The annual $10,000 award for college costs would go to one female and one male public high school senior in New York City who demonstrated evidence of their academic and extracurricular commitment to environmental stewardship within the urban context through their development and execution of sustainability-themed projects—for example, recycling, energy monitoring, parks stewardship, greening. These projects would promote the spirit of civic engagement among fellow students and the community at large in line with Maathai's vision. Maathai would have appreciated the collaboration between the nonprofit sector and city government in a country she visited frequently, MacDonald told me later in an interview.

The ceremony embodied Maathai's personal dedication and civic responsibility. In her speech that day, which she kindly gave to me, MacDonald emphasized Maathai's role as an educator who loved teaching and also loved her students:

For "Prof," as she was known to many of us, education was not only essential for advancing environmental awareness and action, but also for raising critical consciousness so that every one of us, young or old, woman or man, could speak truth to power and change our societies for the better. . . . Wangari would have been extremely curious to see which young man and which young woman received the first awards in 2013 and would have looked forward to meeting them.

MacDonald ended with a quote from Maathai's last book, *Replenishing the Earth*: "I would advise young people to let their experiences take them to the next level and always give 100 percent. That way, when you're old and look back, you can tell yourself that you may not have achieved all you set out to accomplish, but at least you tried your best. You were a hummingbird" (p. 191–2). MacDonald was present when Beninoise singer Angelique Kidjo planted a tree in honor of Maathai in

Brooklyn's Prospect Park in June 2012, and her memory was evoked by Gloria Steinem and others during a "Women Waging Peace" concert in her honor. MacDonald also attended a planting of a tree in Maathai's honor at the United Nations on May 19, 2014.

On my office door at Brooklyn College I keep the poster of a symposium I organized on March 28, 2012, to honor Maathai's memory and work because of my respect for her, and also because she continuously impacts my work. The poster features her picture, a short biographical summary, and details of the symposium. Whoever enters my office, including colleagues, staff, and students, cannot fail to notice it. Often, meetings held in my office begin with questions about who Wangari Maathai was and what made her unique. The interactions lead to stimulating discussions about Kenya, women, and agency. I cannot count the number of people I have urged to view the movie in which Maathai talks about her hummingbird story (Maathai 2011a). Consistently, viewers are struck by her presence and passion in stressing human agency—our ability to make a difference in life.

Few experienced in life what women like Maathai and myself have— concerns over subsistence and welfare, numerous dependents including extended family members, the embracing of education as transformative and enabling, and the constant awareness that much more is required from those to whom much has been given. Maathai always insisted that poverty may mean a lack of resources but not a lack of knowledge and skills.

Although our paths never crossed, I take immense pride in Wangari Maathai as well as countless other women who go to graves unknown and unnamed. Maathai saw clearly that people often held the solutions to the problems they identified and could themselves remake society and reclaim a more humane world. The difficulty of persuading people to undertake causes—environmental conservation and political change—that had short-term difficulties and long-term benefits cannot be underestimated. Yet she undertook that challenge, and did it facing considerable odds. In this light, there are no "small" choices; each one has consequences, even beyond the grave. Maathai planted material and symbolic trees of hope, peace, courage, independence, and social transformation. Her achievements prove that change is always possible.

APPENDICES

1

SPEECH BY CORA WEISS

ON THE AFRICAN AMERICAN STUDENTS FOUNDATION
AND THE AIRLIFT (1959–1963)
AFRICA STUDIES ASSOCIATION
OF THE *AFRICANA LIBRARIANS COUNCIL*
NEW ORLEANS, LOUISIANA, NOVEMBER 19, 2009

It was the height of the Cold War, the height of the civil rights movement in this country, and the height of the anti-colonial movement for independence in East Africa. Kenya would be independent in 1963 and the British would be taking all the civil servants with them, leaving no one to run the government, staff the schools, and build the new nation. There was no school of higher learning in all of East Africa, save for Makerere, which was then a technical school. For those very few who could afford it and sought higher learning, all roads led to London, all paths to Moscow or Peking. Kenya was Britain's client state. In a year, John F. Kennedy would run for president.

Into this confluence comes Tom Mboya, very bright, very young, very dedicated to freedom, and very worried that there would not be enough well-educated Kenyans to assume the roles of nation builders and fill the emptied civil servant positions. Africans thirsted for education.

Tom came to the United States at the invitation of the American Committee on Africa and toured colleges and universities. At every stop following his speech he met with the school authorities and arranged to get promises of scholarships. He would have to go home to Kenya with a bag full of free education, and no way to get the students to take advantage of them.

In New York City Tom met a young entrepreneur who made airplane parts in a small factory in New Jersey. William X. Scheinman was also a gambler, a risk-taker, and he loved jazz. Bill and Tom spent hours together at a jazz club in Harlem, and clearly bonded. Bill started making personal donations to meet Tom's requests for plane fares to the United States for students. Bill's accountant finally suggested that he create a charitable entity so that his contributions could be deductible. The African American Students Foundation [AASF] was born. The object would be to raise funds to provide chartered aircraft to bring the students here, get them to the schools that accepted their applications, and get them home to become Kenya's nation builders. The Foundation had both African and American members of the Board of Directors and agreed that students would be vetted and approved by a team of Africans including Tom Mboya. That was unique. Americans would not say who could or could not come here.

No one ever dreamed how this simple, laudatory idea would rock the boat. No one could ever dream how we could be so attacked for "diluting standards of education" by bringing large numbers of Africans, many from rural areas, to American colleges, which until then had taken in foreign students on a very elite basis. And many, especially all-white Christian colleges in the South, had never admitted an African-American. I have maintained that the Africans became a wedge to open the door to American blacks, with the help of the civil rights movement, of course.

The Airlift, as it was soon called, or just the "lift," as Wangari Maathai says, became a political football in the 1960 Kennedy election; it had an impact on the civil rights movement; it changed the attitude toward foreign student enrolment; and it produced nation builders for the new, independent countries of Kenya, Tanzania, Uganda, and a few other neighboring nations. It also brought together a remarkable group of people in this country who were dedicated to the care and feeding of the students and enhancing their educational possibilities.

But it also caused a storm. In a wonderful letter to *The New York Times*, refuting the *Times'* editorial accusing the Airlift of being more crash than program, Bill Scheinman wrote that the single most important difference between the AASF Airlift and the college programs for African students run by Dean Henry of Harvard, the IIE [Institute of International Education], and the AAI [Africa-America Institute], was that our airlift was initiated by Africans, run by Africans, and the U.S. office was a joint effort with Africans and Americans on the Board. Subsequently, we enjoyed a close working relationship with Gordon Hagberg of the IIE who moved with his wife to Nairobi and was admired and trusted by our African colleagues. I have found long, handwritten letters from him and my equally long replies.

Oscar Kambona, then Secretary General of TANU [Tanganyika African National Union] and Minister of Education, told me that Canada had offered more scholarships than the United States, and complained about the rigid requirements and difficult standards of the AAI and the David Henry Harvard program.

AASF boxes of files, checkbook stubs, newspaper clippings and photographs have been in our garage for nearly 50 years. For the record, Robert Stephens, once a USIA [United States Information Agency] official in Nairobi, came to our house and took a bunch of papers from the files for photocopying. He has written a manuscript about the Airlift which has not been published. But no one has really plowed through the massive amount of information until Tom Shachtman used them as the basis of the *Airlift to America* book, with a foreword by Harry Belafonte, who was on our Board. Those boxes are now in our apartment, and I have gone through most of them in preparation for this discussion and for their shipment to the archives at Michigan State University where you will all soon be able to find the papers to document what I tell you today and more.

So, what do the files tell us?

First, we find hundreds of painfully composed, handwritten, blue air letters, addressed to us and many of the schools from which Tom had received promises of scholarship aid.

There is a report of a Maasai delegation coming to urge Tom Mboya and the U.S. Consul General to accept more members of their tribe.

Then we find fundraising letters; index cards with addresses of foundations across the nation; letters to the editor appealing for summer jobs, home stays, funds for airplane charters. More fundraising letters. In fact, searching for financial support is the biggest activity undertaken by the foundation president, Frank Montero.

An appeal written by Ruth (Mrs. Ralph) Bunche, who was also on our Board, addressed to presidents of hundreds of colleges, reaped remarkable replies offering scholarships.

And [there are] ledgers with carefully handwritten names, addresses, and $1, $2, $3, $5, $10, $25 donations to the AASF. Thousands of them. We have a day ledger from 1959 alone, with 4,458 entries.

Checkbook stubs tell a remarkable history. . . . Bill Scheinman and I were reimbursed for travel to Washington, D.C., to attend a CECA [Council on Educational Cooperation with Africa] meeting (9/29/61). I was reimbursed for a trip to Kenya for a CECA meeting (7/20/61, 9/20/61, 10/11/61). . . . I found reimbursements for student picnic expenses. . . . We worked out of Milton Gordon's office; he owned Lassie, the Hollywood collie, and while the office was rent-free and gorgeous, we rigorously paid for our long-distance telephone calls. One check was for $4.40.

There was a check to my gynecologist for $35 to take care of two of the women students. Some checks to students were marked "emergency advance pending further investigation."

We kept careful records of all stipends we gave to students. One of those students was at the University of Hawaii. We didn't bring [Barack] Obama, Sr., on an Airlift plane—his airfare was paid for by two American women teachers in Nairobi—but once here, he needed books, additional tuition, and maintenance money, which we provided. Barack Obama, Sr., was a member of the Airlift family. In June of 1961 we sent around a form asking every student to whom we gave financial assistance to report on their personal situation.

We celebrated Africa Freedom Day every year. Once it was held at Hunter College on April 17, 1961, and we introduced many of the Airlift students to the speakers—including Tom Mboya, Kenneth Kaunda, Joshua Nkomo, and Hubert Humphrey, and musicians Dizzy Gillespie, Herbie Mann, and Miriam Makeba.

We provided legal defense for students who accused cops of beating them up; and CBS's Ed Joyce took one of our students on an experiment [to see] which apartment for rent would be available for the African and which for Ed Joyce. The whole thing was recorded and made a great radio program on racial discrimination. I organized a small, sad ceremony in a cargo terminal at Idlewild Airport for a student whose body we had to ship home, his death resulting from a hit-and-run driver near the Lincoln University campus, which I always believed to be a racist act. Naftal Gichaba, the victim, started at Greenville [College], IL, and transferred to Lincoln. He was one of a group of students who "hung out" at Arthur and Mathilde Krim's house in Manhattan. Mr. Krim owned United Artists and Mathilde, a biochemist, claims that one consequence of getting to know the African students resulted in her deep interest in seeking the cure for HIV/AIDS.

When the British denied visas to Frank Montero and Peter Weiss to go to Kenya to check on the situation on behalf of the Joseph P. Kennedy Foundation, as a site visit prior to their approving our grant, Frank asked Ted Kheel, noted labor lawyer and President of the National Urban League, to represent us. Ted was the secretary-treasurer of the AASF and brought considerable cachet to our initiative. He took his friend Milton Gordon with him to Kenya, which resulted in our getting free office space in the Seagram Building on Park Ave. in New York City. Ted's report was filled with wonderful examples of the enormous thirst for education he encountered everywhere.

Frank Montero, President of the AASF, was sent on a six-week mission in Jan/Feb 1961 to six countries in East and Central Africa, where he met with leaders of PAFMECA [Pan African Freedom Movement for East and Central Africa], to determine whether the AASF should undertake another airlift in 1961. Four of the six leaders of the PAFMECA countries were on the Foundation Board. Montero returned here to urge President Kennedy to convene a conference on Education for African Freedom, which he had broached during his campaign, to meet the increasing competition of expanding Soviet bloc educational programs for Africans. The African leaders urged that we "see African need through African eyes."

Jackie Robinson, Sidney Poitier, and Harry Belafonte had very little in common politically. They were celebrities, artists, and a baseball player, but they could all agree on signing a fundraising letter to support the Airlift and the students needed warm clothes for the winter, jobs to earn spending money, and hours to spend vacation time. They were all on our Board of Directors. Jackie engaged fellow Republican Richard Nixon in a challenge to give government support to the Airlift; he filled his columns in the *New York Post* with stories of the Airlift students and appealed to his readers for support. Harry Belafonte performed concerts to benefit the Airlift.

We had secretarial services from Sylvia Freirich, Jean Carey, and Mary Isaac, as well as Mary Hamanaka, a Japanese-American whose life began in an internment camp in California. This was the most culturally and racially diversified team you could find anywhere. Remember, it was 1959.

Major findings from the files:

1. The extraordinary letters from the potential students;
2. Letters from Tom Mboya with details about individuals who needed something, someone I was to pay special attention to, bills that needed to be paid; and just plain "hello, how are you, congratulations on the birth of your son, we're waiting to receive you for Uhuru";
3. Newspaper clippings that show the impact this unusual initiative made, including success stories as well as acts of racism;

4. The Kennedy football. The ugly speeches and accusations that filled the air of the Senate, the columns in the papers across the country. Charges and counter-charges.

5. Memos, reports, letters reflecting the extraordinary tension and political attacks that showed the apparent threat our little effort seemed to have for the traditional establishment of organizations dealing with international students and especially students from Africa. We were attacked for "dumping the students," for running a crash education program that was more crash than education, and other not-printable language.

Samples of student letters appealing for scholarship assistance:

The Competent College
PO Box 12331
Nairobi

Dear Sir, I humbly submit this application for a scholarship and admission to your institute in 1961. I am a Kenya African boy who is thirsty for education and who desires madly to join USA institutions. . . . MBL

17 July 1960
Convent, Kiambu

I feel that I should not hesitate to present this application. . . . I am a girl of poor parents who tried hard to educate me till I get in Standard VII. But now due to their poverty they are unable to educate me any more. . . . PW

Riamukiumwe Intermediate School
27 June 1960

I shall be very grateful for you to get me further education. I am sixteen years old. I am an orphan boy who helps himself by earning during the holidays. . . . EK

Kihora Intermediate School

18 September 1960

I am boy of 15 and my parents are very poor and I don't hope to get any help from them. I wish you can admit me in your school in order to help my country and my poor family. MG

5 September 1960

Co. Co-op Society

I write to you to beg a vacancy. . . . I am a poor African wanting to spend his time youth with studies rather than wasting time for nothing. . . . Poverty is on my shoulders. . . . I am hopeless without your help. . . . EM

30 October 1959

I am a Kikuyu in tribe. . . . I have been detained for so long, 5 years since Emergency declared . . . but now I am free. . . . DW

We have hundreds of these painfully written, simply said, earnest, hungry-for-education letters.

LETTERS FROM TOM MBOYA

Tom Mboya is best known as a brilliant labor leader, charismatic politician, eloquent leader of the movement for liberation from colonial rule, [Kenya's] Minister of Labour, Minister for Justice and Constitutional Affairs, and Minister for Economic Planning and Development. But Tom was also a consummate letter-writer, had written, typed, dictated, short messages wishing us all well, longer detailed requests to pay attention to problems he heard someone was experiencing, and, always, pleas to pay bills. All that before being cut down at 39 years of age.

Tom followed the press and wrote letters to the editor. On November 24, 1959, in a one-inch-long column, his letter first expressed his personal and his people's gratitude to all American friends who made the first Airlift possible. He appreciated the interest of the U.S. press; he referred to the grave shortage of facilities for higher education and the urgent need for education. He mentioned the trickle of students sent to Britain, which couldn't meet the country's needs. He said that the United States could meet this need, "regardless of the diplomatic problems and without embarrassment to themselves or to America's allies." And he appealed for help—scholarships, families to take in students, religious groups, and outright grants. He gave the name and address of our AASF.

Personal correspondence between myself and Tom Mboya:

20 February 1962: Thank you for your letter of Feb. 9th, the enclosure has been dealt with as instructed. . . . I hope to see you Friday on my way to Chicago. . . .

27 October 1962: Hope you are well and find time to rest. . . . Congratulations to you both from Pam and myself for Daniel's safe arrival. . . . Love, Tom.

7 November 1962, detailed letter about a student at Winona State University who needs an additional $500: As you will recall I could only raise $500 from this end. If there is anything you can do, don't hesitate to do so.

24 December 1962, return address Ministry of Labour: Thank you for your letter of 17th Dec., very brief. I have noted your remarks and was not unduly worried (about a student).

6 February 1963: My dear Cora, Just greeting for the New Year and to tell you that Stevens Ochieng has written to ask me to thank you for the help he has received from you enabling him to go to Delaware State College, Yours Sincerely, Tom.

I also found letters from the Minister of Education, Mr. L. G. Sagini:

15 August 1962: Dear Cora, Thank you very much for your hospitality, what with your nice parties in your home for all the Kenyan students. Oh, you funny girl. You talk of teaching

Kenya girls how to use contraceptives. Do you know that you are talking to a Catholic? Don't be frightened.

THE KENNEDY FOOTBALL

By now you all know, from President Barack Obama's book *Dreams from My Father*, from the many press accounts, his own speeches, and Senator Edward Kennedy's endorsement, the claim that the Kennedys were responsible for bringing his dad to this country were all a bit wrong. Barack Obama, Sr., came to the United States, probably in the spring of 1959 in time for the fall semester, and as I said earlier, with the help of two American women teaching in Nairobi. Once here, the AASF gave him three grants to help him with tuition, books, and clothing. He went to the University of Hawaii because of Tom Mboya's work in creating the Airlift culture and he and Tom were very close friends. Obama, Sr., went to work with Tom in the Ministry of Economic Development. And, sadly, he was the last to see Mboya before he was gunned down in July 1969. But [let's] back up.

In the summer of 1960, Tom came [to the United States] on a speaking tour and collected dozens of scholarships to take home to offer students who qualified. While here, we arranged for him to meet with Senator John F. Kennedy at Hyannis Port. Kennedy was the Chair of the Senate Subcommittee on Africa. The two bonded quickly, and Kennedy called his brother-in-law, Sargent Shriver, in Chicago who ran the Joseph P. Kennedy Foundation and asked him to cut a check to enable the AASF to charter three planes to bring the students. We had already been turned down by the State Department, and London had made it clear to Washington that Kenya was "theirs" and Washington should keep their hands off.

News reached the Senate where Senator Hugh Scott (Rep. PA) took to the floor and accused Kennedy of using his family's foundation for political purposes to enhance his candidacy for president . . . and the football was in motion. Senator Kennedy's speeches in defense of United States aid to support the educational aspirations of educationally deprived Africans are among his most eloquent. In the absence of U.S. government support, his family foundation would be glad to chip in. Shriver tried to get other major foundations to join as partners; none would agree. Once Vice President Nixon heard about the Kennedy Foundation offer of $100,000, he ordered the State Department to rescind its initial rejection and offer the funds to the AASF, which we refused to accept.

The line-up of players: Senator John F. Kennedy, Vice President Richard Nixon, Secretary of State Christian Herter, Jackie Robinson, Senator Hugh Scott (R-PA), Senator William Fulbright (D-AR), Senator Gale McGee (D-WY), Nixon aide James Shepley, and former Governor Averell Harriman, who charged Sen. Scott with "doing a pretty lousy thing of bringing the Airlift in to politics by making outrageous accusations against Sen. Kennedy." Senator Eugene McCarthy called Senator Scott's blast at Kennedy a "kind of Murder, Incorporated."

There is at least one historian who has a documented theory that Kennedy's engagement with the African Airlift won him the election. He won by a narrow margin, as you remember, and the swing vote, it is claimed, was the African American vote, and that Kennedy's engagement with the AASF influenced that vote. Others believe this is a stretch. It's there for your consideration.

Wangari Maathai, the Nobel Peace laureate, came on what she called the "Kennedy 'lift'"—one of the three planes chartered with Kennedy family funds in 1960.

The editor of the *Pittsburgh Courier*, P. L. Prattis, wrote to us saying "the Airlift is truly participating in history and you are playing both a helpful and dramatic role. Someday something like *Exodus* will be written about this undertaking."

One of the most significant facts of the demographics was that by October 1960 we had brought over 236 men and 53 women students . . . rather revolutionary at the time to have such a good number of women. They were at 145 institutions in 41 states, with 36 in high schools in Canada, Jamaica, Alaska, and the United States.

The files are exhausting to read through, and fascinating. You feel the tension, the attacks, the desperate and relentless search for funds to provide for students' needs as well as additional airplanes. The Council on Educational Cooperation with Africa [CECA]—a gathering of the "warring parties," someone wrote—was a consequence of the Airlift. On the African side, what began as Tom Mboya's vision and initiative, and included Kariuki Njiiri and Gikonyo Kiano, grew to become an East and Central African coalition, PAFMECA, with Tanganyika, Uganda, and the Rhodesias joining. While the majority of students were Kenyan, there are remarkable success stories of young people who returned to their homes in other countries still under colonial rule. Letters express the joy and profound appreciation of the students.

Foundations rejected us with a very few exceptions. I found receipts from the William C. Whitney Fund for $1,000, the Max Ascoli Fund for $500, and the Aaron E. Norman Fund for $1,000.

The bulk of our funds came in 1960 from the Joseph P. Kennedy Foundation, which provided a total of $122,500 (as of August 31, 1961) that covered three chartered planes in 1960 and stipends for maintenance, tuition, and books for students.

The Aaron E. Norman Fund also gave us a grant for $2,000 to send John A. Marcum, Professor of Political Science and Director of the Africa program at Lincoln University, to Africa to investigate student needs and ways of increasing the number of students coming to this country.

Who Were We?

The Board of Directors of the AASF included: Mrs. Chester (Stebb) Bowles, Mrs. Ralph (Ruth) Bunche, Harry Belafonte, Kenneth Kaunda, Theodore W. Kheel, Tom Mboya, Frank C. Montero, Joshua Nkomo, Julius Nyerere, Sidney Poitier, Jackie Robinson, William X. Scheinman, and myself [Cora Weiss].

The Educational Advisory Board included: Father R. J. Henle, Dean of the Graduate School at St. Louis University; Professor Robert A. Manners, Department of Anthropology, Brandeis University; Professor John V. Murra, Department of Anthropology, Vassar College; Kariuki K.

Njiiri, Kenya Education Department; Professor Glen L. Taggart, Dean of the International Program, Michigan State University.

Frank Montero was President; Bill Scheinman was Vice President; Ted Kheel was Secretary-Treasurer; and I [Cora Weiss] was Executive Director and student advisor.

We worked very closely with the American Committee on Africa and its director George Houser, Ida Wood at the Phelps Stokes Fund, and Dana Klotzle, a Unitarian minister who assumed responsibility for the high school program.

There is also a gender dimension to this story. While the African, all-male vetting committee selected a significant number of girls to send for higher education and some for high school, I was Mrs. Peter Weiss. Slowly I became Mrs. Cora Weiss and then just Cora Weiss, as the women's movement came into focus.

All of this information and more can be found in the files. It makes for exciting reading. Frankly, it's rather amazing what a small band of determined people can do on a shoestring.

More information about the Airlift can be found at www.airlifttoamerica. org and Michigan State University's Africa Activist Archive Project at www. africanactivist.msu.edu, where this speech is archived.

2

KEYNOTE ADDRESS BY WANGARI MAATHAI

ON FORESTS FOR PEOPLE, LIVELIHOODS
AND POVERTY ERADICATION
UNITED NATIONS FOREST FORUM AND THE LAUNCH
OF THE INTERNATIONAL YEAR OF FORESTS 2011
NEW YORK, NY, FEBRUARY 2, 2011

Mr. President, Excellencies, Distinguished Delegates, Members of the United Nations family, Representatives of the civil society, Ladies and Gentlemen,

There is a contradiction here; and it is that many forest-dependent communities that live in resource-rich forests are poverty-stricken. There is something inherently wrong and unjust with a global economic system that tolerates dehumanizing poverty in regions that are so resource-rich. Why are leaders so slow to embrace solutions that would deal with such inequalities and injustices?

As a Goodwill Ambassador of the Congo Forest Ecosystem, I thank the British and the Norwegian governments that supported the creation of the Congo Basin Forest Fund, based in the African Development Bank. But it has been very difficult to get more partners to join the Fund.

Without adequate international support for such efforts, it is very painful to see forests degrade, disappear, and threaten the livelihoods of millions of especially indigenous and forest-dependent peoples. It is even more unfair to force the future generations to inherit such a legacy.

In that connection I am grateful that the President of Congo Brazzaville, H. E. Denis Sassou Nguesso, has offered to host a summit on the three river basins (the Congo, the Amazon and the Borneo-Mekong) on 31st May to 3rd June, 2011. This is important for the International Year of Forests in Africa.

Indeed, we are encouraged by reports that there is a decline in the deforestation in the world's great tropical rainforests of these basins. We congratulate the concerned governments, their people and partners. Where there is political will, commitment, transparency, and accountability, there will always be a way to find financial support.

We are all working hard to realize the Millennium Development Goals, especially eradication of poverty. My experience with the Green Belt Movement is that it is virtually impossible to realize many of the other MDGs if No. 7, on sustainability, is only given lip service. Sustainability of resources like trees, forests, and water is "the mother of all other MDGs." Where governments ignore sustainability, they are also only giving lip service to the other MDGs, and it shows!

We know that generating national revenue and improving the quality of life of citizens is often the reason governments tolerate destructive activities like logging, charcoal burning, human settlements, and agricultural activities at the expense of forests and biodiversity. But this often only exacerbates the financial and economic challenges the same nations face when they are later confronted by floods and landslides; dried-up riverbeds, lakes, and water taps; crop failure, starvation, death of both humans and wildlife and the embarrassment of begging for international aid.

In such instances, it is because there is failure to recognize the relationship between our human activities and many disasters that follow. That failure is the reason we are here to continue appealing and encouraging each other to appreciate that, contrary to common mythologies, the gods are not to blame! Many of these disasters are man-made and preventable.

It is not that we do not know. None of us can claim ignorance. We know what to do. Much information is out there in offices and libraries and they are constantly being reviewed in seminars and meetings.

Although many governments, communities, companies, cities, and even individuals are doing their part at their levels, there is need to intensify global partnerships because the threats are real and global.

For example, we must stop undervaluing and taking for granted the environmental services forests and trees provide, especially when they are standing in some remote poor part of the world. They are taken for granted and treated as unlimited. Well, they are finite. Therefore, we need to bring into our dialogues and accounting systems their full value and be willing to pay.

As we negotiate and make recommendations and agreements, there is need to find a balance between the immediate needs of communities and the common good of all, who depend on forests that are sometimes long distances from where they live. Governments have a responsibility to ensure that the ecological services provided by trees and forests are available for the common good of all communities, including the future generations.

In closing, I wish to congratulate governments and organizations—too many to name individually—that have contributed to the success of so many initiatives including encouraging green technologies, jobs, lifestyles, and tree planting activities like UNEP's Billion Tree campaign.

We congratulate the Secretary General of the United Nations, H. E. Ban Ki-moon, the UN-REDD program, and the United Nations Forest Forum for contributing and coordinating all these achievements.

Congratulations to all, and may we have a very successful United Nations International Year of Forests (2011).

Thank you.

3

Nobel Peace Prize Acceptance Speech

BY WANGARI MAATHAI
OSLO, NORWAY
DECEMBER 10, 2004

Your Majesties
Your Royal Highnesses
Honourable Members of the Norwegian Nobel Committee
Excellencies
Ladies and Gentlemen

I stand before you and the world humbled by this recognition and uplifted by the honour of being the 2004 Nobel Peace Laureate.

As the first African woman to receive this prize, I accept it on behalf of the people of Kenya and Africa, and indeed the world. I am especially mindful of women and the girl child. I hope it will encourage them to raise their voices and take more space for leadership. I know the honour also gives a deep sense of pride to our men, both old and young. As a mother, I appreciate the inspiration this brings to the youth and urge them to use it to pursue their dreams.

Although this prize comes to me, it acknowledges the work of countless individuals and groups across the globe. They work quietly and often without recognition to protect the environment, promote democracy, defend human rights and ensure equality between women and men. By so doing, they plant seeds of peace. I know they, too, are proud today. To all who feel represented by this prize I say use it to advance your mission and meet the high expectations the world will place on us.

This honour is also for my family, friends, partners and supporters throughout the world. All of them helped shape the vision and sustain our work, which was often accomplished under hostile conditions. I am also grateful to the people of Kenya—who remained stubbornly hopeful that democracy could be realized and their environment managed sustainably. Because of this support, I am here today to accept this great honour.

I am immensely privileged to join my fellow African Peace laureates, Presidents Nelson Mandela and F. W. de Klerk, Archbishop Desmond Tutu, the late Chief Albert Luthuli, the late Anwar el-Sadat and the UN Secretary General, Kofi Annan.

I know that African people everywhere are encouraged by this news. My fellow Africans, as we embrace this recognition, let us use it to intensify our commitment to our people, to reduce conflicts and poverty and thereby improve their quality of life. Let us embrace democratic governance, protect human rights and protect our environment. I am confident that we shall rise to the occasion. I have always believed that solutions to most of our problems must come from us.

In this year's prize, the Norwegian Nobel Committee has placed the critical issue of environment and its linkage to democracy and peace before the world. For their visionary action, I am profoundly grateful. Recognizing that sustainable development, democracy and peace are indivisible is an idea whose time has come. Our work over the past 30 years has always appreciated and engaged these linkages.

My inspiration partly comes from my childhood experiences and observations of Nature in rural Kenya. It has been influenced and nurtured by the formal education I was privileged to receive in Kenya, the United States and Germany. As I was growing up, I witnessed forests being cleared and replaced by commercial plantations, which destroyed local biodiversity and the capacity of the forests to conserve water.

Excellencies, Ladies and Gentlemen,

In 1977, when we started the Green Belt Movement, I was partly responding to needs identified by rural women, namely lack of firewood, clean drinking water, balanced diets, shelter and income.

Throughout Africa, women are the primary caretakers, holding significant responsibility for tilling the land and feeding their families. As a result, they are often the first to become aware of environmental damage as resources become scarce and incapable of sustaining their families.

The women we worked with recounted that unlike in the past, they were unable to meet their basic needs. This was due to the degradation of their immediate environment as well as the introduction of commercial farming, which replaced the growing of household food crops. But international trade controlled the price of the exports from these small-scale farmers and a reasonable and just income could not be guaranteed. I came to understand that when the environment is destroyed, plundered or mismanaged, we undermine our quality of life and that of future generations.

Tree planting became a natural choice to address some of the initial basic needs identified by women. Also, tree planting is simple, attainable and guarantees quick, successful results within a reasonable amount time. This sustains interest and commitment.

So, together, we have planted over 30 million trees that provide fuel, food, shelter, and income to support their children's education and household needs. The activity also creates employment and improves soils and watersheds. Through their involvement, women gain some degree of power over their lives, especially their social and economic position and relevance in the family. This work continues.

Initially, the work was difficult because historically our people have been persuaded to believe that because they are poor, they lack not only capital, but also knowledge and skills to address their challenges. Instead they are conditioned to believe that solutions to their problems must come from "outside." Further, women did not realize that meeting their needs depended on their environment being healthy and well managed. They were also unaware that a degraded environment leads to a scramble for scarce resources and may culminate in poverty and even conflict. They were also unaware of the injustices of international economic arrangements.

In order to assist communities to understand these linkages, we developed a citizen education program, during which people identify their problems, the causes and possible solutions. They then make connections between their own personal actions and the problems they witness in the environment and in society. They learn that our world is confronted with a litany of woes: corruption, violence against women and children, disruption and breakdown of families, and disintegration of cultures and communities. They also identify the abuse of drugs and chemical substances, especially among young people. There are also devastating diseases that are defying cures or occurring in epidemic proportions. Of particular concern are HIV/AIDS, malaria and diseases associated with malnutrition.

On the environment front, they are exposed to many human activities that are devastating to the environment and societies. These include widespread destruction of ecosystems, especially through deforestation, climatic instability, and contamination in the soils and waters that all contribute to excruciating poverty.

In the process, the participants discover that they must be part of the solutions. They realize their hidden potential and are empowered to overcome inertia and take action. They come to recognize that they are the primary custodians and beneficiaries of the environment that sustains them.

Entire communities also come to understand that while it is necessary to hold their governments accountable, it is equally important that in their own relationships with each other, they exemplify the leadership values they wish to see in their own leaders, namely justice, integrity and trust.

Although initially the Green Belt Movement's tree-planting activities did not address issues of democracy and peace, it soon became clear that responsible governance of the environment was impossible without democratic space. Therefore, the tree became a symbol for the democratic struggle in Kenya. Citizens were mobilised to challenge widespread abuses of power, corruption and environmental mismanagement. In Nairobi's Uhuru Park, at Freedom Corner, and in many parts of the country, trees of peace were planted to demand the release of prisoners of conscience and a peaceful transition to democracy.

Through the Green Belt Movement, thousands of ordinary citizens were mobilized and empowered to take action and effect change. They learned to overcome fear and a sense of helplessness and moved to defend democratic rights.

In time, the tree also became a symbol for peace and conflict resolution, especially during ethnic conflicts in Kenya when the Green Belt Movement used peace trees to reconcile disputing communities. During the ongoing rewriting of the Kenyan constitution, similar trees of peace were planted in many parts of the country to promote a culture of peace. Using trees as a symbol of peace is in keeping with a widespread African tradition. For example, the elders of the Kikuyu carried a staff from the *Thigi* tree that, when placed between two disputing sides, caused them to stop fighting and seek reconciliation. Many communities in Africa have these traditions.

Such practices are part of an extensive cultural heritage, which contributes both to the conservation of habitats and to cultures of peace. With the destruction of these cultures and the introduction of new values, local biodiversity is no longer valued or protected and as a result, it is quickly degraded and disappears. For this reason, the Green Belt Movement explores the concept of cultural biodiversity, especially with respect to indigenous seeds and medicinal plants.

As we progressively understood the causes of environmental degradation, we saw the need for good governance. Indeed, the state of any country's environment is a reflection of the kind of governance in place, and without good governance there can be no peace. Many countries, which have poor governance systems, are also likely to have conflicts and poor laws protecting the environment.

In 2002, the courage, resilience, patience and commitment of members of the Green Belt Movement, other civil society organizations, and the Kenyan public culminated in the peaceful transition to a democratic government and laid the foundation for a more stable society.

Excellencies, Friends, Ladies and Gentlemen,

It is 30 years since we started this work. Activities that devastate the environment and societies continue unabated. Today we are faced with a challenge that calls for a shift in our thinking, so that humanity stops threatening its life-support system. We are called to assist the Earth to heal her wounds and in the process heal our own—indeed, to embrace the whole creation in all its diversity, beauty and wonder. This will happen if we see the need to revive our sense of belonging to a larger family of life, with which we have shared our evolutionary process.

In the course of history, there comes a time when humanity is called to shift to a new level of consciousness, to reach a higher moral ground. A time when we have to shed our fear and give hope to each other.

That time is now.

The Norwegian Nobel Committee has challenged the world to broaden the understanding of peace: there can be no peace without equitable development; and there can be no development without sustainable management of the environment in a democratic and peaceful space. This shift is an idea whose time has come.

I call on leaders, especially from Africa, to expand democratic space and build fair and just societies that allow the creativity and energy of their citizens to flourish.

Those of us who have been privileged to receive education, skills, and experiences and even power must be role models for the next generation of leadership. In this regard, I would also like to appeal for the freedom of my fellow laureate Aung San Suu Kyi so that she can continue her work for peace and democracy for the people of Burma and the world at large.

Culture plays a central role in the political, economic and social life of communities. Indeed, culture may be the missing link in the development of Africa. Culture is dynamic and evolves over time, consciously discarding retrogressive traditions, like female genital mutilation (FGM), and embracing aspects that are good and useful.

Africans, especially, should re-discover positive aspects of their culture. In accepting them, they would give themselves a sense of belonging, identity and self-confidence.

Ladies and Gentlemen,

There is also need to galvanize civil society and grassroots movements to catalyze change. I call upon governments to recognize the role of these social movements in building a critical mass of responsible citizens, who help maintain checks and balances in society. On their part, civil society should embrace not only their rights but also their responsibilities.

Further, industry and global institutions must appreciate that ensuring economic justice, equity and ecological integrity are of greater value than profits at any cost.

The extreme global inequities and prevailing consumption patterns continue at the expense of the environment and peaceful co-existence. The choice is ours.

I would like to call on young people to commit themselves to activities that contribute toward achieving their long-term dreams. They have the energy and creativity to shape a sustainable future. To the young people I say, you are a gift to your communities and indeed the world. You are our hope and our future.

The holistic approach to development, as exemplified by the Green Belt Movement, could be embraced and replicated in more parts of Africa and beyond. It is for this reason that I have established the Wangari Maathai Foundation to ensure the continuation and expansion of these activities. Although a lot has been achieved, much remains to be done.

Excellencies, Ladies and Gentlemen,

As I conclude I reflect on my childhood experience when I would visit a stream next to our home to fetch water for my mother. I would drink water straight from the stream. Playing among the arrowroot leaves I tried in vain to pick up the strands of frogs' eggs, believing they were beads. But every time I put my little fingers under them they would break. Later, I saw thousands of tadpoles: black, energetic and wriggling through the clear water against the background of the brown earth. This is the world I inherited from my parents.

Today, over 50 years later, the stream has dried up, women walk long distances for water, which is not always clean, and children will never know what they have lost. The challenge is to restore the home of the tadpoles and give back to our children a world of beauty and wonder.

Thank you very much.

4

Tribute by H.E. Mr. Macharia Kamau

Ambassador/Permanent Representative of Kenya to the United Nations, in Honour of Prof. Wangari Muta Maathai

New York, NY, October 5, 2011

On Sunday, September 25, 2011, we lost a very special lady. Prof. Wangari Maathai died at Nairobi Hospital after a long, courageous struggle with cancer.

We thank the doctors here in New York as well as in Nairobi, where she sought treatment, for doing all they could to give her a few extra months to be with us and to enjoy her family, her children and her grandchild.

I personally met Prof. Maathai in my previous incarnation as Kenya's ambassador on matters of environment and climate change, and subsequently we met a couple of times here in New York. In recent months, our exchanges had grown warm and personal. I feel deeply that we have lost someone dear and special.

Prof. Wangari Maathai was a champion of peace, equality, democracy and the rights of women. She spoke for the voiceless, the oppressed and the dispossessed. She spoke truth to power in ways in which those in power had no choice but to listen.

The world came to know her as the protector of forests and all that lies therein; the millions who call forest habitats their home, and by extension the animals, the birds, all creatures great and small.

In the context of the global debate on environment, climate change and biodiversity, her message rang loud and true. She reminded us time and again that our forests are indeed the nurturers of our biodiversity and the forests are the lungs which help our earth breath as well as regulate its climate. The forests are life itself. Prof. Wangari Maathai was convinced of this and preached the message to the world.

If Mother Earth, if life itself, had a friend and protector, a Nightingale, a Joan of Arc, it was Wangari Maathai:

Philosopher.

Environmentalist.

Educationist.

Political Activist.

Freedom Fighter.

Mother, Grandmother, Guiding Light.

We in Kenya knew her and experienced her in all her manifestations. As a nation, we were intimate with her. She spoke out for us. She took a beating for us. She was our beacon of hope, sanity and political transformation. She was our shield and defender in the face of dictates from men in power and in conspiracy.

To the world she was the champion of forests, the voice and protector of everything that is green, that is life that is true.

She was our pride, our genius, our Nobel Laureate.

She was *Wangari, Wangari.* The matriarchal name of the Gikuyu lineage of the warriors, the protectors of the people.

We will miss her.

We will celebrate her.

We will emulate her.

We will never forget her.

She will continue to live in all that is green, all that is life, and all that is true.

Peace be upon her wherever she is. And may her family find courage and strength in this time.

Thank you all for coming and God bless.

WORKS CITED AND BIBLIOGRAPHY

All websites accessed July 1, 2014

Abercrombie, Sharon (2011). "Wangari Maathai Helped Us to 'Rise Up and Walk'," *National Catholic Reporter*, October 4, 2011.

Abwunza, Judith M. (1997). *Women's Voices, Women's Power: Dialogues of Resistance from East Africa*. Peterborough, Ont.: Broadview Press.

Adar, Korwa G. and Isaac M. Munyae (2001). "Human Rights Abuse in Kenya Under Daniel arap Moi, 1978–2001." *African Studies Quarterly* 5(1): 1.

African Activist Archive. *The Kenya Airlift, 1959–1963* (Unearthing Africana Collections and Providing Global Access, Part 2) <http://africanactivist.msu.edu/audio.php?objectid=32-12E-24>. (Documents were provided by Cora Weiss during our interview.)

Akiteng, Yangki Christine (2009). "The Road Less Traveled: The Wrong Bus Syndrome—Wrong Driver, Wrong Direction, Wrong Mindset," July 31, 2009 <http://searchwarp.com/swa525346.htm>.

Ampofo, Akosua A., Josephine Beoku-Betts, and Mary J. Osirim (2008). "Researching African Women and Gender Studies." *African and Asian Studies* 7: 327–341.

Amutabi, Maurice N. (2007). "Intellectuals and the Democratisation Process in Kenya." In *Kenya: The Struggle for Democracy*, edited by Godwin R. Murunga and Shadrack W. Nasong'o. New York: Codesria/Zed Books, pp. 197–226.

Anderson, J. E. (1965). "The Kenya Education Commission Report: An African View of Educational Planning." *Comparative Education Review* 9(2): 201–207.

Anderson, John (1970). *The Struggle for the School: The Interaction of Missionary, Colonial Government and Nationalist Enterprise in the Development of Formal Education in Kenya*. London: Longman.

Anderson, W. B. (1977). *The Church in East Africa, 1840–1974*. Dodoma, Tanzania: Central Tanganyika Press.

Arndt, Susan (2000). "Africa Gender Trouble and African Womanism: An Interview with Chikwenye Ogunywemi and Wanjira Muthoni." *Signs: Journal of Women in Culture and Society* (25)3: 709–726.

Associated Press (September 26, 2011). "Tributes Pour in for 'Tree Mother of Africa'," *CBSNews*, September 26, 2011.

Avert (2011). "Worldwide HIV & AIDS Statistics" (statistics from UNAIDS, WHO, and UNICEF for 2011) <http://www.avert.org/worldwide-hiv-aids-statistics.htm>.

Ayiemba, Elias H. O. (1988). "The Kenyan Family and Attitudes Toward Family Formation." In *Kenya's Population Growth and Development to the Year 2000*, edited by Simeon Hongo Ominde. Nairobi, Kenya: Heinemann Kenya, pp. 48–56.

Baldwin, James (1988). "A Talk to Teachers." In *Multicultural Literacy; Opening the American Mind,* edited by R. Simonson and S. Walker. St. Paul, Minn.: Graywolf Press, pp. 3–12.

Barasa, Lucas. (2012). "Kibaki Urges Women to Seek Elective Posts," *Daily Nation*, November 26, 2012.

Bartoo, Vincent (2011). "Conservationists Want Statue Erected," *East African Standard*, October 9, 2011.

Bassey, Nnimmo (2011). "The Trees Will Clap for Her." *Pambazuka*, 550 <http://www.pambazuka.org/en/category/features/76698>.

Bever, Edward (1996). *Africa: International Government and Political Series.* Phoenix, Ariz.: The Oryx Press.

Bindra, Sunny (2012). "Women's Soft Power Good for Leadership," *Daily Nation*, September 29, 2012. See also "How Much Longer Will Women Be Kept Away from the Top Table?," *Sunday Nation*, September 30, 2012.

Boddy-Evans, Alistair (n.d.). "National Council of Women of Kenya," About.com, "African History" <http://africanhistory.about.com/od/glossaryn/g/def-National-Council-Of-Women-Of-Kenya.htm>.

Bogart, Laura M. and Sheryl Thorburn (2006). "Relationships of African American's Sociodemographic Characteristics to Belief in Conspiracies about HIV/AIDS and Birth Control." *Journal of the National Medical Association*, 98(7): 1144–1150.

Boyer-Rechlin, Bethany (2010). "Women in Forestry: A Study of Kenya's Green Belt Movement and Nepal's Community Forestry Program." *Scandinavian Journal of Forest Research* 25(Supp 9): 69–72.

Branson, Richard (2012). "Richard Branson on Why We Need More Women in the Boardroom," *Entrepreneur.com*, September 24, 2012 <http://www. entrepreneur.com/article/224476>.

Bravman, Hill (1998). *Making Ethnic Ways: Communities and Their Transformations in Taita, Kenya, 1985–1950*. Portsmouth, N.H.: Heinemann.

Burgman, Hans (1990). *The Way the Catholic Church Started in Western Kenya*. Nairobi, Kenya: Mission Book Service.

Campbell, Horace (2011). "Wangari Maathai: Reclaiming the Earth." *Pambazuka*, 550 <http://pambazuka.org/en/category/features/76724>.

Catholic Review (2007). "Nobel Peace Laureate: Church Can Do More for Environment," June 5, 2007 <http://catholicreview.org/article/work/economy/ nobel-peace-laureate-church-can-do-more-for-environment#sthash. krKPMbNv.dpuf>.

Center for Reproductive Rights (2007). "Women Suffer Decades of Abuse in Kenya's Health Facilities, According to New Fact-Finding Report," September 8, 2007. <http://reproductiverights.org/en/press-room/women- suffer-decades-of-abuse-in-kenyas-health-facilities-according-to-new-fact- finding-r>.

Central Intelligence Agency. "Kenya," *The World Factbook* <https://www.cia.gov/ library/publications/the-world-factbook/geos/ke.html>.

Chege, Fatuma N. and Daniel N. Sifuna (2006). *Girls' and Women's Education in Kenya: Gender Perspectives and Trends*. Geneva: UNESCO.

Chege, Njoki (2011). "Unbowed, Even in Death," *Eve Woman* in *The Standard on Sunday*, October 2, 2011.

Chesaina, Ciarunji (1994). "The Development of Women's Studies in Kenya." *Women's Studies Quarterly* 3&4: 180–196.

Chimbi, Joyce (2012a). "Women's Issues Within the 2011 Budget," *Kenyan Woman: Advocating for the Rights of Women* (19):1 (July 2011).

—— (2012b). "There is Need for Gender Sensitive HIV Programs," *Kenyan Woman: Advocating for the Rights of Women* (19):1 (July 2011).

Chimbi, Joyce and Rosemary Okello (2011). "Women Stand to Reap Heavily from the Constitution," *Kenyan Woman: Advocating for the Rights of Women* (19): 4 (July 2011).

Church of England Newspaper (2012) "Bishop's Murder Politically Motivated," Conger, <http://geoconger.wordpress.com/tag/alexander-muge/>.

Climate Progress (2011). "The Passing of Nobelist Wangari Maathai: You Cannot

Protect the Environment Unless You Empower People" <http://thinkprogress. org/romm/2011/09/26/328405/wangari-maathai>.

Conway, Lawrence. "'Hell with the Lid Taken Off': The Pictures of Bygone Pittsburgh and Its Residents Choking Under Clouds of Thick Smog," *Daily Mail*, June 7, 2012.

Coray, Michael S. "The Kenya Land Commission and the Kikuyu of Kiambu." *Agricultural History* 52(1) (January 1978), pp. 179–93.

Daily Nation (2011). "Celebrating the Life of a Woman for All Seasons," *Daily Nation*, op. ed., September 27, 2011.

Dater, Alan and Lisa Merton (2008). *Taking Root: The Vision of Wangari Maathai*. Marlboro, Vt.: Marlboro Productions.

Economist, The (2011). "Wangari Maathai, Kenyan Environmentalist and Political Activist, Died on September 25th, Aged 71," October 8, 2011 <http://www. economist.com/node/21531415>.

Education in Kenya. Wikipedia.

Ekisa, Emongor (2011). "Embracing Selfless Leadership Best Way to Honor Maathai," *The Standard on Sunday*, October 2, 2011.

Felski, Rita (2011). "Doing Time: Feminist Theory and Postmodernist Culture." In *Feminist Literary Theory: A Reader* (3rd ed.), edited by Mary Eagleton. Malden, Mass.: Wiley-Blackwell, pp. 37–41.

Florence, Namulundah (2011). *The Bukusu of Kenya: Folktales, Culture and Social Identities*. Durham, N.C.: Carolina Academic Press.

Freire, Paulo (2000). *Pedagogy of the Oppressed* (trans. M. Bergman Ramos). New York: Continuum.

French, Howard W. "The Ritual: Disfiguring, Hurtful, Wildly Festive," *New York Times*, January 31, 1997.

Fustos, Kata (2012). "Violence Increases Risk of Infection for Women in Africa," *Kenyan Woman: Advocating for the Rights of Women* (19):18 (July 2011).

Gaggawala, Paul Onyango (1992). *Towards an Inclusive Society, Theology, and Church: Jesus' Option in the Context of Discrimination Against Women in Africa with Special Reference to Kenya*. M.A. Thesis, Maryknoll School of Theology: Maryknoll, New York.

Gaitho, Macharia (2011). "Farewell to the Indefatigable Fighter for Justice Who Goaded a Rotten Regime," *Daily Nation*, September 27, 2011.

Gathigah, Miriam (2011). "Kenya: Government Funds Free Sanitary Pads for Schoolgirls," *Guardian*, July 29, 2011.

Gecaga, Margaret G. (2007). "Religious Movements and Democratisation in Kenya: Between the Sacred and Profane." In *Kenya: The Struggle for Democracy*, edited by Godwin R. Murunga and Shadrack W. Nasong'o. New York: Codesria/Zed Books, pp. 58–89.

Gettleman, Jeffrey. "Wangari Maathai, Nobel Peace Prize Laureate, Dies at 71," *New York Times*, September 26, 2011.

Gibbs, Walter, (2004). "Nobel Laureate Seeks to Explain AIDS Remarks," *New York Times*, December 10, 2004.

Gorsevski, Ellen W. (2012). "Wangari Maathai's Emplaced Rhetoric: Greening Global Peacebuilding." *Environmental Communication: A Journal of Nature and Culture*, (6)3: 290–307.

Graham, Judith (1993). "Wangari Maathai. Current Biography Yearbook 1993." In *Current Biography Yearbook*. New York: The H. W. Wilson Company, pp. 353–357.

Green Belt Movement <http://www.greenbeltmovement.org/>.

Gwengi, Omondi (2011). "Public Gives Government Report Card Under Current Constitution," *Kenyan Woman: Advocating for the Rights of Women* (19): 6 (July 2011).

Hirschmann, Nancy J. (2008). "Mill, Political Economy, and Women's Work." *American Political Science Review* (102)2: 199–213.

Hobley, Charles W. (1970). *From Chartered Company to Colony: Thirty Years of Exploration and Administration in British East Africa* (2nd ed.). London: Frank Cass & Co.

Holmes, Rachel (2007). "Sowing the Seeds of Change," *The Times* (UK), February 3, 2007.

Hornsby, Charles (2012). "Why Kenyatta's Sunset Years Led to an Orgy of Official Graft," *East African Standard*, May 12, 2012.

House-Midamba, Bessie (1996). "Gender, Democratization, and Associational Life in Kenya." *Africa Today* (43)3: 289–306.

Houser, George M. (1989). *No One Can Stop the Rain: Glimpses of Africa's Liberation Struggle*. New York: The Pilgrim Press.

Ikonya, Philo (2008). "Kenya is Burning: Women's Voices Are Missing in the

Making of the Nation," *The WIP*, March 1, 2008 <http://www.thewip.net/contributors/2008/03/kenya_is_burning_womens_voices.html>.

International Crisis Group (2006). "France and Its Muslims: Riots, Jihadism and Depoliticisation," March 9, 2006 <http://www.crisisgroup.org/en/regions/europe/172–france-and-its-muslims-riots-jihadism-and-depoliticisation.aspx>.

Jungck, John R. (1985). "Wangari Maathai, 'Afforestation of the Desert'." *The American Biology Teacher* 47(2): 76–90.

Kabeberi-Macharia, Janet (1995). "Women, Laws, Customs and Practices in East Africa: Laying the Foundation." *The Law and Status of Women in Kenya*. Nairobi: Women & Law in East Africa.

Kabira, Wanjiku Mukabi (1994). "Gender and Politics of Control: An Overview of Images of Women in Gikuyu Oral Narratives." In *Understanding Oral Literature*, edited by Austin Bukenya, Wanjiku Mukabi Kabira, and Okoth Okombo. Nairobi: University of Nairobi Press, pp. 77–84.

Kanga, Anne (2004). "Taboo Subject Boldly Bared: A Feminist Analysis of Sexual Harassment as a Major Hindrance to Learning Among High School Girls in Kenya." In *Research on Education in Africa, the Caribbean, and the Middle East: A Historical Overview*, edited by Kagendo Mutua and Cynthia Szymanski Sunal. Greenwich, Conn.: Information Age Publishing, pp. 33–57.

Kanjama, Charles (2011). "Strength Can Be Found in the Tender Heart of a Woman," *East African Standard*, October 2, 2011.

Kanogo, Tabitha (2005). *African Womanhood in Colonial Kenya 1900–50*. Oxford: James Currey.

—— (1987). *Squatters and the Roots of Mau Mau*. Oxford: James Currey.

Kaplan, Irving, *et al.* (1976). *Area Handbook for Kenya*. Washington, D.C.: Foreign Area Studies.

Karanja, Stephen K. (n.d.). "Population Control—The Kenyan Perspective." Population Research Institute <http://www.pop.org/content/population-control-the-kenyan-perspective-895>.

Kareithi, Amos (2004). "Kenya: Disease 'A Weapon to Wipe Out Blacks'," *East African Standard*, August 31, 2004.

Kelvin, Karani (2011). "Empowerment Must Rise Beyond Second in Command," *Kenyan Woman: Advocating for the Rights of Women* 19:1 (July 2011).

KENSUP. Kenya Slum Upgrading Project. See UN-HABITAT <http://www. unhabitat.org/content.asp?cid=668&catid=206&typeid=13>.

Kenya—education (n.d.) <http://kenya.rcbowen.com/people/education.html>.

Kenyan Women Professors (2010). Blog for International Women's Day, March 8, 2010 <http://kenyanwomenprofessors.blogspot.com/2010/03/celebrating-international-womens-day.html>.

Kenyatta, Jomo (1962). *Facing Mount Kenya: The Indigenous Life of the Gikuyu.* New York: Random House.

Kibaji, Egara Stanley (2005). *The Construction of Gender Through the Narrative Process of the African Folktale: A Case Study of the Maragoli Folktale.* Unpublished doctoral dissertation. Doctorate in Philosophy in the Department of English at the University of South Africa.

Kiberenge, Kenfrey (2012). "How the City Teenagers Pass from Childhood to Adulthood," *Daily Nation,* December 16, 2012.

Kisii Women (1999). "Africa: Kisii Women on Warpath Over Circumcision," *Daily Nation,* January 12, 1999.

Koinange, Jeff (2009). "Wangari Maathai on the Bench with Jeff Koinange." November 2009 <http://tributetowangarimaathai.blogspot.com/2011/09/wangari-maathai-on-bench-with-jeff.html>.

Kolawole, Mary M. (2002). "Transcending Incongruities: Rethinking Feminisms and the Dynamics of Identity in Africa." *Agenda* 54: 92–98.

Korwa G. Adar and Isaac M. Munyae (2001). "Human Rights Abuse in Kenya under Daniel Arap Moi 1978–2001." *African Studies Quarterly* 5(1): 1.

Krebs, Ronald R. (Winter 2009/2010). "The False Promise of the Nobel Peace Prize." *Political Science Quarterly* 124(4): 593–625.

Kushner, Jennifer Lara Simka (2009). *Righteousness Commitment: Renewing, Repairing, and Restoring the World—Wangari Maathai and the Green Belt Movement.* Unpublished doctoral dissertation, March 2009. Department of Adults in Continuing Education. National Louis University <http://digitalcommons.nl.edu/diss/23>.

Lamb, Gregory M. (2011). "A Nobel Peace Prize Winner Finds Spiritual Values in Planting Trees," *Christian Science Monitor,* January 24, 2011.

Lappé, Anna and Frances Moore Lappé (2004). "The Genius of Wangari Maathai," *New York Times,* October 14, 2004.

Lee, Lois (2009). "Interview with Professor Nira Yuval-Davis: After *Gender and Nation.*" *Studies in Ethnicity and Nationalism* 9(1): 128–138 (April 2009).

Leftie, Peter (2011). "Kenya: Board Reveals Best and Worst Users of CDF Kitty," *Daily Nation*, March 27, 2011.

Letiwa, Paul (2011). "A Month in the Life of a Public University Professor," *Daily Nation*, November 17, 2011.

Lewis, Jone Johnson. "Wangari Maathai," Women's History <http://womenshistory. about.com/od/wangarimaathai/p/wangari_maathai.htm>.

Lone, Salim (2011). "They Shaved Off the Hair of a Woman Who Was Decades Ahead of Her Time," *Daily Nation*, September 28, 2011.

Maathai, Wangari (2011a). "I Will Be a Hummingbird" <http://www.youtube. com/watch?v=IGMW6YWjMxw>.

—— (2011b). "Wangari Muta Maathai: Share Your Condolences" <http:// greenbeltmovement.org.s126284.gridserver.com/> (currently unavailable to the public).

—— (2010). *Replenishing the Earth; Spiritual Values for Healing Ourselves and the World.* New York: Doubleday.

—— (2009). *The Challenge for Africa.* New York: Pantheon Books.

—— (2008). "An Unbreakable Link: Peace, Environment, and Democracy." *Harvard International Review* 29(4): 24–27.

—— (2007). "A Statement to the 18th General Assembly of Caritas Internationalis." Lecture, Synod Hall, Vatican City, June 3, 2007.

—— (2006). *Unbowed: A Memoir.* New York: Anchor Books.

—— (2004). Nobel Peace Prize Lecture. December 10, 2004 <http://www. nobelprize.org/nobel_prizes/peace/laureates/2004/maathai-lecture-text.html>.

—— (2003). *The Green Belt Movement: Sharing the Approach and the Experience.* New York: Lantern Books.

—— (2000). "Speak Truth to Power," an article excerpted from *Speak Truth to Power: Human Rights Defenders Who Are Changing Our World* edited by Kerry Kennedy and New York: Umbrage Editions. Available at <http://www. greenbeltmovement.org/wangari-maathai/key-speeches-and-articles/speak-truth-to-power>.

—— (1996). "The Planet Is Our Common Home; Excerpts, Statement by the Commission on Global Governance." *Women's Studies Quarterly* 24(1/2): 102–104.

—— (1994). *The Bottom Is Heavy Too: Even with the Green Belt Movement.* Edinburgh: Edinburgh University Press.

MacDonald, Mia (2005). "The Prize is Right," *Satya,* January 2005 <http://www.satyamag.com/jan05/macdonald.html>.

MacDonald, Mia and Dani Nierenberg (2004). "Don't Get Mad, Get Elected: A Conversation with Kenyan Activist Wangari Maathai." *World Watch* 17(3): 25–27.

Magesa, Laurenti (1997). *African Religion: The Moral Traditions of Abundant Life.* Maryknoll, N.Y.: Orbis Books.

Makila, F. E. (1978). *An Outline History of Babukusu of Western Kenya.* Nairobi: Kenya Literature Bureau.

Mama Fatuma Goodwill Children's Home (2001) <http://mamafatumas.org/history-vision/>.

Mankell, Henning (2011). "The Art of Listening," *New York Times,* December 10, 2011.

Martin, Jane Roland (2007). *Educational Metamorphoses: Philosophical Reflections on Identity and Culture.* Lanham, Md.: Rowman & Littlefield.

—— (1994). *Changing the Educational Landscape: Philosophy, Women, and Curriculum.* New York: Routledge.

—— (1985). *Reclaiming a Conversation: The Ideal of an Educated Woman.* New Haven, Conn.: Yale University Press.

Martins, Dino (2011). "Tree Planting in Honor of Wangari Maathai," *National Geographic,* October 9, 2011 <http://newswatch.nationalgeographic.com/2011/10/09/tree-planting-in-honor-of-wangari-maathai/>.

Mary Muthoni Nyanjiru. Information at <http://www.answers.com/topic/mary-muthoni-nyanjiru#ixzz2lMn4mD00>.

Mathenge, Oliver (2012). "Kenya Ethnic Bastions on Campus Exposed," *Daily Nation,* March 7, 2012.

Mbiti, John S. (1970). *African Religions and Philosophy.* Garden City, N.Y.: Anchor Books.

Mboyah, Duncan (2011). "Realizing Kenya's Dream from the Sleeping Sickness," African Woman and Child Feature Service, July 21, 2011 <http://www.awcfs.org/new/index.php/women-who-make-a-difference/889-realising-kenyas-dream-from-the-sleeping-sickness >.

McPherson, Kimra (2006). "Tree Advocate Helps Kick Off New Planting," *San Jose Mercury News*, May 1, 2006.

Mengo, Bedah (2011). "University Education in Kenya: Lecturers Are Pushing for an Increase in Their Salaries, Which Will Put Them at Par (or Higher) with Their Counterparts in East Africa," *Coastweek Kenya* <http://www.coastweek. com/3445_lecturers.htm>.

Menya, Walter (2011a). "Wangari Maathai's Last Wishes," *Daily Nation*, September 27, 2011.

—— (2011b). "World Mourns Nobel Laureate Wangari Maathai," *Daily Nation*, September 26, 2011.

Menya, Walter and Daniel Wesangula (2011). "Kenya: Maathai Rejected Lucrative Offers to Ship Her Memoirs to Kenya," *Daily Nation*, October 8, 2011.

Michaelson, March (1994). "Wangari Maathai and Kenya's Green Belt Movement: Exploring the Evolution and Potentialities of Consensus Movement Mobilization." *Social Problems,* 41(4): 540–561.

Mill, John Stuart (1869). "The Subjection of Women." London: Longmans, Green, Reader, and Dyer <https://archive.org/details/subjectionofwome00millrich>.

Minnich, Elizabeth K. (2005 [1990]). *Transforming Knowledge* (2nd ed.). Philadelphia: Temple University Press.

Mitchell, Brian R. (1998). International Historical Statistics: Africa, Asia and Oceania 1750–1993. New York: Stockton Press.

Mojtehedzadeh, Sara (2012). "Boy Steps into Maathai's Shoes at Age 12," *Daily Nation*, September 27, 2012.

Moody, Eric M. (2010). "Book Reviews: Wangari Maathai. *The Challenge for Africa.* New York, N.Y.: Pantheon books, 2009." *African Studies Quarterly* 11(2/3): 155–156.

Moore, Henrietta L. (1999). "What Happened to Women and Men? Gender and Other Crises in Anthropology." In *Anthropology Theory Today* edited by Henrietta L. Moore. Cambridge: Polity Press, pp. 151–171.

—— (1988). *Feminism and Anthropology*. Minneapolis: University of Minnesota Press.

—— (1986). *Space, Text, Gender: An Anthropological Study of the Marakwet in Kenya.* Cambridge: Cambridge University Press.

Moore, Solomon (2012). "Hague Court Charges Kenya Leaders: Deputy Premier,

Former Minister to Face Trial for Post-Election Violence; Wrench in Presidential Race," *Wall Street Journal*, January 24, 2012.

Moran, Andrew (2012). "Kenya's $12 Million Renovation of Parliament Includes $3k Chairs," *Digital Journal*, August 7, 2012 <http://www.digitaljournal.com/article/330275#ixzz2AezyOoJ7>.

Mothers (1999). "Kenya: Mothers in Dire Straits After 'Cut'," *Daily Nation*, November 11, 1999 <http://allafrica.com/stories/199911110036.html>.

MSNBC.com News Services (2010). "'Shocking' Conditions at Kenyan Trash Dump" <http://www.msnbc.msn.com/id/21152506/ns/world_news-world_environment/t/shocking-conditions-kenyan-trash-dump/#.UF3ClfVOhMg>.

Mucai-Kattambo, Victoria and Janet Kabeberi-Macharia (1995). *Women, Laws, Custom and Practices in East Africa: Laying the Foundation*. Nairobi: Women and Law in East Africa, pp. 83–84.

Mugo, Beth (2012). An official report of the event is available at <http://www.kenyaembassy.com/pdfs/BulletinVolume2SeptemberOctober.pdf>.

Muindi, Benjamin (2010). "Scandal of Kenyan Universities Without a Single Professor," *Daily Nation*, November 6, 2010.

Muiruri, Faith (2011). "An Oasis of Hope for Maasai Women's Rights," *Kenyan Woman: Advocating for the Rights of Women* 19:15 (July 2011).

Munene, Ishmael I. (2013). "Our University: Ethnicity, Higher Education and the Quest for State Legitimacy in Kenya." *Higher Education Policy,* 16:43–63.

Mungai, Michael (2011). "Wangari Maathai and Education of Girls in Africa," September 27, 2011 <http://www.huffingtonpost.com/michael-mungai/wangari-maathai-education_b_983492.html>.

Mureithi, Francis (2011). "Koigi Mum: The Wangari I've Known," *Sunday Nation*, October 9, 2011.

Murunga, Godwin R. and Shadrack W. Nasong'o, eds. (2007). *Kenya: The Struggle for Democracy*. New York: Codesria/Zed Books.

Musyoka, Stephen Kalonzo (2011). "We Must Not Lose Sight of Wangari Maathai's Outstanding Inspiration," *East African Standard*, October 2, 2011.

Mutiso, Gideon Cyrus Makau (1975). *Kenya: Politics, Policy and Society*. Nairobi, Kenya: East African Literature Bureau.

Mutua, Martin and Felix Olick (2013). "Threats Over Truth, Justice and Reconciliation Commission's Explosive Report on Past Injustices," *East African Standard*, May 18, 2013.

Mwangi, Evan (2010). "The Incomplete Rebellion: Mau Mau Movement in Twenty-First-Century Kenyan Popular Culture." *Africa Today* 57(2): 86–113.

Mwaniki, Charles (2011). "Neighbours in Nyeri Accept Maathai Won't Be Going Home," *Daily Nation*, October 8, 2011.

Mwaniki, Mebo Kabeta (1973). *The Relationship between Self-Concept and Academic Achievement in Kenyan Pupils.* Ph.D. Dissertation, Department of Educational Psychology, Stanford University Press.

Mwenzwa, Ezekiel Mbitha (2011). "From Center to Margin: An Appraisal of the Constituencies Development Fund (CDF) as a Decentralization Strategy in Kenya" <http://www.eldis.org/vfile/upload/1/document/0711/Paper on Decentralization.pdf>.

Myers, Jimmy (2007). "Nobel Prize Winner's Mission Begets Hope," *St. Joseph News-Press*, January 29, 2007.

—— (2006). "Nobel Winner to Speak in Atchison: Maathai to Return to her Alma Mater," *St. Joseph News-Press*, November 17, 2006.

Nagel, Mechthild (2005). "Environmental Justice and Women's Rights: A Tribute to Wangari Maathai." *Environmental Justice and Women's Rights* 2: 1–9.

Nasimiyu, Ruth (1997). "Changing Women's Rights Over Property in Western Kenya." In *African Families and the Crisis of Social Change,* edited by Thomas Weisner, Candice Bradley and Philip L. Kilbride. Westport, Conn.: Greenwood, pp. 283–298.

Nasong'o, Shadrack W. and Theodora O. Ayot (2007). "Women in Kenya's Politics of Transition and Democratisation." In *Kenya: The Struggle for Democracy,* edited by Godwin Murunga and Shadrack Nasong'o. New York: Codesria Books/Zed Books, pp. 164–196.

NCWK. National Council of Women of Kenya <www.ncwk.or.ke>.

Ndegwa, Alex (2011). "Kenyans Pay Last Respects to Maathai," *East African Standard*, October 9, 2011.

Ndeta, John H. (2013). "Party Primaries Robbed Women of Leadership Chance," *Kenyan Woman: Advocating for the Rights of Women* 34: 2 (February 2013).

Ndung'u, Wambui (2011). "Wangari Inspired Us," *Eve Woman* in *The Standard on Sunday*, October 2, 2011.

Ng'etich, Jacob (2011). "Maathai's Final Wish Granted That No Tree Should Be Felled for Coffin," *Daily Nation*, October 7, 2011.

Ngugi, Mumbi (2001). "The Women's Rights Movement and Democratization in

Kenya: A Preliminary Inquiry into the Green Formations of Civil Society." *Series on Alternative Research in East Africa (SAREAT)*, Nairobi: Unpublished paper.

Ngw'eno, H. (1994). "Education, the Key to a Better Life: Education for Girls Promotes Economic Growth and Reduces Poverty," *Weekly Review*, May 20: 24–25.

Ngwiri, Magesha (2000). "Time We Gave Women a Chance to Be Heard," *Daily Nation*, May 28, 2000.

Nixon, Rob (2006). "Slow Violence, Gender, and the Environmentalism of the Poor." *Journal of Commonwealth and Postcolonial Studies*, 3.2–14.1 (2006–2007), pp. 14–37.

Noddings, Nel (1989). *Women and Evil*. Berkeley: University of California Press.

Nordenberg, Mark (2006). "News from Pitt," October 9, 2006. See <https://groups.yahoo.com/neo/groups/africa-oped/conversations/topics/20924>.

Nwankwo, Clement (n.d.). "The Status of Human Rights Organizations in Sub-Saharan Africa, Kenya." University of Minnesota Human Rights Library <http://www1.umn.edu/humanrts/africa/kenya.htm>.

Nzioka, Patrick (2011). "She Was Our Mother, a Role Model," *Daily Nation*, September 27, 2011.

Obbo, Christine (1980). *African Women: Their Struggle for Economic Independence*. London: Zed Press.

Obonyo, Oscar (2011a). "Julia Ojiambo Reveals Deep Relationship She Shared with Maathai," *East African Standard*, October 2, 2011.

——— (2011b). "Maathai: Prophetess Who Was Never Cherished at Home," *East African Standard*, October 2, 2011.

Ochieng, Philip (2011). "Whence Cometh Another Heroine," *Daily Nation*, September 26, 2011.

Odhiambo, Millie (2012). "Despite Progress, Gap Between Boys and Girls Still too Large in Education," *Daily Nation*, March 25, 2012.

Ogunyemi, Chikwenye Okonjo (1985). "Womanism: The Dynamics of the Contemporary Black Female Novel in English." *Signs: Journal of Women in Culture and Society* (11)1: 63–80.

Ogutu, Evelyne (2008a). "Kenya: Maathai's Protest on Bodyguard," *East African Standard*, January 25, 2008.

——. (2008b). "Kenya: Sanitary Pads Reinvented," *East African Standard*, September 28, 2008.

Okeke, Philomena E. (1996). "Postmodern Feminism and Knowledge Production: The African Context." *Africa Today* (43)3: 223–234.

Okin, Susan Moller (2002). "'Mistresses of Their Own Destiny': Group Rights, Gender, and Realistic Rights of Exit." *Ethics* 112(2): 205–230.

—— (1996). "Sexual Orientation, Gender, and Families: Dichotomizing Differences." *Hypatia* (1): 30–48.

—— (1994). "Political Liberalism, Justice, and Gender." *Ethics* 105: 23–43.

Okoiti, Okiya Omtatah (2011). "Maathai Made Real Courage Fashionable," *Daily Nation*, September 27, 2011.

Okungu, Jerry (n.d.). "The Beauty and Shame of Kenya's Constituency Development Fund." Constituencies Development Fund Board <http://www.cdf.go.ke/9-news/30-the-beauty-and-shame-of-kenyas-constituency-development-fund-cdf.html> and <http://www.cdf.go.ke/allocations>.

Okwany, Rebecca (2013). "Parents Call for KCPE to be Abolished," *Daily Nation* January 2, 2013.

Oloo, Adams (2007). "The Contemporary Opposition in Kenya: Between Internal Traits and State Manipulation." In *Kenya: The Struggle for Democracy,* edited by Godwin R. Murunga and Shadrack Nasong'o. New York; Codesria/Zed Books, pp. 90–125.

Ombara, Omwa (2009). "Lady Justice Nancy Baraza," *Kenyan Woman: Advocating for the Rights of Women* 19: 3 (July 2011).

Ominde, Simeon Hongo, ed. (1988a). *Kenya's Population Growth and Development to the Year 2000.* Nairobi, Kenya: Heinemann Kenya.

—— (1988b). "Population Trends and Health with Special Reference to Kenya." In *Kenya's Population Growth and Development to the Year 2000*, edited by Simeon Hongo Ominde. Nairobi, Kenya: Heinemann Kenya, pp. 108–119.

Ondiege, Peter O. and Robert A. Obudho (1988). "Population Growth and Demand for Rural and Urban Housing." In *Kenya's Population Growth and Development to the Year 2000*, edited by Simeon Hongo Ominde. Nairobi, Kenya: Heinemann Kenya, pp. 120–130.

Onyango-Obbo, Charles (2011). "Tanzania: The Meaning of Wangari Maathai's Life—By a Rogue African Journalist," *Daily Nation*, September 29, 2011.

Oriang, Lucy (2009). "With All This Sex Abuse, Where Shall We Hide Our Daughters?," *Daily Nation*, November 5, 2009.

—— (1999). "Kenya: Ritual or Taboo, the Victim Must Have a Say," *Daily Nation*, November 22, 1999.

Orlale, Odhiambo (2011). "The Fall of a Giant," *Kenyan Woman: Advocating for the Rights of Women* (22): 1 (October 2011).

OSFEA. Orphelins San Frontières <http://www.osfea.com/>.

Oucho, John Oyaro (1988). "Spatial Population Change in Kenya: A District Level Analysis." In *Kenya's Population Growth and Development to the Year 2000*, edited by Simeon Hongo Ominde. Nairobi, Kenya: Heinemann Kenya, pp. 131–139.

Path Press Release (1997). PATH is an international non-profit organization whose stated mission is to improve the health of women and children. See <http://www.bluegecko.org/kenya/tribes/meru/articles-circword.htm>. See also Nation Correspondent (1999).

Pierson, Robert (2011). "Trees and the Forest: Story and Trustori in Quaker Faith in Practice." *Crosscurrents* 61(2): 150–150 (June 2011).

Procter & Gamble (2006; 2013). "P&G Helping Kenyan Girls." <http://www.proudlyafrican.info/Kenya/Procter-and-Gamble-Top-Corporate-Company.aspx>.

Ritchie, Cyril (2011). "Deterred by Nothing, Discouraged by Nothing." *Pambazuka*, 550 <http://www.pambazuka.org/en/category/features/76701>.

Robin, Corey (2011). *The Reactionary Mind: Conservatism from Edmund Burke to Sarah Palin*. New York: Oxford University Press.

Rodney, Walter (1972). *How Europe Underdeveloped Africa*. London: Bogle-L'Ouverture Publications.

Rogoff, Barbara, *et al.*, (2003). "Firsthand Learning Through Intent Participation." *Annual Review of Psychology*, 54: 175–203.

Rono, Joseph Kipkemboi (2002). "The Impact of Structural Adjustment Programmes on Kenyan Society." *Journal of Social Development in Africa* 17(1):81–98 (January 2002).

Rosenfeld, Paul E. and Lydia G. H. Feng (2011). *Risks of Hazardous Wastes*. Oxford, U.K.: William Andrew.

Rosenthal, Elisabeth (2009). "Smuggling Europe's Waste to Poorer Countries," *New York Times*, September 26, 2009.

SACMEQ (Southern and Eastern African Consortium for Monitoring Educational Quality). "Kenya" <http://www.sacmeq.org/education-kenya.htm> and <http://www.sacmeq.org/sacmeq-members/kenya>.

Salo, Elaine, and Amina Mama (2001). "Talking About Feminism in Africa." *Agenda: African Feminisms* 50: 58–63.

Schloemann, Martin (2005). Quoted in "What Luther *Didn't* Say about Vocation." Editorial in *Word & World* 25(4): 359–361 Fall 2005.

Schoofs, Mark (1999, December, 1–7). "Death and the Second Sex," Part 5: "AIDS: The Agony of Africa" series, *Village Voice*, November 30, 1999.

Science Daily (2010). "Hazardous E-Waste Surging in Developing Countries," *Science Daily*, February 23, 2010 <http://www.sciencedaily.com/releases/2010/02/100222081911.htm>.

Sekoh-Ochieng, Jacinta (2000). "Year of Landmark Gains for Women," *The Nation*, December 28, 2000.

Seppala, Pekka (1995). *The Changing Generations: The Devolution of Land Among the Babukusu in Western Kenya.* Helsinki: The Finnish Anthropological Society.

Shachtman, Tom (2009). *Airlift to America: How Barack Obama, Sr., John F. Kennedy, Tom Mboya, and 800 East African Students Changed Their World and Ours.* New York: St. Martin's Press.

Sheffield, James R. (1973). *Education in Kenya: An Historical Study.* New York: Teachers College Press.

Sigei, Julius (2011). "Pomp and Ceremony to Mark Third State Funeral," *Daily Nation*, October 7, 2011.

Simiyu, P. (2012). "Bungoma Leaders Vow to Defend the Embattled DCJ," Westfm, January 14, 2012 <http://westfm.co.ke/mobile/index.php?page=news&id=4355>.

Sipalla, Florence (2011). "Women's Bank Leaves Them Financially Stronger," *Kenyan Woman: Advocating for the Rights of Women* 19: 8 (July 2011).

Siringi, Samuel (2009). "Shocking Details of Sex Abuse in Schools," *Daily Nation*, November 1, 2009.

Smiley, Tavis (2009). Nobel Laureate Wangari Maathai Tribute. Interview by Tavis Smiley, April 21, 2009 <http://www.pbs.org/wnet/tavissmiley/interviews/nobel-laureate-wangari-maathai-tribute/>.

Smith, David (2013). "Kenyan Woman's Pact to Marry Two Men Causes Outrage," *Guardian*, August 27, 2013.

Smith, Philip (2001). *Cultural Theory: An Introduction.* Malden, Mass.: Blackwell Publishing.

Social Education (2006). "Wangari Maathai." *Social Education* 70(4), 13 (May/June 2006).

Steyn, Tisha (2004). "Nobel Winner: AIDS a WMD," *The New South Africa*, October 11, 2004. See <https://thenewsouthafrica.wordpress.com/2004/10/>.

Stolberg, Sheryl Gay (2011). "When It Comes to Scandal, Girls Won't Be Boys," *Kenyan Woman: Advocating for the Rights of Women* 19: 12 (July 2011).

Stone, Judith (2005). "Phenomenal Woman: Wangari Maathai," *O, The Oprah Magazine*, June 2005.

Swainson, Nicola (1980). *The Development of Corporate Capitalism in Kenya 1917–77.* Berkeley: University of California Press.

Taylor, Verta, Nancy Whittier, and Cynthia Fabrizio Pelak (2009). "The Women's Movement: Persistence Through Transformation." In *Feminist Frontiers* (8th ed.) edited by Verta Taylor, Nancy Whittier, and Leila Rupp, New York: McGraw Hill, pp. 515–531.

Think Progress (2011). "The Passing of Nobelist Wangari Maathai: 'You Cannot Protect the Environment Unless You Empower People'," by Climate Guest Blogger, September 26, 2011 <http://thinkprogress.org/romm/2011/09/26/328405/wangari-maathai/>.

Thomas, Mark Roland (2012). "African Debt Since Debt Relief: How Clean Is the Slate?" October 4, 2012 <https://blogs.worldbank.org/africacan/african-debt-since-debt-relief-how-clean-is-the-slate>.

Tignor, Robert L. (1976). *The Colonial Transformation of Kenya: The Kamba, Kikuyu, and Maasai from 1900 to 1939.* Princeton, N.J.: Princeton University Press.

Tripp, Aili M. (2003a). "African Feminisms: A New Wave of Activism." Conference Papers—American Political Science Association, 2003 Annual Meeting, pp. 1–29.

—— (2003b). "Women in Movement: Transformations in African Political Landscapes." *International Feminist Journal of Politics* (5)2: 233–255.

—— (2000). "Rethinking Difference: Comparative Perspectives from Africa." *Signs: Journal of Women in Culture and Society: Journal of Women in Culture and Society* (25)3: 649–675.

Uhuru Park. "Living in Nairobi: Uhuru Park" <http://www.jambonairobi.co.ke/activities/boat-riding/uhuru-park/>.

UNESCO Institute for Statistics. "Education (all levels) profile – Kenya" <http://stats. uis.unesco.org/unesco/TableViewer/document.aspx?ReportId=121&IF_ Language=eng&BR_Country=4040>.

UNESCO Institute for Statistics (2011). UIS Statistics in Brief <http://stats. uis.unesco.org/unesco/TableViewer/document.aspx?ReportId=121&IF_ Language=eng&BR_Country=4040>.

University of Oxford. "Kenyan Environmentalist and Nobel Laureate Launches Billion Tree Campaign in UK," February 12, 2007 <http://www.ox.ac.uk/ media/news_stories/2007/070212.html>.

U.S. State Department (2013). "Secretary Clinton To Announce Launch of Up to $86.5 Million in Public-Private Partnerships," January 30, 2013 <http:// www.state.gov/r/pa/prs/ps/2013/01/203543.htm>.

Valente, Judy (2007). "Wangari Maathai," *Religion and Ethics Newsweekly*, a report by Judy Valente, November 9, 2007 <http://www.pbs.org/wnet/ religionandethics/2007/11/09/november-9-2007-wangari-maathai/4544/>.

Vidal, John (2011). "Wangari Maathai Obituary," *Guardian*, September 26, 2011.

—— (2004). "Rooting for Peace," *Guardian*, October 12, 2004.

Vogel, Gretchen and Malakoff, David (2004). "Kenya's Maathai Wins for Reforestation Work." *Science*, 306(5695): 391.

Voice of Russia (2011). "Mass Riots Spread from London to Other Cities," August 9, 2011 <http://english.ruvr.ru/2011/08/09/54381650.html>; "Mass Riots Hit London," by Radjabisol, August 7, 2011, Newsflavor <http://newsflavor. com/world/europe/mass-riots-hit-london/>.

wa Gacheru, Margaretta (2011). "Committed to Justice for People and Planet." *Pambazuka*, 550 <http://www.pambazuka.org/en/category/features/76700>.

wa Thiong'o, Ngugi (1997). *Writers in Politics: A Re-engagement with Issues of Literature and Society*. Portsmouth, N.H.: Heinemann Educational Books.

Wambugu, Ngunjiri (2012). "Is Nancy Baraza a Victim of Hubris?," *The Star*, January 16, 2012.

Wandibba, Simiyu (1997). "Changing Roles in the Bukusu Family." In *African Families and the Crisis of Social Change,* edited by Thomas S. Weisner, Candice Bradley, and Philip Leroy Kilbride. Westport, Conn.: Bergin & Garvey, pp. 332–340.

Wangari Maathai Institute for Peace and Environmental Studies <http://wmi. uonbi.ac.ke/node/4090>.

Warah, Rasna (2011). "Wangari Maathai: Unbowed and Unbeaten Till the End." *Pambazuka*, 550.

Warigi, Gitau (2011). "Maathai Shunned Elitist Life to Stand for Ordinary People," *Daily Nation*, September 27, 2011.

Wax, Emily (2009). "A Place Where Women Rule: All-Female Village in Kenya is a Sign of Burgeoning Feminism Across Africa," *Washington Post*, July 9, 2005.

WEDO (2010). Women's Environment & Development Organization. "Wangari Maathai & the Green Belt Movement" <http://www.wedo.org/news/wangari-maathai-the-green-belt-movement> and <http://www.youtube.com/watch?v=BQU7JoxkGvo>.

Were, Elizabeth (2012). "Kenya: Plant Trees in Honor of Wangari—Shebesh," *The Star*, June 5, 2012.

Wereschagin, Mike (2013). "Pitt Honors Student: Nobel Prize Winner Who Influenced Kenyan Culture," *TribLive*, September 25, 2013 <http://triblive.com/news/adminpage/4770772–74/kenya-maathai-university#ixzz2gZbn9foA>.

White, Luise (1990). *The Comforts of Home: Prostitution in Colonial Nairobi*. Chicago: The University of Chicago Press.

Winkler, Allan (2004). *Uncertain Safari: Kenyan Encounters and African Dreams*. Lanham, Md.: Hamilton Books.

Wipper, Audrey (1977). *Rural Rebels: A Study of Two Protest Movements in Kenya*. Oxford: Oxford University Press.

Wokabi, Charles (2012). "Kenya: Learning to Finance a Costly Education System," *Daily Nation*, January 12, 2012.

World Bank (2013). "Proportion of Seats Held by Women in National Parliaments (%)" <http://data.worldbank.org/indicator/SG.GEN.PARL.ZS>.

Worthington, Nancy (2003). "Shifting Identities in the Kenyan Press: Representations of Wangari Maathai's Media Complex Protest." *Women's Studies in Communication*, 26(2): 143–164.

—— (2001). "A Division of Labor: Dividing Maternal Authority from Political Activism in the Kenyan Press." *Journal of Communication Inquiry*, 25(2): 167–183.

Wright, Nancy G. (2011). "Christianity and Environmental Justice." *Crosscurrents*, pp: 161–190.

WuDunn, Sheryl (1999). "Japan's Tale of Two Pills: Viagra and Birth Control," *New York Times*, April 27, 1999.

Yuval-Davis, Nira (1997). *Gender & Nation*. London: Sage Publications,

—— (1993). "Gender and Nation." *Ethnic and Racial Studies* (16)4: 621–632.

Zawadi (2010). The Zawadi Africa Matching Fund <http://zawadiafrica.org/wp/> and <http://www.youtube.com/watch?v=x7welZ1AUMc>.

INDEX

About the Publisher

LANTERN BOOKS was founded in 1999 on the principle of living with a greater depth and commitment to the preservation of the natural world. In addition to publishing books on animal advocacy, vegetarianism, religion, and environmentalism, Lantern is dedicated to printing books in the United States on recycled paper and saving resources in day-to-day operations. Lantern is honored to be a recipient of the highest standard in environmentally responsible publishing from the Green Press Initiative.

www.lanternbooks.com

CPSIA information can be obtained
at www.ICGtesting.com
Printed in the USA
FFOW01n2044101114
8689FF